INTERNATIONAL RELATIONS AND THE GREAT POWERS

General Editor: **John Gooch**
Professor of International History, University of Leeds

Titles in the International Relations and the Great Powers series

Britain and the World in the Twentieth Century
by John W. Young

Japan and the World since 1868
by Michael A. Barnhart

Forthcoming

France and the World in the Twentieth Century
by J.F.V. Keiger

Russia and the World since 1917
by Caroline Kennedy-Pipe

The United States and the World in the Twentieth Century
by Michael Dunne

BRITAIN

AND THE WORLD IN THE TWENTIETH CENTURY

John W. Young
Professor of Politics
University of Leicester

A member of the Hodder Headline Group
LONDON • NEW YORK • SYDNEY • AUCKLAND

First published in Great Britain in 1997 by
Arnold, a member of the Hodder Headline Group
338 Euston Road, London NW1 3BH
175 Fifth Avenue, New York, NY 10010

Distributed exclusively in the USA by
St. Martin's Press, Inc.
175 Fifth Avenue, New York, NY 10010

British Library Cataloguing in Publication Data
A catalogue record for this book is available from the British Library

Library of Congress Cataloging-in-Publication Data
Young, John W., 1957–
Britain and the world in the twentieth century/John W. Young.
p. cm.—(International relations and the great powers)
Includes bibliographical references and index.
ISBN 0-340-69174-3.—ISBN 0-340-54013-3 (pbk.)

1. Great Britain—Foreign relations—20th century.
2. International relations—History—20th century. 3. World politics—20th century. I. Title. II. Series.
DA566.7.Y68 1997 97-3796
327.47—dc21 CIP

ISBN 0 340 54013 3 (Pb)
ISBN 0 340 69174 3 (Hb)

Typeset in 11/12½ Bembo by Scribe Design, Gillingham, Kent
Printed and bound in Great Britain by JW Arrowsmith Ltd, Bristol

To my son
David Jack Young

Contents

List of abbreviations

ASEAN	Association of South-East Asian Nations
BEF	British Expeditionary Force
CAP	Common Agricultural Policy of the EEC
CFM	Council of Foreign Ministers
CFSP	Common Foreign and Security Policy of the EEC
CIA	American Central Intelligence Agency
CID	Committee of Imperial Defence
CIGS	Chief of Imperial General Staff
CND	Campaign for Nuclear Disarmament
CO	Colonial Office
Comintern	Communist International
COS	Chiefs of Staff
CRO	Commonwealth Relations Office
DRC	Defence Requirements Committee
EC	European Community
EEC	European Economic Community
EFTA	European Free Trade Association
EMU	Economic and Monetary Union
ERM	Exchange Rate Mechanism
EU	European Union
FCO	Foreign and Commonwealth Office
FO	Foreign Office
GATT	General Agreement on Tariffs and Trade
GC&CS	Government Code and Cypher School
GCHQ	Government Communications Headquarters
GDP	Gross Domestic Product
GHQ	General Headquarters
GNP	Gross National Product
IMF	International Monetary Fund
IRD	Information Research Department
JIC	Joint Intelligence Committee

MI5	British Counter-Intelligence (formerly MO5)
MI6	British Secret Intelligence Service (in 1916–21 designated MI1c; also known as SIS)
MOD	Ministry of Defence
MOI	Ministry of Information
NATO	North Atlantic Treaty Organisation
OAS	Organisation of American States
OAU	Organisation of African Unity
OECD	Organisation for Economic Cooperation and Development
OEEC	Organisation for European Economic Cooperation
OPD	Overseas Policy and Defence Committee
OPEC	Organisation of Petroleum Exporting Countries
PUSC	Permanent Under-Secretary's Committee
PWE	Political Warfare Executive
RAF	Royal Air Force
SIS	Secret Intelligence Service (MI6)
SOE	Special Operations Executive
UDC	Union of Democratic Control
UKUSA	Anglo-American agreements on intelligence cooperation
UN	United Nations
UNESCO	UN Educational, Scientific and Cultural Organisation
UNICEF	UN International Children's Emergency Fund
US	United States
USSR	Union of Soviet Socialist Republics (Soviet Union)

General editor's preface

Great Powers stand at the centre of modern international relations. The history of their inter-relationships once rested entirely on the formal record of diplomacy, and focused exclusively on the statesmen, diplomats and ambassadors who shaped and conducted foreign policy. Today, international historians, while still acknowledging the importance of diplomacy, cast their nets more widely. Power rests on many foundations, both tangible and intangible. National wealth is one ingredient of power, but so are ideology and national politics. Personalities have their influence on policies, so that there must always be a place for the individual in the history of international relations; but so, too, do the collective institutional forces of modern state bureaucracies, the military and naval establishments, big business and industry. Together, in varying combinations at different times, these forces and factors find their expression in external policy.

The policies of Great Powers are shaped by their unique amalgams of internal ingredients; but they also have to act and react in a particular but changing international environment. Their choices of policy are affected by the shifting balance between them, and by contingent events: wars and revolutions sometimes offer them opportunities but at other times represent set-backs to a preferred course. The aim of this series is therefore to present the histories of the Great Powers in the twentieth century from these two broad perspectives and to show how individual powers, trying to achieve their own priorities in the regional and global arenas of world politics, have sought to balance the actions and reactions of their rivals against the imperatives of domestic policies.

Recently, much of the history of the Great Powers has been written in terms of 'rise' and 'decline'. Firmly embedded within that paradigm, Great Britain's progress through the twentieth century has been seen by many as a classic case of decline, as her grasp outran her means. Faced first with industrial challenges from Germany and America, and then from Europe and the Far East, the British economy appeared initially to have been overhauled by others, and then to have collapsed into long-term under-performance. The military demands of two world wars – and particularly Britain's apparent subordination to the United States after 1945 as a consequence of her indebtedness to her ally – seem both to emphasise the gap between means and goals, and to provide an important part of the explanation for her sedate decline into the ranks of the second-rate powers. By the same token, dethronement from her empire both signalled and contributed to Britain's fall from the pinnacle of supremacy which she had occupied at the end of the nineteenth century.

In his contribution to this series, John Young challenges the assumption that, for Britain, the twentieth century saw a gradual but inexorable decline from grandeur. Moving from the machinery of government through economic considerations to broader issues of national politics, he presents a picture of change and adaptation in which Great Britain not only managed successfully to adjust to altering realities, but also helped to shape the new international environment in which she had to live. The process by which imperial retreat was accomplished without a descent into wars of decolonisation, as Empire gave way to Commonwealth, adds force to the argument that change, and not decline, is the more appropriate perspective through which to view Britain's passage across this century. With 1 per cent of the world's population and accounting for 5 per cent of world trade, Britain may not be the power that she was in Victorian times but, as John Young shows, she remains both a wealthy and an influential member of the international community of states.

John Gooch
May 1997

Acknowledgements

I am particularly grateful to Professor John Gooch for inviting me to contribute to the series on 'International Relations and the Great Powers', and to Christopher Wheeler and his staff at Arnold for seeing the project through to fruition. This study makes no pretence to being a work of original research. It draws on the author's work in British, American and French archives and on published volumes of documents, but relies heavily on books and articles written by others, only some of which are referred to in the brief footnotes and the bibliographical essay. Numerous friends, colleagues and students have discussed British foreign policy with me over the years, and I gleaned much useful information on the contemporary position from participation in a Chatham House Study Group on the Future of British Foreign Policy in 1995–96. I have been fortunate to work in two university departments dedicated to the study of international history, at Leeds and the London School of Economics. I would particularly like to thank Roy Bridge, David Dilks, Ed Spiers, Phil Taylor, Geoff Waddington and Keith Wilson from the former, and John Kent, Kate Morris, Alan Sked, David Stevenson and Donald Watt from the latter, as well as Richard Aldrich, Christopher Andrew, Ann Deighton, Mike and Saki Dockrill, Robert Frazier, Lawrence Freedman, Erik Goldstein, Mike Hopkins, Evanthis Hatzivassiliou, Scott Lucas, Callum MacDonald, Effie Pedaliu, Gillian Staerck, Glyn Stone and Geoffrey Warner. At my current university, Leicester, I am also fortunate to work with a small group of international historians, including Stuart Ball, Geoff Berridge, Jan Melissen and Wyn Rees, as well as a number of people interested in European cooperation including Alasdair Blair, Christopher Goldsmith, Phil Lynch and Joerg Monar. I would also like to thank: my deputy, Bob Borthwick, for bearing so many administrative burdens which have helped me write this book whilst acting as Head of Department; my typist, Janet Smith, who has now completed six typescripts for me with care and enthusiasm; and last but not least, my wife Brigette, who has coped bravely with proof-reading, pursuing her own career and new motherhood.

John Young
Loughborough
March 1997

Introduction

The intention of this book is to provide an up-to-date, readable and short introductory text for those studying twentieth-century British external policy, interpreted in a wide sense. Though organised into chapters on the basis of chronological periods, and whilst giving a description of such major events as the outbreak of war in 1914, the Munich conference and Falklands War, the book aims to be analytical in content. It provides a broad outline of the general course of British external policy and major diplomatic initiatives such as the making of the *ententes* before 1914, the policy of appeasement in the 1930s and the creation of the Atlantic alliance after 1945. But it also looks at a wide range of influences which lay behind the country's international behaviour, helped to shape British policy and restricted the country's independence. In particular attention is paid to the following factors, all of which changed over time. First, the formal organisation and informal influences upon the foreign policy making machine in Whitehall, particularly the Foreign Office (its recruitment, organisation and leadership), but also other relevant ministries (such as the Treasury, Board of Trade, the Colonial Office, the Bank of England, intelligence services and defence ministries), as well as the position of the Cabinet, ambassadors, key civil servants and individual ministers – not least the Foreign Secretary and his relationship with the Prime Minister. The 'official mind' and 'bureaucratic politics' of London could do much to shape policy abroad. The second factor is the impact of other elements within Britain, including the City of London, industrialists, parliament, the political parties, pressure groups, academics, the Press and public opinion, and the ability of the government to manipulate these through, for example, the increasing sophistication of propaganda. Background factors such as social attitudes and values will also be examined, especially the desire to preserve liberal democracy, individual rights, economic wealth and external prestige, as well as the pragmatism of British people and leaders, and their ability to operate an 'unwritten' constitution. Such attitudes were not without their contradictions:

democratic control of external policy was always challenged by elitist attitudes in Whitehall; liberal and humanitarian beliefs did not prevent the use of coercion in the Empire; and a supposed non-ideological approach to world affairs was tempered after 1917 by a strong aversion to Communism. Economic, commercial and financial considerations are a third factor, including the creation and demise of Imperial trade preferences, the position of Sterling, the drain on resources caused by the world wars, and the need to apportion resources between international commitments and such domestic needs as health, education and social security. Fourth come strategic factors, such as the island position of the country, the existence of global interests (through the Empire, Dominions and wide commercial and financial interests), the defence of the Channel coast and north-west Europe, and the need for alliances to protect Britain's position. Fifth, technological changes such as the development of dreadnoughts, aircraft and the atomic bomb, and the impact of these on military thinking, will be examined, as well as the increasing sophistication of communications, intelligence-gathering and psychological warfare techniques. A sixth important factor is the development of an 'interdependent world' with global economic structures, international law, the growth of international organisations and, of course, European institutions. It will be seen that Britain felt itself to be very much part of a global economy even in the 1890s: 'interdependence' is far from a recent phenomenon. But over time, especially after 1945, interdependence grew, the British became less able to shape the international environment and more dependent on cooperation with others. The rise of new powers (the US, Japan, China) and of third world states, with the associated change in Europe's position through decolonisation, is another important theme not least because, as has so often been said, Britain's decline was relative not absolute: in 1990 it possessed greater wealth and military power than in 1890, yet relatively speaking had fallen well behind America on both indices and was economically outclassed by Japan, Germany and France. The management of alliances and friendships (the *ententes*, NATO, the Commonwealth) and the response to clear external threats (Germany, Italy and Japan in the 1930s, or Russia – an ideological as well as security menace – at certain points) are other obvious subjects. It will be seen that the challenges from Germany and Russia actually lasted across the century whether they were ally or enemy and that the most persistent and successful challenge to British power came not from declared enemies but from an ally, the United States.

The book therefore goes well beyond narrowly focused 'diplomatic' history and deals with a wide range of 'new' areas opened up by international historians in recent decades (propaganda, intelligence and bureaucratic politics), although sight is not lost of more traditional approaches (defence planning, imperial considerations and diplomatic negotiation). All these factors are blended together in the account. Overarching topics, inevitably, are the (relative) decline of Britain, the end of Empire and the shift in status from a world power to membership of the European Union. The amount of material available on British foreign policy in the twentieth century, from documentary sources and published works, is huge and ever-increasing. In Britain itself public records are now open into the late 1960s. Some areas, especially the appeasement period and the origins of the Cold War, are literally awash with books and articles and it has only been possible to touch on the debates among historians in a very general way. But there is an attempt here to contribute to the debate on British foreign policy and decline in the twentieth century, already familiar from the works of Paul Kennedy, Bernard Porter, Robert Holland, David Reynolds and others. In particular the point is made that the impact of relative decline on British policy should not be traced back too far and that economic factors must not be treated in isolation from other forms of power, such as national prestige, financial strength and the possession of a global network of naval bases.

Before looking at British external policy towards the end of the Victorian era, some points of general background about the country's international position are in order. Exploiting its geographical situation on the edge of Europe, Britain had taken full advantage of the general rise of European fortunes after 1500, when Western European states in particular outmatched the rest of the world in technology, weaponry and social organisation. The country proved more open than most to free enterprise, was more socially cohesive and politically stable than the rest of Europe after 1660, and it developed an effective system of taxation and national debt. Financiers and merchants found it possible to win wealth, social respect and political influence, alongside the old landed aristocracy in the eighteenth century, and encouraged the country's expansion overseas. By 1815 Britain had lost one Empire, in North America, but (alongside Austria, Prussia and, most importantly, Russia) helped defeat Bonaparte's bid for European domination, had won control of India and was the world's first industrial power, making good use of its limited but valuable natural resources of iron and coal. By 1890 Britain formally controlled a quarter of the globe, was the world's largest seapower, handled about a third of manufacturing trade and had huge financial wealth. Britain, like other European powers, possessed Imperial power not only in the form of colonies but also through 'informal' economic exploitation of countries like China. Its island position had long kept it safe from invasion, it maintained its industrial lead (although other powers were beginning to catch up) and the City of London provided the world with credit, insurance and shipping services which other countries were, as yet, incapable of providing for themselves. Despite industrialisation, rapid population growth and profound social changes, Britain generally maintained its stability. Under a conservative but adaptable 'gentlemanly' elite of aristocrats and financiers (extended in the Victorian Age to industrialists and professional groups), Britain slowly developed a liberal, democratic political system whilst preserving respect for traditional privileges, property, personal wealth and the rule of law. National unity, patriotism and public service won more adherents than ideologies, class division and (except in Ireland) regional identities, although the development of such liberal beliefs as rational reform, free trade and national self-determination did alter the outlook of many Britons. Where world affairs were concerned the British were as flexible, pragmatic and non-ideological as they were at home. With such wide-ranging interests and possessions, they sought to preserve their freedom of manoeuvre abroad and were reluctant to enter alliances. Yet they did have a tendency, like most peoples, to believe that the world would be a better place if others behaved like them: in particular free trade, peace and non-intervention in the problems of others were seen as universally beneficial, but actually were rooted in self-interest. There were also certain traditional concerns of foreign policy which governments, not always consistently, maintained: the control of the seas (or at least those most vital for Imperial security), home defence and British trade, demanded a substantial navy, a system of naval bases and the control of such strategic points as Gibraltar, the Suez Canal and Singapore; the defence of India required a large, mainly native army; keeping the Low Countries free from control by another Great Power was seen as essential because of the danger of Belgium and the Netherlands being used as platforms for the invasion of Britain; and there was a long-standing tradition of preserving the so-called 'balance of power' in Europe to prevent any single, aggressive rival from dominating the continent and threatening Britain, as Bonaparte had done. A related fear, seen around 1900 and again, arguably, in the post-1957 European Community, was that a group of continental states might voluntarily unite against Britain. Policy-makers in London, then, had to consider both the European *and* global situations, and fully-fledged 'isolationism', in the sense of a withdrawal from the world, was impossible. In the eighteenth century the struggle with France had involved Britain in a series of costly wars in Europe, India and North America. In the nineteenth century wars were generally avoided and the country had no large land army outside India. But there were considerable differences over which policies to pursue. Whereas a Gladstone might champion caution, negotiation rather than conflict, and cooperation with a 'concert' of European powers, a Disraeli might prefer a patriotic, even jingoistic line and a readiness to fight beyond Europe, in expanding the Empire. Even at the height of Victorian power it was clear that the country, for all its strengths, faced many dangers in the world. Its population was only half that of America's; scientific advancement brought ever-more expensive technological developments; after 1880 new naval and industrial competitors were emerging and large continental states like America and Russia were able to use the swifter communications brought by railways to mobilise their natural resources; the Empire was scattered and might conceivably be threatened by rising local powers beyond Europe, such as Japan; internal unrest might also make the Empire costly to control; and Britain's own need to import food and raw materials made it particularly vulnerable to disorder in the world. However, these challenges had not led to excessive self-doubt, a search for allies or serious suggestions that Britain's *laissez-faire* outlook needed to be changed.

1
Empire and isolation, 1895–1905

The Imperial dilemma

The 1890s have often been seen as a pivotal point for British foreign policy. For eight decades already Britain had played the pre-eminent role in world affairs, underpinned by enormous financial wealth, a front place in the first industrial revolution and, after Trafalgar in 1805, unchallenged naval power. In the mid-nineteenth century Britain seemed distinct from Europe, not only because of its island position, but also because of its domination of global trade, its urbanised, industrial society and its liberal political tradition. The picture was not as untainted as many Britons assumed. They faced little domestic instability, but the lives of much of the population, in the industrial towns or in Ireland, were not happy; in contrast to Russia, Austria and France, there was no secret police but, despite religious and political toleration, the country was far from achieving universal suffrage even for males; and, whatever the rising power of businessmen, the professions and other middle-class groups, considerable power still resided in the hands of a privileged elite of aristocrats and financiers. Neither, on certain indices of power, did Britain count for much: the United States and Russia had far larger populations, and most major European powers had bigger land armies. Britain did not develop such a force because home and Imperial defence self-evidently relied on a strong navy. Abroad even in the 1850s, the country's military limitations were exposed in the Crimean War, and the Indian Mutiny was a serious challenge to Britain's hold on the Empire. The celebrated *Pax Britannica* never actually did bring complete peace to the globe. Nonetheless, Britain stood, in commercial, financial and naval terms, well ahead of its rivals and British leaders easily assumed that if only other states would marry together free trade capitalism and liberal politics, the world would find that such a system guaranteed wealth and, equally important, peace: for the British were only too aware that, despite a frequent need to fight brief colonial campaigns against native peoples, the stability and profitability of their own trade and investments were inextricably bound up with peace. In retrospect, some economic historians consider Britain's *relative* decline, compared to leading competitors like America (which overtook Britain as an industrial power in the 1890s) and Germany, to have begun during the 1870s. But this was not obvious at the time and it is important not to read back too far the idea that Britain was slipping behind other powers. True, industry and trade were troubled by the falling profits and prices of the Great Depression (which lasted for about two decades after 1873) and the 1880s witnessed the violence both of Fenianism in Ireland and strikes in industry. But there were similar problems elsewhere in Europe and the government lacked the necessary statistics to make sophisticated comparisons with major competitors. Right down to 1914 British industry continued to grow, based on textiles, coal and steel, as did financial wealth and such services as shipping and insurance, whilst trade and investment were directed less towards the Empire (though India, as ever, was vital) than towards America, Latin America and China. It can even be argued that the growth of *industrial* competitors was beneficial for British *financial* interests, because the rising manufacturing wealth of other countries helped them pay their debts to the City of London. British industrial leaders did not perhaps innovate, or expand rapidly into such new areas as chemicals and electrics, but this was partly because profits *were* so high. The merchant navy was as large as the rest of the world put together and by 1914 Britain's overseas investments were worth almost £4 billion. The finance houses of the City stood at the centre of a global system of investments and payments, Britain was the world's greatest creditor nation and the Pound Sterling was the world's major currency. There was persistent concern about Britain's ability to pay both for social reform at home and for the defence of the Empire abroad, yet tax levels were lower at the end of the nineteenth century than they had been at the start, during the Napoleonic Wars, and the twentieth century would demonstrate that it was possible to devote a much, much larger percentage of national wealth to social and defence programmes.

The 1890s saw doubts not so much about Britain's current pre-eminence as about the ways to ensure a leading role through the next century. Queen Victoria's Diamond Jubilee in 1897 marked the high point of national faith in an Empire which, covering a quarter of the globe and with over 400 million people (over half of them in India), was the largest ever seen and the essential source of Britain's greatness. It was the Empire which gave Britain, itself populated by only 42 million people, superiority in numbers over the combined Empires of Russia (130 million) and France (100 million), who were then seen as the most potent, likely threat to British security. It provided a focus for national pride, even a focus for national unity among the English, Scots, Welsh and Irish. The formal building of the Empire was driven by commercial, financial and strategic demands, though historians vigorously debate which was most vital and the precise reasons for annexation differed from possession to possession. It was a source of raw materials and, especially in India's case, troops. It was also an outlet for settlement, trade and investment. Yet for all this it was not simply viewed by its creators as an exploitative enterprise. Missionary societies, rather than seekers after earthly glory, had often provided the spearhead of expansion and Victorians liked to see the Empire as part of a religious and 'civilising' mission, albeit by a racially superior people, in which the ideal of service (in the army, church or bureaucracy) played a vital role. Even in 1897, one of the Empire's greatest literary figures, Rudyard Kipling, could hint at doubts about how long it might survive: 'Lo all our pomp of yester-day, Is one with Nineveh and Tyre!' But most Britons showed no outward trace of such pessimism even if there was a sense of defensive-ness and vulnerability in the very act of securing *formal* control over such a vast area. In mid-century, where possible, the British had preferred to exploit global trade through an *informal* system, where the activities of merchants were unimpeded by the territorial claims of other Great Powers. Formal control had been extended to certain areas by 1815, either to keep out competitors (as with the French in India and Canada) or to secure strategic points on shipping routes (such as Malta and Cape Colony). However, such formal control had its costs, demanding gover-nors, civil servants and military garrisons. This was true even though the British tried to run their possessions 'on the cheap', ruling indirectly via local elites, either through traditional channels of chiefs and princes, or through newly educated groups who staffed the lower levels of the civil service. In order to minimise discontent, a policy of 'divide and rule' was practised, local religious and social customs were preserved and major reforms were avoided. There was little attempt to tackle 'normal' levels of poverty, though assistance was given when famine and natural disas-ter caused particular distress; and by providing order, investment and trade the Empire did provide an important element of *mutual* gain for its members. Whilst education was improved and railways built, and whilst the Colonial Office tried to limit the exploitation of colonial peoples by British businessmen, there was no sophisticated policy of 'development' until the twentieth century. This low-cost system of rule helped to minimise taxes on British people and – backed by pro-Imperial propa-ganda, the sense of awe which surrounded British rule, and the ultimate sanction of military force – kept the Empire in reasonable internal order. Thus India, for all its vast population, required less than 1500 British officials to govern it, and in peacetime before 1914 the total size of military forces in the colonies only reached about 320 000 (mostly in India, which had a British garrison of 70 000 and a native army of twice that number).

The Empire was a scattered and ramshackle affair with many different forms of government, including crown colonies, protectorates and self-governing entities. India, a third of which was ruled by local princedoms, was itself a hotch-potch of languages, religions and peoples; elsewhere in East Asia, Britain ruled over Burma, the Malay states and the wealthy Chinese trading outlet of Hong Kong; in the Caribbean, the West Indies sugar islands had long since lost their profitability but their Afro-Caribbean population was not viewed as ready for self-government; in the Middle East, Britain's hold on Egypt relied on a military presence rather than a firm legal base; the settlement colonies of Canada, Cape Colony, Australia and New Zealand had been given a large degree of independence in domestic affairs but remained loyal to the Crown, partly because most of their population (except in Quebec and the Cape) was of recent British stock. White settlers in these 'Dominions', as they became known, had some of the highest living standards in the world and could rely on London to provide for their defence, a beneficial position which provoked increasing complaint from some in Britain. It led the Colonial Secretary, Joseph Chamberlain, to ask colonial leaders, at the Fourth Colonial Conference in August 1902, to provide greater financial assistance to 'the Weary Titan', especially to pay for the Royal Navy. By then the world had reached the end of the 20-year bout of expansion known as the 'New Imperialism', the most important aspect of which was the 'Scramble for Africa', in which the British had extended formal control to much of East Africa and the wealthier, more densely populated areas of West Africa, such as the Gold Coast (later called Ghana) and Nigeria. Latin America, China and the Ottoman Empire continued to be exploited by 'informal' means, with British power in some parts of China verging on sovereign control. Egypt, with control of the Suez Canal, became an essential linchpin of Imperial security but, even together, the rest of the African colonies did not provide more than a few per cent of British trade and investment before 1914. They had been hastily seized, partly it seems as a pre-emptive measure against other European states, partly because of foreign commercial competition and protectionism, partly in the vain hope of achieving a position of complete security.

Ministers and officials in London, concerned by the costs of Empire, by the need for good relations with other European states and the desire to preserve peace and stability (rather than profits), were often reluctant to extend formal control. However, their hand could be forced by their own local representatives, both political and military (the so-called 'men on the spot'), and formal Imperialism was goaded by commercial interests, by patriotic public opinion and by issues of prestige. Changes on the so-called 'periphery' (lands bordering the existing Empire) could also encourage expansion: tribal wars or dynastic instability might lead traders, for example, to demand that the British military enforce order. At the end of the Scramble, Britain had demonstrated its capability of offensive action and kept its lead over its competitors, grabbing more of Africa than anyone else. True, even this could be seen as a retreat, for where British businesses had in the past been able to exploit most of the world as a source of profit, now they concentrated attention on certain parts of the globe. The threat to Britain's belief in *laissez-faire* methods was further emphasised by the growth, in Europe during the Great Depression, of tariff barriers and what the British considered 'unfair' restrictive commercial practices. In response, British traders and investors themselves demanded that *laissez-faire* policies give way to government intervention to protect their interests and guarantee 'fair trade'. Feelings of vulnerability led Imperialists, in both the Conservative and Liberal parties, to consider diverse ideas to bind the Empire together and compete with such large, continental states as America and Russia. The idea of federation as a way to unite and strengthen individual colonies had already been seen in the formation of a Canadian government in 1867 (designed in part to counter the power of the archetypal federal country, the US); it was seen again with the formation of Australia in 1901. However, from the 1870s onwards the idea also grew, in intellectual and political circles, of a complete, Empire-wide federation. This was seen in books such as J.R. Selley's *The Expansion of England* (1884) and in pressure groups like the Imperial Federation Committee (1894). A more practical form of consolidation was the inauguration of government-level conferences between Britain and the settlement colonies, such as that which saw Chamberlain's 'Weary Titan' appeal. Nonetheless, whatever the signs of defensiveness and doubt in British policy, decline and fear can hardly be said to have dominated the nation's mind, and the country's leaders proved capable of determination, resilience and innovation in maintaining their leading position.

Salisbury and 'splendid isolation'

At the end of Victoria's reign, *laissez-faire* was giving way to formal Imperialism abroad and to revivified paternalism, welfare reform and state intervention at home. Rather than ensuring peace and stability, increased commercial competition between states had led to territorial expansion and the danger of conflict. Other powers were jealous of London's position and unwilling to acquiesce in a British-dominated system of world trade, even if the British argued that this brought universal benefits. These powers too were all expanding their navies, forcing Britain in 1889 to adopt a 'two-power standard': where previously the Royal Navy had more battleships than all other countries put together, now it would seek to match the next two largest navies. America, Japan, Italy and Germany were all building ships, as were much older opponents, France and Russia. There was no sign that the situation was about to ease. New 'scrambles' seemed possible in the Ottoman Empire and China. And new power centres had evolved beyond Europe: Japan, by defeating China in 1894–95, had emerged as a major force in the Far East and the US was becoming more assertive across the Atlantic. Meanwhile in Europe itself, the Great Powers had divided into two alliance blocs: Germany and Austria–Hungary had aligned themselves in 1879, soon to be joined by Italy in a 'Triple Alliance'; whilst in 1894 the Franco-Russian alliance was formed. Both blocs included states who were building up large conscript armies at a time when the British Army remained a small, professional force, geared to colonial service. Britain had the world's largest navy, possessed naval bases at strategic points around the globe and could therefore defend the homeland, shipping routes (which carried much of Britain's food) and most Imperial possessions. But militarily the country was puny, incapable of fighting a land war in Europe or even of meeting the Russian Army if it should invade India from Central Asia – a permanent nightmare for the British, given India's wealth. The threat grew from the 1870s onwards as Russian power expanded in the region and competition began for influence in the 'buffer' zone, comprising Persia, Tibet and Afghanistan. States face new challenges all the time and there was no direct threat to Britain's predominant position in the 1890s. The changes at the end of the Victorian era should be seen, not necessarily as the harbingers of decline, but as forcing British leaders to readjust their policies, once more, to new realities. But, when compounded, developments on the global and European levels certainly served to emphasise London's own comparative isolation. The term 'isolation' was extensively used by ministers, MPs and officials between 1895 and 1902, but was never defined in any government document and its meaning has been the subject of great debate. It can be dismissed as an overused cliché, too vague to be of any use in historical analysis. For certain commentators at the time it represented a dangerous situation of friendlessness in the world, but for others, less fearful about Britain's position, it was a welcome phenomenon. The term 'splendid isolation' was first used in the Canadian parliament in January 1896 and was soon adopted by Joseph Chamberlain. He emphasised the continuing power of the Royal Navy and the strength of the Empire as sources of British might, and spoke in 1902 of being 'alone ... in a splendid isolation surrounded by our kinsfolk'. Significantly, however, Chamberlain was also the minister most interested in a German alliance: for him Imperial consolidation and a policy of alliance in Europe were *complementary* ways to ensure British security. Another minister, George Goschen, the First Lord of the Admiralty, saw isolation as providing 'the freedom to act as we choose in any circumstances that may arise',[1] conveniently forgetting that the Empire itself gravely restricted British freedom and that on paper (and contrary to popular assumption) Britain had a series of commitments to foreign powers, ranging from an alliance with Portugal made in 1373 to, most recently, an 1878 defensive guarantee of the Ottoman Empire's Asian possessions. There was also a guarantee of Belgian territorial integrity made jointly with other powers in 1839, which reflected Britain's main strategic interest in Europe: the denial of the Low Countries to a potential invader. Some historians see isolation as the continuation of a well-established British policy of distancing itself from other powers whilst trying to maintain good relations with all; it was simply that, in the 1890s, the creation of alliances by the continental powers made observers see Britain's position as something new. Had Lord Palmerston not said that Britain had no eternal friends or enemies, only interests? Others see isolation as a result of the demise of the mid-century ideal of loose, general cooperation between all the Great Powers, the 'Concert of Europe', in which Britain *had* been ready to play a part. Some see it as meaning the avoidance of any peacetime alliance – and hence believe that isolation ended with the 1902 Anglo-Japanese treaty – but others see it as representing 'aloofness from the European balance of power'[2] and may date it to the Anglo-French *entente* of 1904.

The figure who was most often, mistakenly, identified with 'splendid isolation' was the Conservative Prime Minister and Foreign Secretary, Lord Salisbury. He actually used the term very rarely and it is clear that he *was* ready to work with other powers. True, he did argue that it was constitutionally impossible for Britain to commit itself in an alliance to go to war. He insisted that parliament and fickle public opinion would decide whether Britain would fight, depending on the situation at the time. However, this may have been a device to forestall an alliance with Germany and it did not prevent him from accepting a similar arrangement with Japan at the end of his premiership. Salisbury was increasingly criticised by members of his own party as slow to make decisions, a leader whose lack of vision left the country vulnerable to foreign pressure when a policy of alliances had become more appropriate. He was certainly cautious and, whilst maintaining Benjamin Disraeli's policy of portraying Conservatives as the patriotic party, was much less belligerent and jingoistic than either Disraeli or Palmerston. With a remarkable overall grasp of foreign issues, and a detached, analytical mind, Salisbury recognised the need to balance Britain's aims in the world against its lack of a large land army and the existence of strong rivals. However, just as he was suspicious about the shift to democracy at home, so he refused to panic over the scale of the challenges which colleagues like Chamberlain claimed to see abroad. Salisbury recognised, for example, that Britain remained well ahead of other powers in naval and financial power, and that it was unlikely that other Great Powers would combine in a consistent anti-British policy. After all, the Triple Alliance and Franco-Russian alliance were divided against each other by long-standing rivalries, particularly Austro-Russian competition in the Balkans and French resentment over the loss in 1871 of Alsace-Lorraine to Germany. If Britain took sides in such disputes it might actually increase the dangers of a war which would damage trade and create a new, even more threatening environment. Yet, whilst preferring a 'free hand' to a policy of entanglements, Salisbury was no simple isolationist. An exponent of secret diplomacy and *realpolitik* and possessing a remarkable sense of timing, Salisbury had already shown, as premier between 1886 and 1892, that he was capable of an active policy to protect British interests and soften antagonisms. Concerned over the potential Russian threat to the Ottoman Empire and to India, and recognising that cooperation with France was impossible (because of the rage in Paris over Britain's 1882 occupation of Egypt), he had aligned himself at that time more with the Triple Alliance. He made the so-called Mediterranean Agreements with Austria and Italy in 1887, to maintain the status quo in the region, and exchanged territory with Germany in the Zanzibar-Heligoland Treaty of 1890. Both, however, were limited agreements, carrying little danger of conflict.

The policy-making machine which Salisbury directed gave him personal control not only over the general outline of policy but also much of its day-to-day execution. In 1895, just as there were no alliances with other Great Powers to tie the Foreign Secretary's hands, so there were no strong international organisations to restrict British actions. Such organisations as existed were for practical purposes (like the International Postal Union) or had a humanitarian role (like the Red Cross). The first Hague Conference on international disarmament, in 1899, led to agreements on the peaceful resolution of disputes, voluntary arbitration and rules of warfare, but nothing which really restricted states' behaviour. There had been *ad hoc* conferences of several Great Powers in the recent past, most notably the Congress of Berlin in 1878, but apart from Britain's own Imperial conferences 'multilateral diplomacy' was a pale shadow of what it became after 1945. At home, Salisbury could depend on Conservative Party discipline and his own reputation as a 'safe', trustworthy leader to minimise disputes over foreign policy in parliament. So-called 'blue books' of diplomatic documents were published to keep parliament informed on the foreign policy front. The fact that, especially after 1880, these usually included only inoffensive, uninformative documents, and that most serious diplomacy was carried out in secret, was of little concern to most MPs. There was virtual national unanimity on the need for a strong navy, and one of the few pressure groups which existed in the sphere of security policy was the Navy League, formed in 1894. Like all pressure groups it used pamphlets, public speakers and links to the Press and individual MPs to argue its case that British naval pre-eminence must be maintained to defend the Empire, its trade and communications. In contrast, a pressure group in favour of a conscript army was not formed until the new century. Significantly, old-style progressive, humanitarian pressure groups in the international area (such as worked for the abolition of slavery) had faded by the 1890s and new groups were concerned with the defence of chauvinistic interests. Public opinion as a whole, though often cited by British leaders as an impediment to action, was difficult to measure, diverse and not very sophisticated: many people did not have the vote; there were no opinion polls; those who supported patriotic bodies like the Navy League seem to have been matched by supporters of Liberal radicalism, socialism and Irish nationalism who questioned the Empire, militarism and power politics; and when there was a 'popular outcry', as over the Armenian Massacres of 1895 or war with Russia ten years later (both discussed below), the understanding of 'national interest' was extremely simple-minded. Public opinion could only crudely be measured through a mixture of mass demonstrations, by-election results, pressure group campaigns and the views of the Press. The last group too was very diverse, though changing in its make-up in the 1890s. Influential 'quality' newspapers, like the *Manchester Guardian* (the prime example of a provincial, liberal newspaper) or *The Times* (sometimes mistakenly seen as a reflection of 'official' opinion), faced competition after 1896 from a new, cheaper, national, London-based and generally pro-Conservative Press, spearheaded by the *Daily Mail* of Alfred Harmsworth (later Lord Northcliffe). This, followed by the *Daily Express* in 1900, found a mass readership among the patriotic and increasingly literate lower middle classes.

One influence on policy which was certainly waning was that of the monarch. The Crown had long since handed its power over war and peace, treaties and territorial exchanges to ministers meeting in Cabinet. Queen Victoria insisted on being consulted about external policy, provided sensible advice on many issues and, through her dynastic relationships, carried some weight in foreign capitals. But she reinforced, rather than contested, government policy. Her son, who became Edward VII in 1901, known as the 'Uncle of Europe', was the last monarch to show an active interest in policy-making but his actual impact was minimal. Within government, the Cabinet had general oversight over policy and could challenge the Foreign Secretary, but it discussed overseas issues infrequently, its members were usually not expert in the field and it lacked a strong specialist committee on the subject. Below Cabinet level the policy-making machine in the Imperial, foreign and security fields was potentially complex. Depending on the issue under discussion, departments which might have an influence included the Foreign Office, War Office (army), Admiralty (navy), Treasury (where expenditure and taxes were concerned), Board of Trade (for international commerce), Colonial Office, India Office, as well as the Viceroy of India, other colonial governors and, increasingly, certain colonial governments. The poor coordination of this policy machine was not unusual: in Paris too there was a struggle for influence between colonial, military and foreign services; in Germany before 1914 the army, navy and Foreign Office frequently pursued contradictory policies. However, in the Foreign Office all high-level policy decisions were still taken by the Foreign Secretary who was invariably (until 1905) an aristocrat. Even senior officials like the Permanent Under-Secretary, Thomas Sanderson, were used virtually as clerical staff, though towards 1900, as the volume of work steadily increased, they were allowed more initiative and could express views, at least on lower-level political matters, to Salisbury, who was never one to involve himself in details. He could trust officials to follow the lines of policy he set out, even though he sometimes only worked in the Office for one afternoon each week. The Foreign Office staff (numbering only 132 officials in 1914) was still separate from the diplomatic service (54 officials in 1914) who worked overseas. Ambassadors, as 'men on the spot', carried on a private correspondence with the Foreign Secretary about matters affecting their particular country and *could* have an influence on policy through the decisions they took. Separate too were the commercial and consular services who were viewed very much as second-class bodies by the Office. The structure of the Office only slowly grew in sophistication: until the late 1890s there was only one department to deal with the whole of North and South America and East Asia. Although officials sometimes worked in line with businesses and banks to secure foreign trade concessions against foreign competitors (in China for example), the Office was determined not to be drawn into disputes by commercial and industrial interests and, under the 1886 Bryce Memorandum, ruled out involvement in private business matters. International economics was to be left to the untrammelled workings of free trade and leading officials felt commercial matters to be rather sordid. The Office was criticised by Liberal radicals as secretive and socially exclusive and its officials certainly led a leisurely life-style, not even starting work until 11.00 a.m. Even in the 1890s some still worked with quills and ink, although the first typist arrived in 1889 and the first telephone nine years after that. In pursuing what they interpreted as the national interest, Foreign Office officials tried as best they could not only to ignore pressures from the business community, but also the public, Press and even parliament. Successful diplomacy was held to rely on discretion and secrecy among its initiates, whilst public scrutiny and open debate might damage national interests.

Global crises and the Boer War

When the Conservatives returned to power in June 1895 they succeeded a Liberal administration which had been torn apart by Imperial and defence issues. The veteran leader, Gladstone, resigned in 1894 over the high levels of naval spending demanded to match the Franco-Russian threat in the Mediterranean. Radical followers of Gladstone had criticised British embroilment in Uganda, but Gladstone himself groomed the Imperialist Lord Rosebery to succeed him and Rosebery, in a short and ill-starred premiership, duly annexed the East African colony. Soon after retiring, however, Gladstone re-emerged as a moralising force in foreign policy by criticising the vicious persecution which the Ottoman Sultan, Abdul Hamid II, launched against his Empire's Armenian minority in 1894–96. For decades a prime aim of British foreign policy had been to prevent the Ottoman Empire from disintegrating. In particular London did not wish to see an extension of Russian power through the Straits at Constantinople, which guarded the route from the Black Sea to the Mediterranean. The Crimean War had been fought by Britain and France to prevent such a development. But all attempts to encourage reform in Turkey had failed and the Armenian Massacres now alienated British public opinion totally from the Sultan. Even the unflappable Salisbury feared that the Ottoman Empire might soon come to an end. Despite strenuous efforts, he could not persuade the other Great Powers to cooperate in forcing a liberal reform programme on the Turks. Furthermore, with France (and its Mediterranean fleet) now Russia's ally, the Royal Navy admitted that it could not prevent the Russians seizing the Straits. Worse still, there were doubts about Britain's ability to match the French and Russians in a wider war which might potentially spread to Africa and India. Russia could no longer be deterred by the threat of a local war on its periphery (such as the Crimean War), for the Royal Navy would find it impossible to penetrate the Black Sea or the Baltic. In November 1895 several Cabinet ministers refused to support Salisbury when he advocated a tougher line against Russia and the following year the Prime Minister himself told the Tsar that Britain would not alone oppose a Russian occupation of Constantinople, should the Ottoman

Empire break up. In fact the Empire survived for another two decades. But the important point for Britain was that the old policy of maintaining Turkey against Russia had effectively come to an end and London was now less interested in Balkan politics and less influential in Constantinople. The City had been reluctant to invest in the Ottoman Empire since the Ottomans defaulted in their debts in 1875. Furthermore, in 1896 the Mediterranean Agreements were allowed to lapse.

If the Ottoman Empire had broken up in the 1890s, the British were determined to protect their interests in Egypt (still nominally under Ottoman suzerainty), the key to the 'Imperial lifeline' from Britain to India. To the south of Egypt the Nile valley was not yet in British hands. A decade before, General Gordon had been killed at Khartoum by followers of the Mahdi, who ruled over the Sudan. Many Imperialists hoped to avenge the humiliation (which had reminded Victorians that they were not all-powerful) and secure control, not just over the Nile valley, but the whole of eastern Africa, from Suez to the Cape. An advance by General Herbert Kitchener into the Sudan finally proceeded in 1898 and led to complete victory over the Mahdists at Omdurman on 2 September. However, by coincidence, Kitchener's victory came just after a French expedition, under Captain Jean Marchand, reached the Nile at Fashoda. The French, already bitter rivals of Britain for influence in West Africa, had built the Suez Canal in the 1860s, had never accepted Britain's occupation of Egypt and hoped that Marchand's arrival on the Nile might lead to an international conference which would force the British into concessions. Salisbury was equally determined that, whilst he hoped to settle the Fashoda crisis peacefully, he could not put Britain's position in Egypt at risk. The French were bluntly informed that the Sudan had 'passed to the British and Egyptian Governments by right of conquest. Her Majesty's Government do not consider this right is open to discussion'[3] and the diplomatic crisis provided Salisbury with a diplomatic victory as complete as Kitchener's military triumph. Whatever the nationalist outcry in Paris, the French Foreign Minister, Theophile Delcassé, was only too aware of his country's weakness in the confrontation with London: Kitchener's army was far superior to Marchand's force; the Russians were preoccupied with Far Eastern problems and had no desire to back their ally in a dispute in Africa; and if it came to a simple Anglo-French war the Royal Navy had twice as many battleships as the French. On 3 November Delcassé agreed to withdraw. Four months later the two countries signed an agreement which acknowledged British dominance over the whole Nile valley. Bilateral relations between them remained poor for some time but, significantly, there was now no concrete territorial issue over which they need confront each other again. The Fashoda crisis boosted Salisbury's reputation and proved that, whatever doubts some might have about isolation, Britain was still capable of acting successfully on its own. Together with the consolidation of British territory in Nigeria and the Gold Coast, expansion down the Nile seemed to make African policy an area of particular success for the government.

The success at Fashoda was soon offset, however, by events at the other end of Africa, where less restrained individuals than Salisbury influenced British policy. Cape Colony had been won from the Dutch in 1815 but many local Dutch settlers – the Boers – had left to establish two countries of their own further north, the Transvaal and Orange Free State. In the early 1880s Gladstone's government, influenced by the Prime Minister's belief in self-determination, had effectively recognised the independence of the Transvaal after a short struggle, leading the Boers to believe that Britain lacked the will to prosecute a long war against them. Over the following years, however, motives for British intervention in the Boer Republics multiplied. As with Egypt there was a desire to control the region neighbouring Cape Colony for security reasons. In southern Africa there was a danger of European intervention not from France but from Germany which, after 1894, posed as a defender of Boer independence. For some Conservatives, a strong policy in south Africa reinforced their reputation as defenders of the Empire, whilst exposing Liberal divisions. The real dramatic change, however, came after the discovery of gold in the Transvaal in 1886, making it the richest area in Africa and an even more tempting prospect for Imperial expansion. As the town of Johannesburg mushroomed in size, many British settlers, known to the Boers as 'Uitlanders', joined the gold rush. The Boers refused to give them equal political rights for fear of seeing the Transvaal elect a pro-British government. But by denying such rights the Boers created a further reason for British resentment. It was in order to tap the Uitlanders' discontent that, on 29 December 1895, the Prime Minister of Cape Colony, Cecil Rhodes, with the knowledge of Joseph Chamberlain, tried to spark off an uprising in the Transvaal by launching the Jameson Raid. No uprising occurred, however, and Dr L.S. Jameson's men were captured by the Transvaal authorities on 2 January 1896. This underhand episode simply boosted the confidence of the Boers whilst provoking criticism of British Imperialism throughout Europe. The German Kaiser, Wilhelm II, even sent a message of congratulations to the Transvaal leader, Paul Kruger, an action which did more than anything else to highlight British differences with Germany in the 1890s, though it was not necessarily as crudely anti-British as it appeared. In fact the Kaiser probably hoped that if he emphasised Britain's isolation he might be able to draw it into an alliance with Germany against France and Russia, or at least win some colonial concession. By August 1898

Germany was ready to abandon support for the Transvaal in return for a secret British agreement that, should the Portuguese Empire (which was in financial difficulties) collapse, Germany would obtain part of it. The following year, to complete the diplomatic isolation of the Transvaal, the ever-pragmatic British made a treaty with the Portuguese (who controlled nearby Angola and Mozambique) guaranteeing their Empire's integrity! The terms of the agreement did not strictly contradict the earlier treaty with Germany but, taken together, the two moves highlighted British deviousness where southern Africa was concerned.

Meanwhile, in 1897 a new British High Commissioner, Alfred Milner, had arrived in Cape Colony. Rhodes had been forced to resign after the Jameson Raid but Milner, the new 'man on the spot', was his match in pressing a firm, pro-Imperial policy whilst the Colonial Secretary, Chamberlain, also pushed the Boers hard. Chamberlain evidently hoped to settle differences with the Boers without war, but on 9 October 1899, after months of tense, slow negotiations over Uitlander rights, the Transvaal government issued an ultimatum: the British must withdraw their troops from the border and submit points of difference to arbitration. Three days later, the British having failed to reply, *both* Boer Republics declared war. Whatever the problems caused by Milner and Chamberlain, the Cabinet was united in believing that Britain's whole position in south Africa, as well as national prestige, was at stake. Also, although Liberals would have preferred a peaceful settlement, popular opinion seems to have favoured the war. But at the outset the Boers were better prepared for a mobile campaign over a large country than local British forces which, despite the rising tension and warnings from the War Office's Intelligence Department (a small, undervalued group), had only been lightly reinforced. As a result, to the shock of the British people, not only did the Boer armies lay siege to the towns of Kimberley, Ladysmith and Mafeking, they also inflicted three defeats on the British during the so-called 'Black Week' of 9–16 December 1899. General Redvers Buller was made a scapegoat for these setbacks and sacked, to be replaced by two heroes of earlier colonial conflicts, Lord Roberts and Kitchener. In Britain the Yeomanry and Volunteers, intended as forces for home defence, had to be called up for foreign service, and the defence budget leapt in order to create an army of 300 000, about four times the size of those of the Boers. In 1900 the war seemed to progress well: Kimberley and Ladysmith were relieved in February and Mafeking, whose defenders were led by Robert Baden-Powell, in May – an event which led to national jubilation in Britain; Bloemfontein, capital of the Orange Free State, was taken in May, and Pretoria, capital of the Transvaal, the following month; in September Kruger fled into exile and October saw the government successfully exploit the apparent victory in the 'Khaki Election'. There had been considerable criticism of the war from the Liberals' radical wing, as well as from Irish Nationalists and the new Labour Party. These dissenters blamed the conflict on financial and economic interests, elements which were to become the main target of left-wing critics of foreign policy during the twentieth century. This allowed Chamberlain to claim 'a seat gained by the Liberals is a seat lost to the Boers',[4] a crude assertion which overlooked the splits in the Liberal Party and the fact that most merely criticised the government's management of the war, not the struggle itself. In any case the Conservative's election proved short-lived for, rather than coming to terms, the Boers decided to launch a guerrilla war, avoiding the sieges and pitched battles of 1899–1900 (which in retrospect were unwise tactics for them) and concentrating on 'commando' raids. Faced by the novel challenge of a guerrilla war – one which would become more common over the following century – Kitchener adopted ruthless methods, burning farms, destroying crops and enforcing martial law on Dutch settlers in the Cape. Most notoriously he forced Boer civilians into 'concentration camps' where they were unable to aid the commandos. Some 28 000 Boers, mainly children, died in the camps of malnutrition and disease, inducing the Liberal leader, Henry Campbell-Bannerman, to accuse the government of using 'methods of barbarism'. Kitchener's tactics bore fruit on 31 May 1902, however, when in the Treaty of Vereeniging the Boers accepted British rule in return for an amnesty and a promise of local self-government. Over the following years southern Africa was reconstructed with British financial support. A group of enthusiastic young officials, known as the 'Kindergarten', worked under Milner to reform the administration, education and landownership. But government policy continued to attract Liberal criticism, especially with the 'Chinese slavery' episode of 1903–5 when Chinese labourers, working on short contracts in harsh conditions, were employed to tackle a labour shortage in the Transvaal mines. Local self-government was finally restored to the Transvaal by the Liberal government in 1906. This apparently magnanimous policy succeeded in preventing further Boer unrest and actually won many, like Jan Smuts, to British control. Finally, in 1910, London was able to fulfil the old dream of forging South Africa into a single federation but, as elsewhere in the Empire, the success of flexible British rule lay in the mutual benefits it brought to colonial inhabitants. In the South African case, local power resided in the hands of an elite of white settlers, mostly Boers, who paid little attention to native African rights.

The end of the Boer War left the Conservatives facing considerable unpopularity, a large national debt and high income tax. But there was a strong determination to tackle the diverse difficulties which the war had exposed and a drive for 'national efficiency' now began. An obvious problem was the unpreparedness of the army and amateurism of British war planning, which were the subject of a number of official reports and considerable public disquiet, rather as occurred during the Crimean War nearly half a century before. The army, it had been revealed, was only readied either for home defence or the reinforcement of small-scale colonial wars. Not only was it unfitted for a European campaign (which had been virtually ruled out as a possibility in the 1891 Stanhope Memorandum) but neither could it face a large-scale colonial war, such as might occur simultaneously against Russia and France. Another problem was that many British men had been found physically unfit for military service. To remedy these problems the Norfolk Commission of 1903 recommended compulsory military training. This followed the formation in 1902 of the National Service League to argue for conscription, which by 1911, under the Presidency of Lord Roberts, numbered 90 000 members. The League argued that a large army *was* now needed for home defence and it found influential allies among journalists such as *The Times'* military correspondent, Colonel Repington. The beginning of Officer Training Corps in schools and universities after 1906, and the creation of Baden-Powell's Boy Scout movement in 1908, were also part of the reaction. Yet conscription was not popular with most of the public, nor with the Treasury, which was now anxious to reduce defence expenditure. Even excluding the costs of the Boer War, military and naval expenditure had grown by a half between 1895 and 1902. A proposal by the Secretary for War, St John Brodrick (1900–03), to form a standing army of 120 000 proved stillborn and a proper army reform had to await the next Liberal government. The War Office's Intelligence Department was actually run down in size. The Conservatives were rather more successful in improving military planning, however. In 1895 a Defence Committee of relevant Cabinet ministers in the field had been formed (succeeding the earlier Colonial Defence Committee), but it was unable to provide proper coordination of the army, navy and foreign policy, partly because it excluded the military and naval chiefs. In any case it met only intermittently and did not keep proper records. In December 1902, five months after Arthur Balfour had succeeded Salisbury as Prime Minister, a more powerful body, the Committee of Imperial Defence (CID) held its first meeting. It included the First Sea Lord, the army's Commander-in-Chief and the Prime Minister, with the last assuming the chairmanship after September 1903. In its early meetings it particularly studied the danger to India if war broke out with France and Russia: the estimate that 100 000 men would have to be sent to the subcontinent was hardly welcome and underlined the need to try to neutralise the Russian threat diplomatically. The CID provided a link between military and naval planners and ministers, and also sometimes included representatives from the colonies. Following the Esher Committee Report of 1904, the CID was given a permanent Secretariat, the first Cabinet Committee to be treated this way. The Report also led to a continental-style General Staff being created, with a Chief of General Staff in place of the old Commander-in-Chief.

Another vital area of concern highlighted by the Boer War was Britain's continuing isolation. Salisbury pointed out that, notwithstanding its lack of allies, Britain, with the help of military contingents from the Empire, had won the war. Once again the other Great Powers had failed to unite against her. Although the Russians had suggested a joint attempt by the powers to force a settlement on the British, and although the French had hoped to exploit the situation to reopen the Egyptian issue, no outside intervention occurred. It was possible for Britain to buy Germany off with more minor colonial concessions, notably the partition of Samoa in the Pacific in November 1899. Yet many Britons were stunned by the Europe-wide condemnation of the Boer War. Concern over isolation was intensified by the fact that, preoccupied in southern Africa, Britain had been unable to act forcefully in the Far East at a time when the rest of the world's attentions focused on that region. Britain had long had the primary commercial position in China, and had no desire to see the country divided formally into territorial spheres. The ideal situation for Britain was that Chinese territorial integrity should be preserved but that the Peking government should allow the country to be exploited by all-comers, offering trading, loan and railway concessions according to the principle of the 'open door'. Failing that, London could accept a commercial (but not political) division into spheres of interest which left British businesses prevalent along the rich Yangtse valley. By the mid-1890s, however, other countries, most importantly Russia, were threatening to launch a 'scramble' which might result in a territorial division of China. In 1895 Japan demanded large territorial concessions from China after defeating her in war and the Chinese were upset that Britain did nothing to prevent this. Instead the French and Germans joined Russia in the 'Triple Intervention', which forced Japan to give up some of her claims. The Russians and Japanese then began to compete for influence in Korea and Manchuria. In 1891 Russia had already begun to build the Trans-Siberian railway from Europe to the naval base of Vladivostok on the Pacific, and it was due to be completed in 1903, improving Russia's ability to move armies to the Far East. The Russians were also interested in Manchuria because of harbours, like that at Port Arthur, which were open all year round: Vladivostok in contrast was ice-bound over winter. In 1897–98 the situation became more complex. Germany won control of the port of Kiaochow, and Russia obtained a 25-year lease from China of Port Arthur. Only the US seemed interested in preserving the 'open door', but she was preconcerned with tensions with Spain in the Caribbean, and so the British were left in an exposed position. In March 1898 they obtained a lease over the port of Weihaiwei. But two months earlier, in order to prevent a further carve-up of China, Salisbury had been ready to contemplate 'an understanding' with Russia whereby in disputes concerning China or the Ottoman Empire, 'the Power least interested should give way to and assist the other'.[5] Preoccupied with events in Africa, and well aware of the wide-ranging threat which Russia presented in the Far East, Central Asia and the Straits, Salisbury was concerned that arguments over Turkey and China could lead to Great Power conflict. This was clear in this famous speech of 4 May 1898 when he talked, in Darwinian terms, of 'living nations' competing over the remains of 'dying' ones. Yet it took another 11 months before Britain reached an agreement on commercial spheres in China with the Russians which recognised the latter's predominance in Manchuria whilst leaving the Yangtse to Britain. Salisbury's hopes for a wider agreement with Russia (though it can be considered another example of flexibility and an indication of the future course of policy) came to nothing and some government ministers were critical of his attempt to make deals with Britain's most powerful rival. When the Boer War broke out the Russian danger in East Asia only seemed to become greater. During the Boxer Rebellion of summer 1900, when Chinese xenophobes besieged the foreign legations in Peking, 50 000 Russian troops were moved to Manchuria. By then Joseph Chamberlain and others had already begun to explore the possibility of an alliance with Germany.

Britain's diplomatic revolution?

It is obvious why the idea of an alliance with another major power became popular for some British leaders at the beginning of the twentieth century. An alliance could help to defend Imperial interests, minimise defence costs, deter other countries from attacking Britain and improve the chances of winning a war if one broke out. Against these arguments had to be weighed the cost of tying British fortunes to another power and the danger of actually arousing other enemies by such a move, perhaps even *provoking* a conflict, when Britain was more interested in reducing frictions and preserving the peace. Isolation might have its own perils, but it might be less dangerous than war. Clearly much depended on who exactly Britain chose to align itself with and what the terms of the agreement were. Chamberlain first 'unofficially' explored the possibility of an alliance with the German Ambassador in March 1898 at the time of the lease of Weihaiwei. Salisbury was ill at the time and the acting premier was his son-in-law, Balfour, who *was* well-disposed to the idea of alliances. But it was soon clear that there were major differences between the British and Germans about an alliance. The British primarily needed German support to protect British interests against Russia in the Far East, had no wish to become involved in defending German interests against the Franco-Russian alliance in Europe, and did not want to make large-scale concessions to Germany in the colonial sphere. But, as Salisbury realised, the Germans wanted an alliance for virtually the opposite reasons, desiring colonial gains and support in Europe. Furthermore, they saw Chamberlain's clumsy approach and a speech by him in May (in favour of a racially based alliance with Germany and America) as evidence that, in due course, the British would accept an alliance on Berlin's terms anyway. In 1898–99 there were, of course, Anglo-German colonial agreements concerning the Portuguese colonies and Samoa but Salisbury was sceptical even about these and doubted that the policy could be taken further. So far as the Ottoman Empire was concerned, the British feared German economic and political penetration in addition to that of Russia. The January 1899 Anglo-Kuwait agreement reflected British fears over potential German influence in the Persian Gulf, viewed as vital to Indian defence. The Boer War led to considerable anti-British feeling in Germany, whilst Germany – which had only emerged as a European power a generation before – was seen in Britain as a formidable and growing commercial rival, a semi-autocratic state with an expanding population whose leaders' ambition of a *Weltpolitik* (world policy) could threaten the British Empire. The erratic and blustering behaviour of the Kaiser, with his talk of obtaining a 'place in the sun', could only add to such fears even if, convinced of the legitimacy of their own Empire, the British could hardly condemn the German ambition of possessing one. Both countries' war plans were based on the danger of conflict with France and Russia and Anglo-German antagonism before about 1906 has too often been exaggerated by historians. Nonetheless, as early as 1896 the German Navy, then only the world's sixth largest, had begun to study a possible war against Britain, and 1897 saw the appointment of Admiral Alfred von Tirpitz who, in the naval laws of 1898 and 1900, began a vast expansion of German warships which by October 1902 was of concern to the Royal Navy.

In November 1900 Salisbury, now in physical decline, handed the Foreign Office to Lord Lansdowne. Alongside the death of Queen Victoria, two months later, it seemed the end of an era, though Salisbury remained premier until July 1902. Lansdowne was a former Viceroy of India and rather unsuccessful Secretary of War, very much in the aristocratic tradition of pragmatism in foreign policy. He had come to believe in the need for alliances, but had no preconceptions or prejudices about who exactly to ally with; indeed he has often been criticised for lacking a comprehensive outlook on Britain's global position, being led by events and so flexible that no consistent policy can be detected in his actions. In March 1901 he discussed a secret 'defensive' alliance with the German Ambassador but, as in 1898, the prime aim for Britain was to meet the Russian threat in the Far East and especially, now, Manchuria, whereas the Germans mainly wanted a British commitment to support them in Europe. Such a step could only increase the danger for Britain of war with France and Russia, and Salisbury remained ardently opposed to it, pointing out that the burden 'of having to defend the German ... frontiers against Russia is heavier than that of having to defend the British Isles against France'.[6] At the end of the year, Lansdowne gave up all idea of such an alliance which soon ceased to be a viable proposition. He himself saw grave difficulties, both in defining when a 'defensive' alliance should come into operation and in aligning British foreign policy with that of Germany to the extent necessary to maintain such a relationship. Only in retrospect might 1901–2 be seen as a 'watershed' after which it was 'possible to detect a growing British conviction that there existed a "German threat"'.[7] Chamberlain, however, was among those who increasingly did believe in such a threat. In spring 1903 he led opposition to British financial involvement in the project for a Berlin–Baghdad railway which would harden German influence in the Ottoman Empire.

By then, in the Far East, Britain had found an alternative partner to match Russian power. In April 1901, as the last bid for a German arrangement failed, Japan approached Britain for an alliance. Lansdowne was evasive at first and during 1901, like Salisbury a few years before, vainly tried to reach a general understanding with Russia. In October, however, he took the Japanese proposal to the Cabinet and, although Britain and Japan could hardly have been considered close friends even one year before, a treaty between them was soon drafted. Signed on 30 January 1902, the five-year Anglo-Japanese alliance helped to counter Russian power in the Far East in a way the Germans were unwilling to do. On its own in the region the Royal Navy was inferior to the combined Russian and French fleets. The Japanese treaty allowed Britain to concentrate on planning for a naval war in European waters, leaving its new ally to handle East Asia, where London's Imperial position would be preserved intact. Lord Selborne, the First Lord of the Admiralty, had decided in January 1901 to concentrate on matching only French and Russian naval strength in the world (ignoring that of America and Japan) and he became a key advocate of the new alliance. The vital element in the treaty was an undertaking that if either Britain or Japan were attacked by one power in the Far East the other would remain neutral; if either were attacked by *more* than one power they would each go to the other's assistance. The principal value of the alliance to Japan was that it would deter France from backing its ally Russia in a Far Eastern war. But there was no cast-iron guarantee that France would not go to war and Arthur Balfour, for one, questioned the wisdom of signing a treaty which could encourage hawkish views in Tokyo and perhaps drag Britain into a conflict with both Russia and France in defence of Japanese interests. For Britain such a war could rapidly assume global proportions. Balfour believed an alliance with Germany still made better sense, because the Germans would be a more potent force in a global conflict. Japan seemed to some to win most from the new arrangement, for whereas Britain had recognised her primary position in Korea, Tokyo made no commitment to defend India. Also, whereas Britain wished to maintain Chinese territorial integrity, Japan had expansionist ambitions there. Yet the treaty aroused little popular or Press interest. Salisbury questioned it, but not as vehemently as he questioned a German alliance, and ministers saw it not as a revolution in British diplomacy but as a shift in their traditional, pragmatic policy of meeting specific pressures as they arose.

It has been said that the essential aim behind Britain's readiness to work with other powers around 1900 'was to reduce the United Kingdom's vulnerability to a war on her imperial circumference, and to free resources to meet ostensible threats closer to home'.[8] But it is not obvious that the British recognised a menace 'closer to home' at precisely this time. The German threat had not yet assumed great importance. True, the Franco-Russian combination spelt naval problems for Britain in the Channel and Mediterranean, but it also involved a threat in the colonies and on the Indian frontier. Rather, the country seems to have felt challenged in several areas as it came to terms with the existence both of a *global* balance of power and a new power-political constellation in Europe. In trying to cope with this situation, foreign policy had to take new turns. What is true is that the British were far better prepared, for practical and psychological reasons, to resolve their difficulties *beyond* Europe (through measures like the Japanese alliance) than they were to become involved in European disputes. This was emphasised by the development at this time, not of an alliance, but of a much friendlier policy towards the US, which after decades of competition with Britain had consolidated its control over half a continent. The policy of friendship came despite the fact that, in some ways, the US represented a potential threat. America, like Germany, was a growing commercial and financial power, a major competitor for trade in South America, an expanding naval power (with the second largest navy in the world, if measured by tonnage, in 1907) and a possible menace to British possessions in the Caribbean as well as to Canada, whose 3000 mile border with America was virtually indefensible. Even at the height of Victorian power, compromises with America had been necessary, notably the 1846 Oregon Treaty and withdrawal from most of the Central American coast in the 1850s. In 1895–96, at the same time as the Jameson Raid, the US had intervened in a border dispute between Venezuela and the colony of British Guiana in South America. The US mistakenly feared a policy of British expansion in the area and President Grover Cleveland asserted that the 1823 Monroe Doctrine (against European colonialism in the Americas) gave Washington the right to mediate in the dispute. Britain refused to recognise the Monroe Doctrine but accepted mediation anyway and won a judgement in its favour in 1899. The crisis upset both the London and New York stock-markets and showed that most British leaders had no desire to clash with America. A war with her would be costly and could gain Britain little. Britain had huge investments in the US itself and America was a major trading partner, especially as a supplier of food. There were, furthermore, close historical, linguistic and cultural ties to the US. Several British politicians, including Chamberlain, had American wives and both Chamberlain and Balfour, though not Salisbury, were among those who asserted the importance of the Anglo-Saxon racial link. When America went to war with Spain in 1898–99, seizing the Philippines and land in the Caribbean, the British did not join in the widespread European condemnation of Washington, but rather welcomed the creation of a second Anglo-Saxon empire, which could take up the 'white man's burden'. In turn the US took a benevolent view of British policy in southern Africa and the following years saw a real improvement in relations. In November 1901, its position further weakened by the Boer War, Britain signed the Hay-Pauncefote Treaty which gave America the sole right to build a canal in Panama from the Atlantic to the Pacific. This ended previous plans to build such a canal jointly and was accompanied by a withdrawal of the Royal Navy from the Caribbean, where in effect British interests were now protected by the US. In late 1902 the Royal Navy joined Germany in a blockade of Venezuela to protect commercial and financial interests, but Britain backed off when the mission aroused US concern. Then, in 1903, to the annoyance of the Canadians, the British agreed to a settlement of the Canadian-Alaskan border in America's favour, a move which was rapidly followed by the resolution of other long-standing local disputes over fishing and sealing. The policy of Anglo-American friendship was maintained over the following decade with few upsets. Meanwhile US relations with Germany grew worse, particularly because of more strong-handed German attempts to enforce debt payments from Brazil (1906) and Haiti (1911).

Whatever the improvement in relations, US friendship was little use to Britain beyond the backwater of the Caribbean. A far more important development, and one which some see as a real revolution in British diplomacy, was the *entente* with France of 8 April 1904. France, of course, was seen only a few years before as a likely enemy in war and was allied to Russia, the most serious menace to Britain's Imperial position. One particularly important hope that lay behind the *entente* was that an amicable France might help to restrain Russian ambitions. A policy of cooperation with Russia had, after all, been envisaged by Salisbury and Lansdowne as an alternative to alliances against her: the important point was to gain influence over Russian policy. Yet the *entente* was far from being a full, Japanese-style alliance with a commitment to mutual assistance in time of war; nor did it mark a greater readiness to become involved in European politics. It was rather a settlement of Anglo-French colonial differences over a range of matters such as Newfoundland fisheries and colonial borders in tropical Africa, but with the essential points involving North Africa. In particular the French gave up their claim to share in the control of Egypt, in return for a British commitment to support French primacy in Morocco. Achieving this settlement was a long, difficult process. The French Ambassador, Paul Cambon, first began to explore the possibility of a colonial deal in 1901. France was overstretched at this time, as Paris tried to maintain both a colonial Empire and a European Great Power role. It wished to assert a leading position (alongside Spain) in Morocco but knew the Russian alliance was of little use where African issues were concerned and feared opposition from London, which had the largest share of Moroccan trade. In fact, faced by so many problems elsewhere, the British had little desire to oppose French ambitions in Morocco. For a long time after the Fashoda crisis Delcassé held out the hope of winning British concessions in Egypt and it took time too for Lansdowne and the British Cabinet to accept that a far-reaching deal with France was desirable. A symbolic improvement in relations came with the state visit of Edward VII to Paris in May 1903, soon followed by the French President's arrival in London. Even then the pace of formal negotiations was slow and the final, rapid settlement in early 1904 was encouraged by the outbreak of war between Russia and Japan. This raised the danger of both Britain and France being drawn in to support their respective allies. Anti-Germanism, it is important to note, was not a major feature of the original *entente*, at least on the British side.

Once signed, the *entente* was widely welcomed in Britain by the business community, Press and all shades of political opinion, including the radical wing of the Liberal Party which had always regretted the breach with France – a fellow liberal democracy – over Egypt. Not only did the *entente* resolve the old Egyptian quarrel and other colonial disputes, it also reduced the danger of British and French involvement in the Far Eastern war and (an important point in both London and

Paris) laid the basis for a possible improvement in Anglo-Russian relations. There was a tense moment in October 1904 when the Russians sank some British trawlers on Dogger Bank, in the North Sea, having mistaken them for Japanese torpedo boats. But the outcry in Britain over this incident soon died down and the Russians agreed to pay compensation. The *entente* 'was designed to eliminate an enemy rather than make an ally,'[9] and like the Japanese alliance its main intention was to deal with problems beyond Europe. Its success in easing British difficulties was emphasised by the surprising series of defeats which Russia soon experienced at the hands of Japan. Most importantly at Tsushima Bay in May 1905, the Japanese totally destroyed the Russian Baltic fleet which had sailed half-way round the world to face them. Four months later the Asian power was able to win control of Korea and domination over Manchuria in a peace treaty. Meanwhile, in August 1905 Britain and Japan renewed their alliance. They now agreed to go to each other's aid if either were attacked by only *one* other power and, to British satisfaction, the terms were extended to cover India: thus the Russians knew that if they invaded India or launched a war of revenge against Japan, they would face a war against both Japan *and* Britain. The result of these developments was to leave Britain feeling as secure as it had for a decade, and perhaps much longer. The Royal Navy's superiority over the Franco-Russian fleets had been restored and five battleships could now be withdrawn from the Far Eastern station. There was little threat to India in the immediate term and the danger either of a Russian attempt to seize Constantinople or of a Russian-led scramble for China had both receded. Furthermore, by the end of 1905 Russia itself was in turmoil, as the Tsar's government faced widespread domestic unrest. The unexpected results of the Russo-Japanese War served to underline the importance of far-off, chance events to British policy-makers. Such events could at one time create challenges, and at other times relieve them. But these same events also showed how, in the emerging era of global communications and world empires, developments in one region could have an impact on the other side of the planet. For the defeat of Russia also served to weaken the position of France, which had only just signed the *entente* with Britain. The *entente*, though not intended by Balfour's government as an anti-German device, had caused grave concern in Berlin, not least because it seemed to ignore German interests in Morocco. And in 1905 the German government decided to test the strength of the new Anglo-French friendship by stirring up a dispute over Morocco. This crisis, coinciding with Russia's defeat and the demise of Balfour's government, marked a seminal moment in British foreign policy before the First World War.

Notes

1 Howard H., *Splendid Isolation. A Study of Ideas Concerning Britain's ... Foreign Policy During the Later Years of ... Salisbury* (London, 1967), 19–21.
2 Taylor A.J.P., *The Struggle for Mastery in Europe* (Oxford, 1954), 400.
3 Gooch G.P. and Temperley H. (eds), *British Documents on the Origins of the War, 1898–1914* (1927–38), Vol. 1, 164.
4 Quoted in Brooks D., *The Age of Upheaval: Edwardian Politics* (Manchester, 1995), 23.
5 Gooch G.P. and Temperley H. (eds), *British Documents*, Vol. 1, 8.
6 Gooch G.P. and Temperley H. (eds), *British Documents*, Vol. 2, 68–9.
7 Kennedy P., *The Rise of Anglo-German Antagonism, 1860–1914* (London, 1982), 251.
8 Holland R., *The Pursuit of Greatness: Britain and the World Role, 1900–1970* (London, 1991), 30.
9 Bourne K., *The Foreign Policy of Victorian England, 1830–1902* (Oxford, 1970), 182.

2
Ententes *and Anglo-German rivalry, 1905–1914*

On 31 March 1905 Kaiser Wilhelm II landed at the Moroccan city of Tangier and declared there should be an international conference on the country's status. Berlin's concern over French attempts to assert predominance in Morocco was understandable, given Germany's substantial economic interests there. But understandable too were British and French worries that Germany might establish its own position in the eastern Mediterranean with, perhaps, a port on the Moroccan coast. Lansdowne was determined to resist this and promised diplomatic, though not – significantly – military support to France. The Foreign Office and armed services believed wider issues were also at stake. As the German government knew, a challenge to France over Morocco was effectively a challenge to the new Anglo-French *entente*. The problem was that, if the *entente* were to be saved, Britain must lead in taking an assertive line. For France's principal ally, Russia, was faced by defeat in the Far East and internal turmoil, and was uninterested in African problems. More worrying, the French government was extremely nervous in the face of the crisis and did not know whether it could trust Britain. To the dismay of Lansdowne, Delcassé was forced out of office on 6 June, which raised doubts about French reliability. The following month German successes continued when the Kaiser and Tsar met at Björko in Finland, and the beleaguered Russian agreed to a draft alliance with Berlin. In fact, although such an alliance had been suggested for some time as a way to secure Russia's European border, freeing it to concentrate on expansion in Asia, nothing came of Björko. The Tsar's ministers opposed the idea, arguing that Russia could not afford a breach with France: this would shift the balance of power markedly in Germany's favour and, besides, the Russians needed French loans. Nonetheless, when the powers agreed to the Kaiser's demand for a conference on Morocco, to meet in January 1906, it still seemed likely to result in German triumph. By the time the conference opened the Conservatives were no longer in office, and the decision whether to resist Germany fell to the Liberals.

Domestic policy-making in the Grey era

Since its victory in the Khaki Election the government had become very unpopular. The guerrilla war in southern Africa and the rising taxes associated with it began the decline. The same factors tarnished popular faith in the Empire which had reached a peak in Victoria's last years. Then, in 1903, came Joseph Chamberlain's divisive campaign for an Imperial Customs Union, designed to give the Empire a preferential position in trade with Britain. This proposal was designed to meet several challenges facing Great Britain at home and abroad: how to consolidate a far-flung Empire and defend Britain's global position; how to compete with new powers like Germany and America, who protected their own domestic markets behind tariff barriers; and how to meet domestic demands (seen in the appeal of the embryonic Labour Party and 'New Liberalism') for costly social reform programmes such as old age pensions. Among Conservative supporters, the landed interest and some industrialists wished to protect British agriculture and industry from foreign competition. Chamberlain, a former radical, who had broken with the Liberals over Irish Home Rule in 1886, wished to consolidate the Empire and use tariffs to pay for reforms which would keep the working classes loyal to the Conservative Party. He was also concerned to maintain Britain's healthy foreign trade. Thus 'tariff reform' seemed to offer a way to revitalise the government after the Boer War and contribute to the drive for 'national efficiency' by fusing Imperialism and domestic reform. In May 1903 Chamberlain made his first speech advocating preferential Imperial trade in Birmingham, and in September he quit the Cabinet to pursue his campaign. Instead of inspiring the Conservatives with a new cause, however, he brought division and doubt. In the popular psyche, it was strongly believed that free trade was the foundation stone of British wealth. Most business people and financiers in the City thought that Britain, with its island position and high percentage of global trade, must remain 'open' to the outside world; Britain's export and investment levels seemed buoyant in the early 1900s under existing policy and were growing in *absolute* terms. The working classes on the other hand liked free trade because it kept food prices down (this also allowed businesses to keep wages low), hence the success of the Liberal campaign, in the 1906 election, against Conservative 'stomach taxes'. There were other ways to deal with British problems in the world: domestic weaknesses might be tackled by such measures as education reform; genuinely 'unfair' trade practices could be answered by specific retaliation; Imperial unity, rather than being bolstered, might be put at risk by tariff reform, since colonial governments showed little interest in economic or political centralisation under London's control. The Conservatives themselves were soon divided on the issue, some joining the Tariff Reform League, others the Unionist Free Food League (both formed in July 1903), though Chamberlainites soon had a majority in the constituencies, among MPs and in the Conservative Press. The Conservative leader, Balfour, tried to pursue a middle way, only to find his government increasingly paralysed. When he resigned as Prime Minister in December 1905 it was in the hope that the Liberals would prove too divided to survive in power long.

The controversy provoked by tariff reform highlighted the dilemmas facing Britain at the start of the twentieth century. At one extreme certain groups might advocate alliances, Imperial consolidation, greater armaments and a drive for national efficiency through social reform as the way to preserve national greatness, but at the other many wished to continue the world of low taxes, free trade, reliance on the navy for defence, non-intervention by government at home and a 'free hand' abroad. Debates on these issues cut across both main parties. Certainly in the Liberal Party there were divisions on domestic policy between Gladstonian advocates of low tax, *laissez-faire* policies and 'New Liberal' advocates of social reform, interventionism and higher taxes. There were arguments too on foreign policy between Imperialists and radicals centring on levels of defence spending and the readiness to run risks in international crises. These differences had been exposed in the Boer War of course. But many Liberals did not fall into either category and, having been excluded from office for most of 20 years, the party proved eager to patch up its differences to hold power. Its leader, Henry Campbell-Bannerman, quickly called an election which produced a landslide victory in January 1906. He appointed a number of 'Liberal Imperialists' to key positions including Herbert Asquith as Chancellor of the Exchequer, Richard Haldane as Secretary for War and Edward Grey as Foreign Secretary. But overall a balance was struck in Cabinet between different elements in the party and the Imperialists could not easily command a majority. Nor were they a united group: thus, whilst most backed a policy of alliances, some (including ex-premier Lord Rosebery) were critical of the restrictions these put on British independence. Grey was to serve in his position until 1916, longer than any other Foreign Secretary of the twentieth century. His policies, especially his support for the *ententes* with France and Russia, have provoked controversy among historians. Although, in contrast to all his recent predecessors, he was in the Commons rather than the Lords, Grey was from a wealthy landowning family which had already produced a Prime Minister. He was torn between political duties and a deep love of ornithology and fishing. But his protests that he would rather be on his country estate disguised a deep commitment to his political career. In any case later foreign secretaries might envy both the amount of time he did spend on his estate (he was generally in the Foreign Office three days a week) and the few times he had to journey abroad: he had made only two such visits, both to the Empire, before 1905 and his first visit to Europe was on the brink of the First World War! Sometimes accused of insularity, it is equally possible to argue that Grey's lack of travel made him more objective about the world he dealt with. He had already served as a junior minister in the Foreign Office in 1892–95 and whilst in Opposition he supported most of Lansdowne's policies, including the Japanese alliance, friendship with America and the *entente cordiale*.

Critics of Grey have argued that he became too closely committed to the *entente* with France, which had not been intended as an alliance and did not *formally* become one under the Liberals, but whose maintenance he stubbornly erected almost into a moral cause. Although he claimed Britain was not committed to aid France in 1914, in effect he abandoned British independence and upset the balance of power even as he sought to maintain it by throwing Britain into the scales. Even if unintentionally, he alienated the Germans, who saw him as a Machiavellian practitioner of *realpolitik*, directing the *entente* against them whilst claiming to be open to agreement. Radical critics in his party and the Press, concerned at the direction of British policy, accused Grey of falling under the influence of an anti-German 'clique' in the Foreign Office. Certainly there were officials who believed Germany was the most serious menace to Britain's world position. These included Grey's two Permanent Under-Secretaries, Charles Hardinge (1906–10), who believed agreement with Berlin to be virtually impossible, and Arthur Nicolson (1910–16). However, the key 'anti-Germans' were Louis Mallet, Grey's Private Secretary in 1905–7, Francis Bertie, who became Ambassador to France, and Eyre Crowe, the Chief Clerk between 1906 and 1912 (who, ironically, had a German mother). Grey was the first Foreign Secretary who it was possible to accuse of falling under the influence of officials, because Foreign Office reforms strengthened their influence over day-to-day decisions. In response to the growing complexity of foreign policy and the volume of paperwork in the Office, a new Registry system was introduced on 1 January 1906. This put clerical work, such as the recording and copying of telegrams, in the hands of Registry staff, freeing higher-level officials to play an active role in defining policy. Yet the impact of this reform should not be exaggerated. Lansdowne had already allowed officials growing political influence and, long after 1906, the diligent Grey continued to take key decisions himself, often against his officials' advice. Ambassadors continued to communicate with him via private letters, by-passing the Registry system, and the Foreign Office continued to suffer from telling inefficiencies. For example, keen to distance itself from popular sentiment, the Office did not create a press office (such as existed in France and Germany) until 1914. Grey, a shadowy figure to the public, left contacts with the Press between 1907 and the war to his Private Secretary, William Tyrell, despite the growing appreciation of the need to shape newspaper opinion in the government's favour. Then again, Grey's policies in themselves served to neutralise criticism from Conservatives and the patriotic Press. Not only did he build on the inheritance from Lansdowne, removing fears that Liberals would pursue a defence-cutting, neutralist, 'little Englander' policy; Grey also consulted Conservative leaders regularly and Balfour even joined a subcommittee of the Committee of Imperial Defence. Bitter arguments between the two main parties therefore focused on domestic issues, although there was an inevitable connection between Conservative criticisms of social spending and their calls for higher defence spending. 'Pensions or Dreadnoughts?' read one *Daily Mail* headline.[1]

Most criticism of Grey, then, came from elements within his own party. Radicals were despondent, not only about Foreign Office influence, but also Imperialism, secrecy in policy-making, the influence of business and balance of power diplomacy. They were involved after 1907 in groups critical of improved relations with the autocratic Tsarist regime, like the Society of the Friends of Russian Freedom and the Persia Committee (concerned with Russian infringements on Persian independence). Radicals also formed the Foreign Policy Committee in 1911 to press for fuller parliamentary control of foreign policy and a friendlier policy towards Berlin. They had sympathy from the Labour Party which in 1911 organised its own conference on disarmament. Leading radical thinkers included E.D. Morel, who led the Congo Reform Association's campaign against Imperialism in central Africa; J.A. Hobson, whose book *Imperialism* (1902) argued that war inevitably resulted from Imperial rivalries which, in turn, were the product not of individuals but of the capitalist system; and Norman Angell, whose *The Great Illusion* (1910) argued that no country gained from Imperialism or war (since colonies and conflict were expensive even to the victors) and that a better international system would be based on global cooperation and free trade. Even taken together such pressure groups and thinkers were few in number and unable to control policy. Radical MPs were unwilling, when it came to a crisis, to bring down the government – which in any case could rely on Conservative MPs to vote for a strong external policy. More worrying to Grey was the sympathy for non-interventionist, pacific policies in the Cabinet which helped prevent a formal alliance with France. Generally he was able to avoid Cabinet interference in day-to-day policies, helped by Campbell-Bannerman and his successor as premier in 1908, Asquith. Foreign and security policy seemed to be decided, as under the Conservatives, by a small group of individuals. However, this is not to say that Grey had great freedom in the policies he pursued. Indeed, the case mounted by his defenders is that he, like Lansdowne, faced *limited* choices because of Britain's small army, scattered Empire and divisions in the country about policy. Grey himself never wanted war – apart from anything else, he believed it would lead to social revolution – and his ideal diplomatic aim after 1905 was to stay close to France, and later Russia, without driving Germany into desperate actions. But this delicate balance was hard to achieve, especially when these other three powers were determined to realise their own foreign policy aims by (at times) risking conflict. British support for France in pre-war crises was significant for boosting French confidence, and thereby strengthening the European opponents of Germany. But the fact that Liberal divisions prevented Grey wholeheartedly supporting an Anglo-Franco-Russian combination meant that France, Russia and Germany were never certain of Britain's position if war came. An important debate thus surrounds Grey's freedom of manoeuvre. Was he at the mercy of impersonal forces, or could he have chosen an alternative policy and preserved British independence in full? In general it might be said that ministers could not maintain both British independence and a low-cost defence policy once Europe had divided into two armed blocs. If Britain wanted to dwell in isolation it must have larger armed forces; if it would not pay for armed forces it must have allies – or very close friends. After 1905 the dilemmas already faced by the Conservatives simply became more intense, especially because Germany threatened both to upset the European balance and to become a major naval power, and it might be said that Grey carried on an inherited trend when he chose to solidify the *entente.* The limits of British power at this time were not much worse than they had been for decades. Its naval pre-eminence and financial wealth commanded great respect. Yet as time went on Grey and his colleagues could have been more honest – not least with themselves – about the contradictions which had grown between the traditional elements of British policy, especially their need to pursue an active role in European diplomacy and the implications of their commitments to France.

The Moroccan crisis and the naval race

Grey, concerned with the balance of power in Europe rather than the situation in north-west Africa, was quick to decide the *entente* must be strengthened in the face of Germany's challenge in Morocco. On 3 January 1906 he warned the German Ambassador that British opinion would not allow France to be defeated in war. Then, on 15 January, the Foreign Secretary gave official sanction to military staff talks between

London and Paris, which had already tentatively begun. Significantly, although War Minister Haldane knew of this step and Campbell-Bannerman was aware that moves were afoot, the Cabinet as a whole was not told for fear it would object. This was a vital moment, which may be seen as the start of British planning for conflict with Germany. Yet Grey desperately hoped there would not be war. True, he wished to check German ambitions and was already thinking of some arrangement with Russia to strengthen the anti-German front. But he was not crudely Germanophobe. He believed Germany would back down and refused Ambassador Cambon's requests for a full defensive alliance. The military talks with France did not advance much. In the short term Britain's most important visible action was the tough diplomatic line taken by Arthur Nicolson, its representative at the Algeciras Conference between January and April 1906 where the Germans were unable to prevent effective French primacy in Morocco. The outcome was that France (along with Spain) was given the right to police most Moroccan ports, though Germany received some succour from the fact that two ports – Tangier and Algeciras – were to be policed by an international force. Nicolson's stance gave confidence to France, impressed the Russians and showed the Germans they could not divide the *entente*. It was also the first time British public opinion found a specific reason to express growing antagonism towards Germany.

As seen in the previous chapter, popular suspicion of Berlin in Britain after about 1902 was partly based on the perception of a *general* threat to British primacy, presented by Germany's commercial expansion, growing population, autocratic government and talk of *Weltpolitik*. This was despite the fact that Germany's colonial empire (at under a million square miles) was paltry: Russia and America were greater *potential* threats to Britain beyond Europe. But Russia was weakened after 1905 and American policy did not actually trouble London. Germany's presence on Britain's doorstep intensified the sense of threat from her and the scale of German *growth* was daunting. Britain and Germany by 1914 were, on one level, excellent trading partners, Britain invested in Germany and its colonies, and Germany was Britain's second best export market. But they were also commercial rivals in Latin America, China and Turkey, and Germany was especially strong in steel production and two new industries, electricals and chemicals. Even on crude contemporary economic statistics it was obvious that Germany was outperforming Britain. Germany's share of world industrial output grew from less than 9 per cent in 1880 to 15 per cent in 1914, while Britain's fell behind, from 23 per cent to 14 per cent. (Again, however, America did best, rising from 15 per cent to 32 per cent.) But it was not just growing German economic power which troubled London. There was also deep concern about what policy Berlin intended to follow. Under Bismarck in the 1880s it was possible to believe that Germany was a satisfied power, ready to maintain the European balance and with only limited colonial ambitions, all of which suited British interests. But under the Kaiser policy was more irrational, the ambitions for *Weltpolitik* more disturbing and the danger to the European balance particularly troubling. 'It was German *policy*, not German *power*, that led the British to identify her as a danger to be countered. And it was German policy in Europe that really mattered ...'.[2] Distrust of Germany in the Foreign Office received its most celebrated exposition in the Crowe Memorandum of 1 January 1907. This sometimes vague document was noteworthy for seeing a *potential*, rather than an actual, threatening policy by Germany. It opposed concessions to Germany, arguing that it was a blackmailer who would keep asking for more. The former Permanent Under-Secretary, Thomas Sanderson, wrote his own memorandum refuting Crowe's arguments and arguing that Germany was not always anti-British. And Grey, though he saw Crowe's memorandum as a cogent statement of the German threat, had no desire deliberately to antagonise Berlin. Berlin equally had no desire to drive Britain further into the hands of France and Russia, who already presented a formidable combination. The Moroccan crisis had been intended to drive a wedge into the *entente*, not consolidate it. Yet the Germans, believing themselves to be faced by 'encirclement' and anxious to find their 'place in the sun', had botched the Moroccan episode and continued to stir suspicion in Britain, nowhere more so than in the development of their navy.

Given their position as an 'island race' who imported half their food, naval dominance was something almost all Britons were determined to maintain and Germany's threat to it was bound to arouse suspicion. There can be no doubt that German naval growth was targeted at Britain. Admiral von Tirpitz, who masterminded the expansion, and may privately have hoped, one day, to equal the Royal Navy, pursued what he called a 'risk theory': Germany might not match the Royal Navy's total size, but as the British were only too aware, the Royal Navy could not be everywhere at once, so if Germany built a medium-sized, but technologically advanced fleet it could threaten a local defeat of the British. To some extent, Tirpitz's argument was a reasonable one. A naval threat might alter London's policies. After all, Britain apparently abandoned the Caribbean in the face of local US naval expansion and decided to enter an alliance with another rising naval power, Japan. The German Navy was not necessarily designed to fight Britain, but rather to win concessions from her, even to induce her into an alliance. Tirpitz himself saw the dangers of antagonising Britain because there was bound to be a 'danger zone' in the German programme when the navy was too small to fight the Royal Navy but large enough to make the British consider a pre-emptive strike. In 1904 and later the Germans feared a 'Copenhagen' – a repetition of Britain's sudden annihilation of the Danish fleet a hundred years before. The Admiralty and British Press were already concerned about Tirpitz's policies and urged that the Royal Navy be expanded. What followed showed the 'risk theory' to be seriously flawed. For the British were not ready to ignore a threat to their homeland, especially when the German Press boasted about it. The British argued that, whereas the Royal Navy was unable to pose a direct menace to Germany, the German Navy *was* a serious threat to Britain because it could carry the formidable German Army over as an invasion force. It was also felt that, in contrast to Britain, Germany did not need a large navy, given that its political and economic interests were focused on the continent. London of course began to neutralise other naval threats by the policy of alliance (Japan), friendship (America) and *entente* (France), and was further helped by the destruction of the Russian fleet at Tsushima Bay. The First Sea Lord after October 1904 was 'Jacky' Fisher, a formidable individual who was able to concentrate more battleships in home waters to meet any threat from European powers, relying on cruiser squadrons to defend the Empire. As a result Tirpitz's 'danger zone' threatened to last indefinitely, with Germany never able to fight the British at sea. Once again Britain's resilience and material strength were confirmed.

The Liberal government inherited a naval expansion plan, the 'Cawdor Programme', from the Conservatives but there was opposition to this from critics of power politics, those who preferred to spend on social reform and Gladstonians who simply disliked public spending. With the German threat not proven in many minds, the Cabinet agreed to naval spending reductions. But before long there were pressures to reverse this decision thanks to the Moroccan crisis and a most important but costly advance in naval technology, the launch in February 1906 of HMS *Dreadnought*. This 'super-battleship' had a formidable arsenal of ten 12-inch guns and oil turbine engines which drove it along at 21 knots. It could catch any enemy, fight at long distances and stay out of range of torpedoes. There is evidence that Fisher believed the future lay with an even faster, less well-armoured ship, the battle-cruiser, which was also developed at this time and was ideal for hunting raiders which dared to prey on British merchant ships around the world. There is evidence too that he saw a Franco-Russian combination as a possible threat: the French had already developed commerce raiders whereas Germany, which lacked a global system of naval bases, had not. But the 'dreadnought revolution' caught the public imagination. In a sense, the *Dreadnought* seemed an unwise move: it made existing battleships redundant and gave Britain's rivals a chance to match her. But there were signs that other countries, including Italy and America, were planning a 'super-battleship' anyway and the decision to build *Dreadnought* was a bold step to keep Britain in the forefront of naval development. Fisher was an advocate of innovation and technology in place of the navy's obsession with tradition and size, and he promised he could cut the costs of the navy while making it more efficient. He was ready to scrap older ships, improve leadership and gunnery skills and take account of new weapons like mines, shells and torpedoes. He also grasped the potential significance of submarines. On the other hand he had serious flaws including a desire to concentrate decisions in his own hands, a characteristic which alienated other naval officers, and a reluctance to draw up a proper war plan. Only in 1912 was the Naval War Staff created to coordinate intelligence gathering and war mobilisation. Significantly the Cabinet did try to avoid a naval arms race being sparked by the dreadnought revolution, through a multilateral negotiation with other powers. The second Hague Conference of 1907 can be seen as an early attempt by some politicians to resolve Britain's external problems through a wider international agreement. Their aims in this were quite selfish: (as so often in the twentieth century) international action was designed to meet *national* interests. In particular London hoped to preserve the current naval balance and to protect merchant ships in war, both points from which it would gain. Whilst radicals had idealistic hopes for wide-ranging disarmament at the conference, professional diplomats were pessimistic. It was clear that the Germans were not ready to accept an arms agreement which effectively 'froze' Britain's naval supremacy, just as the British were unwilling to give that supremacy up. The Kaiser's response to Fisher's challenge was simply to build more ships. At the same time suspicion of Germany was rekindled by other actions, notably the Kaiser's *Daily Telegraph* interview of October 1908 in which he admitted most Germans were ill-disposed to Britain, and the short-lived Casablanca crisis the following month which rekindled Franco-German antagonism in Morocco. By then, however, Grey had strengthened Britain's diplomatic hand by concluding a second *entente*, with Russia.

The Russian *entente* and the defence of Empire

It is often claimed that under Grey, still more than under his predecessors, attention began to focus more on European than Imperial concerns. The *ententes* with France and Russia can be seen as attempts to resolve Imperial problems in order to concentrate on the threat nearer home from Germany. Yet it can also be argued that the Russian convention 'was devised in the interests of England's Imperial position, not for the sake of the balance of power in Europe'.[3] It helped extinguish the wide-ranging threat which Britain faced from the combination of France (strong in the Channel, Mediterranean and West Africa) and Russia (in Central Asia). Then again, European and Imperial concerns were surely linked: Britain wished to preserve security in both spheres. The attempt to resolve difficulties with Russia was an idea stretching back to the mid-1890s, whose moment came because of Russia's defeat by Japan which made St Petersburg less adventurist and more willing to deal with Britain. One reason for the Russian *entente* was undoubtedly fear of Germany, as well as a desire to put relations with France on a surer footing. After all, Britain's alliance with Japan was largely directed against France's ally Russia, providing potential for German trouble-making. Almost as he came into office Grey told the Russian Ambassador that he favoured agreement with St Petersburg and on 20 February 1906, at the height of the Moroccan crisis, wrote, 'An entente between Russia, France and ourselves would be absolutely secure. If it is necessary to check Germany it could ... be done.'[4] Key supporters of the new *entente* were Permanent Under-Secretary Hardinge, who had served in Russia, and the Ambassador to St Petersburg after May 1906, Nicolson. Russia – unlike Britain – had a large army which could directly threaten Germany. There were doubts about the enterprise from those centrally concerned with the defence of India. The India Office, Viceroy and War Office were disturbed by Russian meddling in Tibet, Afghanistan and Persia, the areas of the 'Great Game' of competition for influence between Britain and Russia. The construction of Russian railways meant that large armies could be carried to the Himalayas and, even if they did not invade India, they might encourage Indian resistance to British rule. It would take reinforcements of perhaps 100 000 men to defend India and the Cabinet was not ready to pay the cost. In 1903 the Conservatives were upset when the Viceroy, Lord Curzon, sent an expedition into Tibet and offended the Russians. One reason why Grey was able to neutralise criticism of the Russian convention from the India Office and radicals, however, was that the Office was in the hands of a Gladstonian, John Morley, who wished to reduce defence spending and realised that this demanded agreement with Russia. Campbell-Bannerman too was keen on an agreement to avoid 'an Asiatic avalanche'.[5] Talks on the Convention began in June 1906 and faced numerous difficulties, including British fears of upsetting Japan, the enduring preference of some Russians for a deal with Germany and the complexity of settling the 'Great Game'. The Convention of 31 August 1907, like the *entente* with France, only directed itself at issues *outside* Europe. It recognised Afghanistan as lying in neither party's sphere of influence. The British promised not to meddle in Tibet's domestic affairs in return for a Russian promise not to extend their influence there. And in the most difficult area, Persia, there was a division into British, Russian and neutral spheres. The India Office was pleased because it specifically protected its interests in the Persian Gulf, but Curzon, now in the House of Lords, was a leading critic of concessions to Russia. The Convention had little to say on other old concerns, the Far East (the key area of Anglo-Russian differences before 1905) and security in the Straits (although here London effectively accepted Russian predominance). One key point, however, was that it improved France's confidence about standing up to Germany. It is worth underlining the about-turn the Convention represented compared with the situation in 1900 of tension with the Franco-Russian alliance and possible agreement with Germany. At the same time the British prevented any Russo-German combination, which both Sanderson and Hardinge had earlier feared, and which could have marked a formidable challenge to British power. It also bears repetition that the *ententes* were not alliances, they gave Britain some influence in Paris and Moscow but involved no automatic commitments to these powers, and Britain was in a strong position *vis-à-vis* both its partners: France, defeated at Fashoda and vulnerable to German pressure in Morocco, needed British diplomatic support, and Russia was in a much-weakened state after 1905.

The new *entente* was never as cordial as that with France; in British eyes it was designed as much to control Russia as cooperate with her, and it was difficult to put into effect. In 1908 Grey only gave limited support to Russia in a Balkan crisis. Russia's rival, Austria, seized control of Slav-populated Bosnia-Herzegovina (which the Austrians had occupied for decades but was nominally Turkish). The Russians, traditional defender of the Slavs, felt humiliated and the Germans, who had initially shown little concern over the Anglo-Russian Convention, used this crisis to drive a wedge between Britain and Russia. They partly succeeded because Britain and France proved unwilling to back Russia to the point of war; neither were they keen to see Russia compensated by concessions in the Straits. More serious problems arose in Central Asia. Once Russia began to recover from the Japanese defeat she became more assertive, threatening armed intervention in Persia in 1909 to end political upheaval there, and reaching an agreement with Germany in August 1911 which gave Russia's blessing to the Berlin–Baghdad railway. There was increasing concern in the Foreign Office about Russia's trustworthiness and by 1914 relations seemed little better than before the Convention. Even Nicolson was perplexed, though he believed the best way to control Russia was not by resistance to her ambitions but by a full alliance with her. Tentative naval talks between them began in May 1914, but marked only the first attempt to give the Convention a military dimension. Meanwhile in the Far East, the British position seemed more secure after the Russo-Japanese War but the situation was fraught with danger, especially in China where Britain had larger investments than any other power and the inept Imperial government was toppled in 1911. In July 1911 the British again renewed the Japanese alliance, this time for ten years. London even made concessions to Japan, recognising the latter's annexation of Korea and agreeing that the treaty need no longer cover Indian defence. In renewing the treaty Grey risked upsetting the US and Imperial governments in Canada, Australia and New Zealand, who were fearful of Japan's increasing power in the Pacific and wished to restrict Japanese immigrants. The alliance was still vital to Britain, not because of the Russian menace, but because the Royal Navy still could not protect British interests in East Asia. Only over the next few years did London become concerned that Japanese expansionism might be the greatest threat to these interests.

In addition to the Russian Convention, historians have seen the Liberals' army reforms as marking a shift from an Imperial (primarily Indian) to a European focus in security policy. This view was first put forward in the memoirs written by Haldane who in 1907 introduced an army reform bill which merged the three irregular, home defence forces – the Militia, Yeomanry and Volunteers – into a Territorial Army of 300 000. The reform came after years of debate since the Boer War and had many beneficial points. It avoided conscription, was cheap, and provided both a reserve for the army and a force for home defence, freeing the regular army to fight elsewhere. And increasingly it seemed 'elsewhere' meant in Europe. As early as 1903 war with Germany was tentatively studied, with ideas for an amphibious raid on Heligoland. At that time France and Russia were still seen as the most likely enemies, the army planning colonial campaigns against France while the navy ensured Britain was safe from invasion. During the Moroccan crisis, however, the military felt it must plan actively for a 'continental commitment', to meet such contingencies as a German invasion of Belgium. Fisher argued that the army should be used as an adjunct to the navy, which would carry it on raids against the German coast, but Asquith was not impressed by such ideas and in 1911 the CID became more favourable to plans for a British Expeditionary Force (BEF) to be sent across the Channel after war broke out. Yet, again, the idea of an inexorable shift towards a continental commitment must not be accepted uncritically, nor must Haldane's reforms be seen as pointing solely towards this. (It was in Haldane's interest to argue such a case in his memoirs because, during the war, he was accused of pro-German sympathies.) In fact the size of the *regular* Army was still governed by the need to provide colonial garrisons and the size of the *Territorial* Army was in turn dependent on the number of regulars.

The significance of colonial concerns was further emphasised in 1909 when the head of the army became the 'Chief of *Imperial* General Staff' and the Dominions agreed to standardise military structures and equipment to allow joint mobilisation in defence of the Empire. In 1914 the BEF, though highly professional and mobile, numbered only 150 000, too small to make much difference in the continental struggle. Some generals even doubted it should cross the Channel. Most spending continued to go on the navy, which could protect Imperial communications and outmatch Germany at sea, but was of no use in land campaigns. Indeed, many Imperialists argued that the Empire and navy, if nurtured, would make Britain powerful enough to stand aside from European conflicts. It cannot be said that Liberals solved the problem of coordinating security policy. Not only was there continuing rivalry between the army and navy over Grand Strategy, but the CID met less frequently and Grey did not properly coordinate his foreign policy (based on the French alliance) with Britain's military capability (which, as just seen, was of limited usefulness to France). In 1914 he seems to have had little grasp of military realities on the continent.

Even if colonial defence remained of great concern, outside the 'Great Game' in Central Asia the Empire provided no major security crises for Grey's 'Imperial Foreign Office'. In South Africa the Boers largely reconciled themselves to British rule. And although native unrest made itself apparent through the odd riot or terrorist incident in India and Egypt, it was easily held at bay. In Egypt in 1906 Lord Cromer ruthlessly punished unrest at Dinshawi by imprisonment, flogging and executions, even though the trouble had been sparked by British troops. Liberal opinion in Britain was offended but Grey took the view that British prestige must be upheld. The following year Cromer, who if nothing else had been an efficient administrator, was succeeded by Eldon Gorst. In contrast to Cromer, Gorst believed local nationalism to be a legitimate phenomenon and tried to build support from middle-class Egyptians who, it was felt, would support modernisation policies, which included development of a cotton industry and attacks on corruption. But Egyptian nationalists continued to see Britain as an undesirable, alien ruler and in 1910 one assassinated the pro-British Prime Minister, Boutros Ghali. Soon after this Gorst died, to be succeeded by Kitchener, under whom a firm policy returned. In India too there was some attempt to depart from the coercion and paternalism of Viceroy Curzon, who was succeeded in 1905 by Lord Minto. The Secretary of State, Morley, believed in 'order plus progress'. He approved Minto's steps to control the Press and ban certain anti-British societies, but also passed the Indian Councils Act (1909), designed to win over educated native opinion by creating a representative element in provincial government. Yet the Morley–Minto reforms were very limited in effect. Designed to bolster British authority, they ruled out an Indian *national* parliament and as part of a process of 'divide and rule' gave separate representation to Moslems, a step which helped foster a separate Moslem identity. Morley, despite his Gladstonian credentials, had little respect for the (admittedly elitist) National Congress Party, which had been formed by educated Indians in 1885. But whatever the limits of reform, nationalists did nothing to disrupt the great Delhi Durbar of December 1911, when George V was enthroned as Emperor of India.

Under the Liberals Britain did not press on vigorously with plans for greater Imperial coordination to improve the Empire's strength and self-sufficiency. The 1907 Colonial Conference decided that Imperial leaders should meet at regular intervals in future to discuss problems and policy. The same year the settler colonies of Canada, Australia, New Zealand and South Africa formally became titled 'Dominions' and, largely in response to Australian pressure, a Dominions Department was formed as a sub-unit of the Colonial Office. In 1909 the Round Table movement became the most powerful pressure group so far to form in support of Imperial consolidation, but at the first of the new Imperial conferences, in 1911, most representatives were dismissive of ideas for an Imperial parliament put by Joseph Ward, the premier of New Zealand. (At that time New Zealand was the Dominion which felt most closely attached to Britain, perhaps because geographically it was furthest away.) Consolidation was seen as a two-way process in which the Dominions would help pay for Imperial defence in return for a say in policy-making. Yet, clearly, if Britain was to share policy-making with Dominion governments, it might work against London's own interests, for Dominion governments, as seen in the 1911 debate over renewing the Japanese alliance, had their own strategic concerns. Because of this, one development which the Colonial Secretary, Lord Elgin, opposed was the foundation of individual Foreign Offices in the Dominions. Nonetheless, in 1906 Grey effectively paved the way for such a development when he allowed a Canadian official to be attached to the British Embassy in Washington. This followed growing Canadian concern over Britain's tendency to placate America at Canada's expense. The prospect of the Dominions pursuing their own security policies raises the issue, hotly discussed by historians, of whether the Empire really was an asset to Britain. Only the bare lines of this debate can be sketched here. It has long been recognised that, on the negative side, most British trade and investment before 1914 was not with the Empire (which took about a third of both) but with the US, Europe and South America; the return on investments from African colonies was not good; and most British emigration was not to the Dominions but the US. In all its colonies Britain's power was restricted by the need to placate elite groups on whom local authority relied and preservation of the scattered Empire created extremely difficult policy choices, for example about who to ally with and how large the navy should be. It also intensified divisions in Whitehall over the interests to which Britain should give priority: the Foreign Office, India Office, Colonial Office, armed forces, and others had their own perspective. Colonies had to be governed and policed; ultimately they could sap resources through rebellion. They sapped resources too because Britain bore most costs of Imperial defence which, on some calculations, were higher than the defence budgets of France and Germany. Yet on the positive side there can be no doubting the value of India to the British economy, or of the Dominions as settler colonies, and, as has just been seen, most British possessions were quiescent in the Edwardian era. Even without formal Empire Britain would have needed to defend its global commercial and financial interests and, as an island power, would have required a substantial navy to protect its food imports. The colonies provided a network of naval bases as well as local troops and, in some cases after 1909, Dominions and colonies did pay to build dreadnoughts. The rise in defence costs, from about £30 million in 1890 to nearly £70 million 20 years later, was largely due not to Imperial demands but to technological advances, and the cost of defence, at a few per cent of national income, was far lower than it was 70 years later, when the Empire was no more. London can even be said to have achieved the aim of maintaining a low-cost defence because comparisons with continental powers should take into account the loss of man-hours in industry which Germany and France faced through conscription. The full value of colonial resources, fighting men and bases would only properly be seen after Britain went to war in 1914. Then again, arguably, the need to defend the Empire proved an ultimate liability because it was that which led to the Japanese alliance (which carried some risk of war with France and Russia) and later to the *entente* with France (which it can be argued eventually drew Britain into a global conflict).

The second Moroccan crisis and Anglo-German *détente*

Following the Russian Convention, the British public remained preconcerned with the German threat and such fears intensified following the German naval expansion of 1908 which threatened to overtake Britain in the number of dreadnoughts within four years. During 1908 most of the Cabinet, including two leading radical figures, Lloyd George (Chancellor of the Exchequer) and Winston Churchill (at the Board of Trade), supported reductions in the naval estimates and in July Lloyd George even made a public call for talks with Germany. But the Germans themselves did not wish to bargain and by February 1909 the Cabinet had become more divided as panic spread over (baseless) rumours that Germany might secretly be building more battleships than it claimed. The Admiralty wanted to build six new dreadnoughts, with an option on two more, but radicals wanted only four and Churchill, believing the German threat was exaggerated, threatened to resign. Another factor was public pressure, stirred up by Conservatives, the Navy League and the Press using the slogan 'We want eight and we won't wait'. A special Cabinet committee was set up and emerged with a clever compromise: to please the radicals, only four dreadnoughts would be ordered; but, to the satisfaction of their opponents, four more would be ordered if necessary. They actually were ordered in July. Almost 80 Liberal MPs voted against the decision, but with Conservative support approval was overwhelming. That year, in an important development, the government finally solved the problem of how to pay for both naval and social spending, when Lloyd George's 'People's Budget' introduced large increases in income tax. The budget initiated an intense period of enmity between the main parties on domestic policy but also, arguably, began a long-term, uneasy compromise in British political life about public expenditure. The Right could be satisfied that security issues would be safeguarded, the Left that social spending would be, even if there was debate over where the balance should lie. In Germany in contrast tax reform failed in 1909 and thereafter most German defence spending went on the army. In effect, Germany had lost the naval race with Britain and began to plan for war with Russia and France. The German Navy was little use except for prestige and as an affront to Britain it was a positive disadvantage. Thus the new German Chancellor, Theobald von Bethmann-Hollweg, offered talks on a naval agreement, but exploratory conversations showed that, as before, the Germans wished to extract too high a price for any deal. They would only avoid further *increases* in naval spending if Britain promised neutrality in war: current levels of German naval expansion would continue and Britain would effectively have to abandon the *ententes*. Contacts continued and, despite the scepticism of Grey, a Cabinet committee was set up in 1911 to study policy towards Germany. At that point, however, relations were upset by another crisis over Morocco.

Morocco re-emerged as a troublespot in spring when a local revolt led the French, rather provocatively, to send a military force to the city of Fez. The Germans were enraged and, as in 1905, chose a dramatic action to demonstrate their feelings, sending a warship, the *Panther*, to Agadir in July. At first the Cabinet, itself displeased over French behaviour, favoured concessions. But Berlin adopted a tough negotiating stance, demanding territorial compensation from France in the Congo. The

Foreign Office was determined to support the *entente*, especially since Russia refused to back France strongly. Foreign Office motives were summed up by Nicolson, in a document which reflected fears both of Germany and the Franco-Russian alliance: Britain must not 'give France any grounds for believing that our adhesion to the Triple Entente is ... weakening' because she 'would never forgive us ... This would mean that we should have a triumphant Germany, and an unfriendly France and Russia', and in turn would necessitate 'increased naval estimates, while the cessation of our intimate relations with Russia would render our position in Central Asia ... insecure'.[6] There is no more succinct description of why the Foreign Office wished to preserve the *entente cordiale* in the decade after 1904. But also at stake, purely and simply, was prestige, as the Germans seemed to believe that the Moroccan problem could be resolved without reference to Britain. To disabuse them of this, the Cabinet approved a speech by Lloyd George, delivered at the Mansion House, in which he declared that Britain must be consulted on all vital international issues. Such a public warning was given because the German Ambassador to London carried little weight with his government. The speech encouraged the French to avoid concessions in the Congo, bitterly offended the German public and upset British radicals. An Anglo-German war seemed possible and behind the scenes other significant moves were afoot. On 23 August the CID decided to favour the army's desire for a 'continental strategy' in war, sending the BEF to Europe. At the same time General Henry Wilson, recently appointed Director of Military Operations, reinvigorated military staff talks with France and Anglo-French naval talks also began. Typically, however, these important decisions were taken without reference to the full Cabinet and, when ministers outside the CID learnt of them, there was a revolt. In November it became clear that even if Lloyd George and Churchill were moving towards the 'strong *entente*' camp, most ministers were concerned over the growing commitment to France. To keep the government united it was agreed that staff talks with France should *not* carry any commitment to intervene in war. This was a critical moment for Grey, reminding him that even if he had a high degree of day-to-day initiative and even if much of the population saw Germany as 'the enemy', he could not set the lines of foreign policy without reference to the Liberal Party and Cabinet. Yet it came just as the French and Germans resolved their differences over Morocco, without major French concessions. Once more it seemed that if Britain stood close by France, the Germans would back down. And even if one accepts that Britain did not count for much in the European *military* balance, it clearly had the wherewithal to command *diplomatic* respect. Once again, German bluster had simply driven Paris and London closer together.

After the second Moroccan crisis, Grey did adopt a more conciliatory line towards Germany whilst continuing to distance British policy on certain issues from that of France and Russia. There was a period of *détente* in Anglo-German relations which belies the claim that 'by 1910 it was fairly clear that sooner or later Britain and Germany would be at war'.[7] Both countries feared Russian ambitions in certain regions and acted together during the Balkan Wars of 1912–13 to prevent an Austro-Russian conflict. With the naval race won and facing considerable domestic problems, the British became less obsessed with the German threat. It should also be remembered that Grey had never wanted war with Germany, but rather to prevent it dominating the continent. Grey's ideal was to secure the old aim of British statesmen in Europe, a 'balance of power' between the Germans and the Franco-Russian alliance which would prevent the need for direct involvement on the continent. He believed it required a flexible British policy to achieve this and objected to the use of the term 'Triple Entente' to describe links between Britain, France and Russia. Other ministers were even keener to reach agreements with Germany and there was a marked improvement in relations between the Colonial Office, under William Harcourt, and its German equivalent: the idea that colonial rivalries led to war in 1914 is now discounted by most historians. Nonetheless, the extent of this *détente* must not be exaggerated. Although the two sides reached an agreement on the Baghdad railway in June 1914, there was no time to ratify it before the war. A new, modest agreement was also negotiated on the Portuguese colonies but never published. By 1912 popular suspicions were too deep to be quickly eradicated. Certain elements of the Press, notably the *Daily Mail*, continued to take a jingoistic line, accepting (with a warping of Darwinian logic) that there would be an 'inevitable' struggle between Britain and Germany for world supremacy. One aspect of the Press campaign was the pre-war invasion and spy 'scares', also fuelled by books like Erskine Childers's *Riddle of the Sands* (1903) or William Le Queux's *The Invasion of 1910* (1906). By 1910 some newspapers were reporting upwards of 10 000 German spies in Britain and the 'scare' affected official policy. In July 1909 a revamped Secret Service Bureau was set up by the CID to spy on Germany and help the anti-subversive Special Branch (established in 1883 by Scotland Yard) uncover German agents in Britain, and 1911 saw a number of important developments which, unknown to most of the population, seriously undermined civil liberties. Most importantly, the Agadir crisis was used to rush an Official Secrets Act through parliament, supposedly as a measure against foreign-employed spies, but actually preventing anyone divulging government secrets without authority. The same year saw the inauguration of the 'D' notice system, under which newspapers agreed not to publish certain stories designated by the

War Office, and the police unofficially began to keep a register of Germans living near naval and military installations. Thus a supposed *foreign* menace was used to expand secrecy, censorship and intelligence work *within* Britain. British intelligence at this point cannot be described as very efficient. Accurate intelligence on German naval capabilities (for example in submarine warfare) seems to have been collected by Mansfield Smith-Cumming's external espionage service only to be ignored, whilst at the height of the Agadir crisis the Admiralty could not discover the location of the German fleet! The Imperial counter-intelligence service MO5 (part of the War Office) was underfunded, poorly led and likely to believe the most preposterous spy stories. Its chief, Vernon Kell, 'was so paranoid about invasion that ... he spent part of his summer holiday at a potential landing spot'.[8] When war eventually broke out, MO5 could only find 21 genuine spies, who were quickly imprisoned, but 50 000 'enemy aliens' were either interned or sent home.

The most substantial point of difference between Britain and Germany remained naval issues. In February 1912 Haldane – who was well-disposed to *détente* with Germany – with the blessing of Grey, Lloyd George and Churchill, went to Berlin to explore the possibilities of a naval agreement. Again the Germans were only interested in a deal if Britain promised neutrality in war, and the mission was undermined by a new German expansion of shipbuilding. Soon after, Churchill, now at the Admiralty, launched his own initiative, proposing a 'naval holiday' by which Britain would desist from building dreadnoughts in the coming year if Germany did. Such moderation helped calm radical fears of an 'anti-German' policy and reconciled parliament to building more ships. He repeated the offer twice in 1913 but only succeeded in stirring up German ill-feeling over what were seen as attempts to frustrate a legitimate aspiration for naval power. Despite *détente*, the March 1912 naval estimates in Britain were clearly aimed at the German threat: the target was no longer the two-power standard but a 60 per cent superiority over Germany in dreadnoughts (actually, in 1914, Britain had 22 such vessels and the Germans 13). Furthermore, the navy was to be concentrated even more in home waters. Indeed, in effectively the most important British commitment to France so far, it was agreed in 1912 that the French should handle maritime security in the Mediterranean (facing the potential threat from Germany's allies, Austria and Italy) whilst the Royal Navy protected the English Channel. This agreement, supplemented by an exchange of letters between Grey and Cambon which promised consultation in times of crisis, made Britain morally responsible for the security of the northern French coast. To some concern in the Foreign and War Offices (both worried over influence in the Mediterranean and Near East), Britain's Mediterranean Fleet was withdrawn from Malta to

Gibraltar. Shortly afterwards, the Kaiser and his advisers agreed to plan war on two fronts, against Russia and France. By boosting French confidence in the two Moroccan crises and thereby strengthening France's value to Russia, Britain can be said to have helped influence this decision. It can also be argued that, by settling differences with Russia in 1907 Britain helped ensure that Russian ambitions focused on the Balkans, where tensions soon became intense. Indeed, the Grey–Cambon letters and German war plans had in a sense mapped the route to war 18 months later. Such a war was certainly not inevitable, but the 1912 Anglo-French naval decisions – taken just as the naval race with Germany was decisively won – were a fateful step, of questionable necessity, which compromised the country's independence more than the original *entente* had done.

The 1914 crisis

In May 1914 Nicolson wrote that, since arriving at the Foreign Office (FO), he had not known such a calm atmosphere. When, in late June, the heir to the Austrian throne was assassinated by a terrorist who had received aid from Serbia, Grey did not see the need for grave concern. Cabinet discussions were dominated by problems in Ireland (where civil war threatened to erupt), Britain had effectively abandoned interest in the Balkans in 1896 and recent crises in the area had successfully been overcome, partly because Germany and Britain had worked to restrain Austria–Hungary and Russia. It was apparent in the 1908 crisis that Grey had little desire to see Russian advances in south-east Europe or to go to war because of Austro-Russian rivalry. Since then Britain had helped ensure that the Turkish Empire in Europe was dismantled peacefully during the Balkan Wars of 1912–13. But Grey did not fully appreciate the ambitions of local powers, like Serbia, or the fears of Austria–Hungary (which believed its Empire might collapse in the face of Balkan nationalism). Also, the Foreign Office did not appreciate either the mutual antagonism gathering on the continent over the rapid build-up of armed forces. Thus whilst the Austrians feared dismantlement, France and Russia feared German hegemony, and Germany feared 'encirclement' – a worry strengthened when Berlin learnt of the Anglo-Russian naval talks. The recent *détente* between London and Berlin, distrust of Russia and fear of French bellicosity helped create a situation where Britain relied more on Germany than its *entente* partners to prevent war. Until late in the crisis, Grey believed that so long as Berlin was not harassed, a (mythical) 'peace lobby' in Germany would restrain the Austrians, just as Bethman-Hollweg hoped for British neutrality. FO officials were much less sure of this. The Cabinet did not even discuss the crisis until 24 July, the day after Austria–Hungary issued a tough ultimatum to Serbia. At that time ministers simply approved Grey's efforts to achieve a peace conference among the powers, efforts rejected by Germany and soon overtaken by the decision of one power after another to mobilise. Just as the Austrians were determined to punish Serbia, so the Russians were determined not to face another humiliation like 1905 and 1908. The Germans could have restrained Austria, but some in Berlin believed that since war was likely to come anyway, 1914 was the best time if Germany wanted a victory: after all the Russians planned by 1917 to have an army of 2 million men. When on 28 July – two days after Austria declared war on Serbia – the Russians mobilised, the Germans had little choice but to follow quickly. For the German war plan, the Schlieffen Plan, was based on the proposition that Germany must fight France *and* Russia, and called for a massive invasion of France to be launched *first*, in the hope of achieving a victory on the western front, before the German Army dealt with the Russian giant. 'If ... the Germans had marched eastwards', one historian has written, 'the situation might have been transformed' and Britain would not have gone to war.[9] But the Schlieffen Plan turned a regional crisis into an all-European one and shifted Britain's focus from Balkan squabbles to security concerns nearer home, in Belgium and the Channel.

As late as 29 July, Grey considered that if an Austro-Russian war broke out, 'It would be a question of the supremacy of Teuton or Slav ... and our idea had always been to avoid being drawn into a war over the Balkan question'.[10] It would be difficult to justify participation to the Liberal Party and public. That day the Cabinet decided to maintain a 'free hand' and avoid giving assurances, either that they would join the war or that they would stay out. Radicals and the Labour Party were opposed to intervention; Norman Angell hastily founded the Neutrality League; and the Governor of the Bank of England begged Lloyd George to 'keep us out of it. We shall all be ruined if we are dragged in.'[11] Everyone knew, however, that if Britain did join in, it would be on the side of France, and Grey, who had backed France in all crises since 1905, privately warned the German Ambassador that 'if the issue did become such that we thought British interests required us to intervene we must intervene at once'.[12] This warning was enough to worry Bethman-Hollweg, leading him to offer restraint: if Britain could delay Russia's mobilisation, Germany would control Austria. By the time the British appealed to Russia, however, it was too late. Mobilisation timetables could not suddenly be thrown into reverse. Britain, unlike the other powers, cannot be accused of pursuing a bellicose line during the July crisis, but British internal divisions and procrastination arguably carried their own price, making France uncertain of support. On 30 and 31 July the Cabinet, increasingly divided between interventionists, undecideds and neutralists, again refused to make commitments and on 1 August a distressed Asquith feared the government would break up.[13] Grey reminded Cambon that there was no written agreement to come to France's aid and said – importantly – that much would depend on the course of public opinion. Cambon, however, argued, equally correctly, that Britain was under a moral obligation to support France because the 1912 naval agreements left the Royal Navy to defend the Channel. There can be little doubt that Grey and the Admiralty were sympathetic to Cambon's case, and on 1 August – in another important action taken without Cabinet approval – Churchill mobilised the navy. Grey also rejected a German idea that Britain should remain neutral if Berlin promised not to land on the northern French coast: such an undertaking was little use if France collapsed and Germany could dictate a European settlement. At the decisive Cabinet meeting on 2 August a number of factors came into play which tipped the balance in favour of intervention. These included Grey's explanation of the moral commitment to France (of which most ministers were unaware), his threat to resign if this were not fulfilled, fear of a German fleet in the Channel and the danger of seeing France destroyed as a Great Power. Important too may have been the knowledge that, if the Liberal government collapsed, the Conservatives were ready to assume office and take Britain into war anyway. There also seemed to be a shift in public attitude as German ambitions in the West became apparent. In order to carry out their invasion of France, the Germans intended to march through Belgium, of whose integrity Britain was a guarantor. On 2 August Berlin issued an ultimatum, demanding that its army be allowed to traverse Belgium unhindered; the following day there was a massive pro-war demonstration in central London. France too had considered breaching Belgian neutrality and the invasion of Belgium was probably not the most vital reason for Britain going to war. But it did play a decisive role for some ministers, since it emphasised Germany's aggressiveness, highlighted the danger to British security and gave a moral cause for which to fight. With only two resignations from the Cabinet Britain declared war on 4 August. In addressing the House of Commons Grey added two other reasons for action. One was that war would damage British commercial and financial interests whether she stayed in or out; the second was that if Britain did not fight it would be despised by the victors. It was better therefore to enter the war, help ensure Germany's defeat and stay close to the French and Russians who, in the long term, remained potential threats themselves. The speech informed the public for the first time about British commitments to France, yet said little about Russia or the Balkan crisis which sparked the conflict.

Although Lloyd George later claimed the government 'stumbled' into war, historians agree there were rational reasons for entry. The exact nature and balance of these is, however, in dispute. Those who see entry as the logical result of Grey's interpretation of the *entente* with France have a strong case, but must address the fact that until early August even Grey feared that public opinion would not allow Britain to fight. Those who argue that war was primarily directed against a German bid for European hegemony in the Napoleonic style – which Britain must always resist – also have a case, given the nature of the Schlieffen Plan. But on other evidence such an interpretation of German policy is debatable and, right to the end, some key figures still had equal fears of Russia. When, at dinner on that fateful 2 August, Lloyd George was asked 'How shall we feel if we see France overrun by Germany', he commented 'How will you feel if you see Germany overrun ... by Russia?'[14] Some argue that if Grey had presented 'a clear and credible threat of British intervention' at an earlier point, war need not have occurred, since this would have been enough to deter Berlin.[15] But there are a number of flaws in such an argument. First, it ignores the fact that until 2 August the Cabinet and public opinion were genuinely divided. For the same reasons that Grey had been unable to turn the *entente* into an alliance, he was unable in July 1914 to say he would support France. Second, it supposes Britain *could* present a credible threat – sufficient to deter Germany – without a large army. Third, it assumes Grey was quite ready to fight in 1914, when in fact he was not. By seeking to restrain Austria *and* Russia, Grey in fact adopted the old British aim of preserving the peace. Peace not war (whatever form it took) was the real British interest: here lies the heart of Anglo-German differences for the Germans *were* ready to go to war to achieve certain ambitions. Finally it assumes that uncertainty about British policy gave encouragement to German aggression. Certainly it worried the French. But some in Cabinet reckoned that 'if both sides do not know what we shall do, both will be less willing to run risks':[16] again the aim was to prevent either side taking a bellicose line, and uncertainty about British intentions could be seen as a positive factor. German political leaders certainly had no right to assume that Britain would remain neutral. Indeed considerable evidence pointed against this, whatever the procrastination in London. Not only had Grey stood by France in previous crises, but Berlin should have known that if anything would induce Britain to enter the war, it was an unprovoked attack on France and Belgium. Yet that is what the Schlieffen Plan represented in 1914. German political leaders were led into this by the military (who were less surprised that Britain went to war).

The 1914 crisis can be seen as the last chapter in a story where Britain tried to keep the peace by shifting its diplomatic stance and preserving its own freedom to manoeuvre. Since the mid-1890s British policy had been 'designed to prevent war generally, while at the same time safeguarding Britain's interests against *all*-comers' – but especially Russia and Germany.[17] Yet despite such successes as victory in the naval race, and despite the maintenance of Britain's overall pre-eminence among the Great Powers, policy choices had become more restricted and foreign secretaries found it more difficult to steer a safe course. The need to defend the world's largest Empire; the creation of new navies and of conscript armies; the rise of armed blocs in Europe; and the need to strike a balance between patriotic and radical viewpoints – all these factors helped push Britain down a road where isolation was left behind. London sought to neutralise certain threats by a process of conciliation (as with the US after 1896 or Russia after 1905) or ran the risk of war by committing itself to other powers who, it was hoped, could defend certain British interests (as with Japan after 1902 or France after 1904). The *entente cordiale* was originally intended as a limited commitment but took on greater importance over time, partly as a way to meet German ambitions and partly as a step to cooperation with Russia, and the 1912 naval commitments to France proved especially significant. Britain could not do everything at once. No country ever could. And old interests, for instance in the Balkans and the Straits, became unimportant. It was not so much a relative industrial and commercial decline *vis-à-vis* other powers that was the problem. The three principal 'rising' powers were America, Germany and Japan, but of these the first was no real threat and the last was an ally. The real problem for British diplomacy was the policy pursued by Berlin, upsetting the European balance and proving ambitious beyond the continent. Especially after Russia's defeat in 1905 and the contemporaneous Moroccan crisis, the German threat loomed larger. Its navy was viewed as a menace. Its ambition of *Weltpolitik* aroused fear, even though Russia was a more serious danger outside Europe and was led by a more autocratic government. After 1912, with the naval race won, Anglo-German *détente* was possible, while Anglo-Russian relations worsened. By then Germany was effectively neutralised as a threat to the Empire. Yet in the Foreign Office, Berlin, with its confusing and volatile behaviour, was not seen as susceptible to a policy of cooperation and, in any case, the *ententes* with France and Russia had enormous importance in their own right, as guarantees of British safety world-wide. As a result, whenever crises occurred there was 'an instinctive reaffirmation of the importance of the *ententes* whether the threat came from Germany or from Britain's *entente* partners'.[18] Whether the *ententes* were primarily seen as anti-German devices or important links in themselves made little ultimate difference: both readings pointed to support for France in 1914. This support revealed that Britain could no longer defend its interests through a 'free hand' and created the situation which the *ententes* had been intended to avoid. Britain was forced to fight a war which tested its character and resources to the limit.

Notes

1 Quoted in Morris A., *The Scaremongers: The Advocacy of War and Rearmament, 1896–1914* (London, 1984), x.
2 Martel G., 'Rethinking the Decline and Fall of Great Britain', *International History Review*, **13**(4), 1991, 685.
3 Wilson K., *The Policy of the Entente* (Cambridge, 1985), 77.
4 Bourne K., *The Foreign Policy of Victorian England, 1830–1902* (Oxford, 1970), 479–81.
5 Wilson J., *CB: A Life of Sir Henry Campbell-Bannerman* (London, 1973), 545–6.
6 Gooch G.P. and Temperley H. (eds), *British Documents on the Origins of the War, 1898–1914* (1927–38), Vol. XVII , 386.
7 Holland R., *The Pursuit of Greatness: Britain and the World Role, 1900–1970* (London, 1991), 48.
8 Hiley N., 'The Failure of British Counter-Espionage against Germany, 1907–14', *Historical Journal*, **28**(4), 1985, 861.
9 Steiner Z., *The Foreign Office and Foreign Policy, 1898–1914* (London, 1969), 224.
10 Gooch G.P. and Temperley H. (eds), *British Documents*, Vol. XI, 180.
11 McEwen J. (ed.), *The Riddell Diaries* (London, 1986), 85.
12 Gooch G.P. and Temperley H. (eds), *British Documents*, Vol. XI, 182–3.
13 Brock M. and Brock E. (eds), *H.H. Asquith: Letters to Venetia Stanley* (Oxford, 1982), 140.
14 McEwen J. (ed.), *Riddell Diaries*, 87.
15 Sagan S., '1914 Revisited', *International Security*, **11**(2), 1986, 168.
16 Ekstein M. and Steiner Z., 'The Sarajevo Crisis'. In Hinsley H. (ed.), *British Foreign Policy under Sir Edward Grey* (Cambridge, 1977), 401.
17 Neilson K., *Britain and the Last Tsar: British Policy and Russia, 1894–1917* (Oxford, 1995), xii.
18 Bartlett C.J., *British Foreign Policy in the Twentieth Century* (London, 1989), 19.

3
Great War and Imperial crisis, 1914–1924

The impact of war

Whatever its relative industrial decline compared to America and Germany, in 1914 Britain easily had the world's greatest Empire, its most powerful navy and largest volume of overseas investments. The country had faced several security challenges in recent decades, including the Franco-Russian alliance, Boer War and naval race with Germany, but financial strength, diplomatic skill and national prestige helped overcome them. The rise of American power might have been daunting in industrial terms, but did not threaten Britain. In 1914, however, the use of differing diplomatic strategies, whether it be coercion or alliance, deterrence or *détente*, had broken down as ways to ensure peace. The difficulties for London should not be exaggerated. Every power had problems adapting to the challenge of a lengthy, far-flung conflict, fought with advanced weapons and demanding the mobilisation of whole societies in 'total' war. Hardly anyone predicted such a long, destructive conflict: the initial expectation was that it would be 'over by Christmas'. Thanks to the war some powers ceased to exist or found their political institutions overturned. Britain at least preserved its liberal constitution and capitalist economy, albeit in much-altered forms; and it emerged on the winning side, able to fulfil such aims as the destruction of the German Navy, the preservation of France and restoration of Belgium. Yet British leaders had been right to expect that a large-scale conflict would be costly even if the country emerged victorious. Britain suffered about 750 000 dead in the war, a further 1.8 million were maimed and the whole country suffered the numbing psychological impact of such losses which, among other results, made it more difficult to pursue a tough, confident foreign policy afterwards. On the material side, despite the original hope of maintaining 'business as usual', and high profits for industrialists who turned to war production, Britain lost commercial markets not only in Central Europe but also in Latin America and East Asia, notably to America and Japan (the powers who gained most from the war in relative terms). British manufacturers suffered because non-European countries developed their own industries. Britain's declining power compared to the US was most marked in the area of 'invisible' trade and financial might. Although able to pay its own war effort and able to rebuild its investments afterwards, Britain used up dollar securities and gold at an alarming rate, especially after 1916. The national debt mushroomed. London also acted as 'banker' to the Allied cause, lending £1750 million to support the war but borrowing about £1000 million from America (and £350 million from other sources). By 1918 America had become the world's largest creditor nation and demanded repayment of its loans in full, but Russia, having fallen to Bolshevism, refused to repay its loans (totalling over £550 million) to Britain. Other countries found it difficult to settle debts with London, placing Britain in an unenviable financial position for a time. The conflict spelled the end of other pre-1914 suppositions about the world. The Empire was racked by crisis for several years afterwards; the balance of power in Europe was completely upset; and at home the Victorian world of low taxes and *laissez-faire*, already compromised, was gone forever. Government intervention, to organise the economy for war, reached a massive scale. Businessmen had to accept price controls, but were compensated with lucrative government contracts; trades unions accepted wage controls and 'no strike' agreements, but were rewarded with greater consultation by ministers. Coal mines, railways, merchant shipping, scientific research: all had to be centrally directed for the purposes of war. Despite the efforts of Chancellor of the Exchequer, Reginald McKenna, to hold down spending in 1915–16, the cost of maintaining the armed forces grew to almost £2000 million in 1918, 20 times pre-war expenditure. Overall, government spending took more than half the country's gross national product (GNP). Payment for this not only meant utilising external assets but quadrupling income tax, the use of food taxes and (in order to keep down inflation, which doubled in any case) high interest rates.

Britain was obviously less prepared than other Great Powers for a large-scale land war. Historically, although it had sometimes fought continental campaigns, Britain usually pursued a 'blue water' strategy, relying on naval power, economic blockade and small-scale land operations to achieve its aims. In the First World War these strategies still had some use, but the term 'world war' was a misnomer, for the conflict was decided in Europe. The navy, though valuable for blockading Germany, had only a limited role to play. In the solitary large-scale sea battle, at Jutland on 31 May 1916, the navy, which had not faced another substantial fleet for decades, lost more ships but prevented the Germans breaking onto the high seas. The homeland was never threatened with invasion, but neither could British admirals lead an assault on the well-fortified German coast. The navy easily mopped up the few German surface 'raiders' and looked after the mundane business of transport duty, but the German submarine menace proved difficult to tackle. In February–June 1917 the U-boats threatened to starve Britain and the situation was only eased thanks to the use of convoys, an innovation originally criticised by the Admiralty. The corollary of the navy's secondary role in defeating Germany was a declining impact on policy. Instead, the major influence came from the army, represented (not always harmoniously) by General Headquarters (GHQ) in France, and the War Office and Chief of Imperial General Staff (CIGS) in London. The power of William Robertson as CIGS in 1915–18 became known as the 'Robertson dictatorship'. Generals (or 'brass hats') even became sophisticated and successful in influencing the Press and, through them, public opinion, in order to win arguments with the politicians (or 'frocks'). This was the first time in 60 years that Britain fought any kind of land war in Europe; its army was tiny compared to conscript forces on the continent; and its industry, other than shipbuilding, was not geared to defence needs. One leading figure who quickly foresaw that war might last years was the veteran Lord Kitchener, recalled to high office as Minister of War. He started to raise a volunteer army – one million signed up by Christmas 1914 – to supplement the British Expeditionary Force, which had been despatched to France in August only to share in the retreat of Allied armies from Belgium. As the western front settled into the stalemate of trench warfare, Kitchener conceived the scheme of building a huge British army, to provide the country with a decisive role in battles which would resolve the conflict in two or three years' time. He shared Prime Minister Asquith's hopes of doing this gradually, with limited disruption to British social and political life. Yet Kitchener was no more able than anyone else to understand the scale of the Great War and during 1915 it became clear that a substantial army could only be created if the country abandoned its aversion to high taxes and, most controversially, conscription. This was a difficult decision for Liberals who nursed beliefs in *laissez-faire* and individualism which were ill-suited to 'total' war. In January 1916, after considerable pressure from the Press, conscription was introduced for single men aged 18–41. Married men followed four months later. Over 16 000 'conscientious objectors' refused to be conscripted and were imprisoned, but this number was relatively small: eventually Britain mobilised about 7 million men and the Empire contributed 3 million more.

In other areas too it was a case of slow adjustment to wartime realities, with increasing popular realisation that the diplomatic manoeuvres of July–August 1914 had resulted in a conflict which affected all areas of national life. At the start of the war the annual output of artillery shells, for example, was half a million tons per annum, but by 1918 had grown to 75 million. A critical point was the May 1915 'shell scandal', which followed complaints from GHQ about the supply of artillery shells. The scandal coincided with one of the war's major military failures, the Gallipoli expedition (discussed below). It also coincided with the disappearance-cum-resignation of 'Jacky' Fisher, who had been recalled as First Sea Lord, only to experience a clash of character with the navy's civilian head, Churchill. The shell scandal, stirred by the Press, reflected the military's dissatisfaction with Kitchener, and seemed to justify Conservative criticisms of Asquith's war policy. One result was the appointment of Lloyd George as Minister of Munitions. He took extensive powers to direct industry and manpower. The second result was the formation of a coalition, including Conservatives and Labour members, portrayed as the embodiment of national unity at a critical time. But Asquith was careful to keep Liberals in a dominant position and continued to direct the war in what Conservatives saw as a lackadaisical way. For all his patience, grasp of detail and political adeptness, he lacked energy, innovation and the ability to inspire others. In wartime it was easy to criticise his active social life and lack of interest in military or international issues. He found it increasingly difficult to hold the coalition together and was weakened by the death, in June 1916, of his closest military adviser, Kitchener, who was replaced at the War Office by the energetic Lloyd George. Over the following months the morale of the nation was sapped by the death of over 100 000 servicemen in the Battle of the Somme. Asquith still nominally commanded a majority of MPs, but parliament's ability to control government declined sharply during the war and, in December 1916, behind-the-scenes machinations led to his being replaced by Lloyd George whose new Cabinet was dominated by Conservatives. These included the leader Andrew Bonar Law and ex-premier Balfour (as Foreign Secretary, succeeding the long-serving Grey). At the same time the Liberals divided, never to dominate government again. The administration survived the war, troubled only by the Maurice Case of May 1918, another potential 'shell scandal', which failed to erupt, partly because Asquith bungled his attack and partly because Lloyd George, in contrast to his predecessor, was careful to draw the Press barons like Lord Beaverbrook closer to the decision-making process. Yet the new government had few new ideas about running the war. Douglas Haig, who took over at GHQ in December 1915, believed in a war of attrition as the way to defeat the Germans and show them war did not pay. True, the so-called 'Westerners', like Robertson, Haig and most Conservatives, were challenged by 'Easterners', including Lloyd George and the Admiralty, who argued it was possible to sidestep the deadlocked western front and defeat Germany by attacking her allies,

Austria–Hungary and Turkey. But Gallipoli and other 'eastern' campaigns failed to produce dramatic results and, between July and November 1917, another bloody offensive was launched in France, in the vain hope of achieving a 'knock-out blow'. Passchendaele cost over 300 000 further British casualties and paved the way for Lloyd George to replace Robertson by a more amenable CIGS, Henry Wilson. As the war dragged on in 1917–18, with the Russian government already a victim of revolution, there was some concern in Britain about rising social discontent, witnessed by a growing number of strikes; there was interest too in negotiated peace. Yet morale and national unity eventually held up, despite food shortages, conscription and heavy demands on workers. Thanks to Germany's invasion of Belgium, Britons always felt themselves to be morally in the right. Wartime propaganda upheld the image of 'Prussian barbarism'; the number of casualties helped stiffen the resolve to achieve victory; and social problems were alleviated by wage increases, measures to prevent profiteering and promises of a 'land fit for heroes' once the sacrifices were over. When Germany sued for an armistice in November 1918 pent-up exasperation with war burst out in a determination to punish the defeated powers – notwithstanding the fact that victory had come suddenly, by a narrow margin, with many German people (misled deliberately by their military leaders) expecting a moderate settlement.

Foreign policy making and the 'new diplomacy'

Foreign policy did not come to an end with war. Grey, demoralised by the July crisis and increasingly confused about his role, believed diplomacy must dedicate itself to achieving victory. His Foreign Office staff grew five times over during the war and took on an increasing range of tasks, which demanded major organisational changes, beginning with the formation of a large War Department to handle political problems generated by conflict. One delicate issue was to prevent neutral states – including, until 1917, America – from trading with Germany. The British insisted on their right, during wartime, to blockade an enemy and trade controls were therefore stiffened in March 1915. But practically enforcement was difficult, upset neutral opinion and even caused controversy among British businessmen, who wished to continue trading with Germany (on non-military items) using neutral go-betweens. In 1916 a special Ministry of Blockade was established in the FO under the Conservative Robert Cecil. An important, new area of activity for the FO (though not their counterparts in Germany or France) was propaganda, to influence foreign opinion in Britain's favour. A News Department was formed to provide 'factual' news items for the foreign

Press, and a secret War Propaganda Bureau was set up to disseminate 'disguised' forms of propaganda. It was especially important to influence US opinion. America's financial importance and military potential were self-evident, but isolationist sentiment, as well as the anti-British propaganda of Germans and Irish-Americans, had to be countered. Yet the FO was never at ease with such 'underhand' work and there was pressure from the War Office and Admiralty for a more vigorous propaganda campaign. In February 1918 a Ministry of Information was set up under Lord Beaverbrook, with a separate Department of Enemy Propaganda under another Press baron, Lord Northcliffe. Both had their own agents abroad and, to the dismay of the FO, began to influence foreign policy by, for example, influencing the definition of war aims. It was partly to reassert its position that the FO developed the Political Intelligence Department which provided information on the possible shape of a peace settlement. This department was principally made up, not of professional diplomats, but of academics.

The Ministry of Information was only one wartime development which called into question the Edwardian predominance of the FO in foreign policy making. The Prime Minister believed in personal diplomacy, and meetings with foreign leaders became a frequent occurrence. He also relied on his own advisers and distrusted traditional networks, claiming 'diplomats were invented simply to waste time'.[1] His own office in Downing Street, the so-called 'garden suburb', played an important role in foreign policy, and was influenced by pro-Imperial thinking, because of characters like Philip Kerr, the Prime Minister's Private Secretary and editor of the journal *Round Table*. Another novel, but long-lasting, factor in Whitehall was the Cabinet Secretariat, set up in December 1916 to rationalise decision-making by recording Cabinet decisions and issuing clear instructions to departments. Its head, Maurice Hankey, had been Secretary of the Committee of Imperial Defence (CID). Other members included Leo Amery, another member of the Round Table, and Mark Sykes, who was important in defining Middle East policies. The pre-war civilian administration had to give way to a more sophisticated system, able to draw on military expertise and take notice of the Dominions. The number of ministerial committees mushroomed to 102 in 1916 and 165 in 1918. Again, Lloyd George's arrival marked an important turning point, with the formation of a War Cabinet of five ministers without departmental responsibilities. It excluded the Foreign Secretary Balfour (though he was often invited to attend) and further sidelined the FO by sending its own members (who included the South African leader, Jan Smuts) on overseas missions. Balfour tolerated the situation because he believed it his duty to defer to Lloyd George, on whom it seemed hopes of victory rested. Less happy was Charles Hardinge, recalled as Permanent Under-Secretary of the FO in 1916. One other growing activity, of significance to foreign policy, was intelligence work. Before the war British policies on internal surveillance, code-breaking and censorship were far less developed than on the continent. Vernon Kell's MO5, with only nine officers in 1914, grew to several hundred by January 1916, when it became known as MI5, and at the end of the war numbered about 850. Having made it virtually impossible for German spies and saboteurs to operate in Britain and the Empire, MI5 became active against such potentially subversive groups as pacifists and strikers: the latter group, it was feared after 1917, could be sympathetic to Bolshevism. In this work, MI5 in Britain had to cooperate with the Special Branch, under Basil Thompson, which itself grew tenfold during the war to about 700 staff. But there was always rivalry between the two organisations, although at the end of the war it seemed Thomson had gained predominance: in 1919 he took the grand title of 'Director of Intelligence' with responsibility for counter-intelligence in the whole Empire – only to fall from office in 1921 after the complete failure of intelligence work in Ireland. The number of censors in the War Office grew from one to nearly 5000 and 'D' notices were widely used to control the Press. The wartime evolution of code-breaking began in October 1914 with the Admiralty's Room 40, which utilised the Post Office and the Marconi Company to intercept German messages. Diplomatic codes too were broken enabling the British, in their greatest coup, to intercept and decipher the February 1917 Zimmermann Telegram, which exposed German contacts with Mexico and helped bring the US into the war. The War Office had its own section MI1b, involved in deciphering work, but for much of the war engaged in wasteful competition with Room 40, both departments refusing to share material. After 1916 Mansfield Smith-Cumming (known as 'C') headed another War Office offspring, MI1c. Emerging from the foreign section of the pre-war Secret Service, it operated agents abroad, handled counter-intelligence outside the British Empire, became active against the Bolsheviks in Russia and in 1921 became known as the Secret Intelligence Service, MI6.

The FO also faced a growing popular belief that it was partly responsible for the war. Before 1914 radical opinion had been critical of the FO's exclusiveness, of secret negotiations and the operation of the international system. When conflict came, Norman Angell's warnings seemed proven correct: war *was* mutually destructive, in economic and human terms, but that did not stop Great Powers engaging in it. A month into the conflict a group of radical MPs and intellectuals, like Angell, formed the Union of Democratic Control (UDC), with E.D. Morel as Secretary. Already, one of their number, Lowes Dickinson, had spoken of creating a 'League of Nations'. It became of central importance to the idea of 'new diplomacy', although at first no one was sure what such a League should do. Some of Grey's critics, like Ramsay MacDonald, who resigned as Labour leader after opposing the declaration of war, feared the League might even become a vehicle for Great Power diplomacy. This fear was not perhaps surprising, since Grey himself took an interest in the League, partly because he himself was disillusioned by the 'old diplomacy' and partly to impress the American President, Woodrow Wilson. The UDC developed a number of ideas similar to Wilson's, designed to end the pre-war international system where, despite increasingly *interdependent* economic relations, order depended on mutual fear. The UDC argued that instead of relying on the balance of power and secret diplomacy, states should solve problems by talking openly; sovereignty must be tempered by a recognition of mutual interest; arms races must give way to disarmament; territorial changes should be made with the consent of those affected; at home foreign policy should be placed under proper parliamentary control; and a League of Nations should supervise the system. Aggressors could be dealt with by economic or even military sanctions, collectively enforced. This 'new diplomacy' was based on a belief that ordinary people around the world had little reason to quarrel and that the 'anarchical' nature of an international system (or other impersonal factors such as Imperialism or capitalism) was to blame for conflict. There was talk among radicals in the immediate term of 'Peace by Negotiation' and 'Peace without Victory', which seemed sufficiently dangerous to the war-effort for Morel to be imprisoned. The proposals of the elitist, left-wing UDC rested uneasily beside the general desire for a vengeful peace but nonetheless began to permeate popular thinking and government. In 1917, with no end to the conflict in sight, the UDC's influence grew out of all proportion to its membership. At the same time, a few MPs proved ready to vote for pro-peace resolutions in parliament and the Labour leader, Arthur Henderson, resigned from the War Cabinet in August, after the government refused to allow British representatives to attend a Socialist convention in Stockholm which would also be attended by Germans. Some Conservatives even feared an alliance of Labour, trades unions and the UDC behind a Bolshevik-style policy of nationalisation at home and internationalism abroad. Others in government had already begun to study the idea of a League of Nations more seriously. In December 1916 Britain and its allies stated their support for a League; in May 1917 Smuts supported the League publicly; and in January 1918 Robert Cecil persuaded a sceptical Balfour to set up the Phillimore Committee to study how a League might operate. By November 1918 the few British leaders interested in the subject had developed ideas which would determine the shape of the new body. Thus Cecil was keen to create a strong bureaucratic structure backed by American power, which would prevent a repetition of the 1914 crisis by forcing states to accept arbitration and conciliation in times of crisis, and Jan Smuts drew up a blueprint for the League's organisation, including a Council of major states. There were differences in government over the exact shape and role of the League. Lloyd George, though sympathetic to disarmament and the peaceful settlement of disputes, disliked an ambitious, formal structure which might restrict British independence. The Prime Minister preferred a consultative organisation, dominated by the Great Powers, ideally represented by heads of government. Whatever the differences, however, and however few the real enthusiasts for a League were in Whitehall, it was clear at the end of the war that *realpolitik* and balance of power were out of fashion, that ministers must at least pay lip service to the 'new diplomacy' and that the League, in some form, would be an important international institution. To provide it with popular support enthusiasts formed the League of Nations Union, which soon boasted Grey and Cecil among its 3000 members.

The diplomacy of war

Diplomacy changed its role during war, from the peaceful management of relations with other states to more specific purposes, including tempting neutral states onto the Allied side (or dissuading them from joining the enemy), dealing with attempts at mediation, and ensuring smooth inter-allied relations. Just as during the pre-war decade London had sought to limit the threat posed by *both* the Franco-Russian alliance and Germany, so in wartime it was vital not to make concessions to the French and, more especially, the Russians which were detrimental to British interests. Officials like Francis Bertie hoped to direct Russian ambitions away from India and the Persian Gulf to the Straits, hence Anglo-French agreement in November 1914 that Russia should obtain Constantinople when the conflict was won. In fact war exposed Russia as a giant with feet of clay and in March 1917 the Tsarist regime collapsed. At first this did not seem a harmful development: Western democrats were never happy with such an autocratic ally and hoped for a new, liberal Russia. Instead, the Bolsheviks seized power in November 1917, made peace with the Germans in March 1918, and thereby freed the Kaiser's army to launch a massive offensive in the West. More reliable as a military ally was France, but jealousy between the generals on both sides dogged the relationship. A single command structure, under France's Marshal Ferdinand Foch, was only formed in April 1918, in the face of the last German offensive and British retreats. London and Paris were able to agree on the division of some spoils of war, such as the German colonies of Togoland and Cameroon, but they differed on other elements of a peace settlement. Another ally which proved troublesome was Japan, which went to war in 1914, rapidly seized German possessions in China and the Pacific and expanded its trade in Asia, Australasia and Canada at Britain's expense. Japan became particularly embarrassing in January 1915 when it made the 'Twenty-one Demands' against China. The demands forced China to agree to a range of Japanese territorial and commercial rights, verging on a protectorate, and upset Britain, the US and the Pacific dominions, who all feared Tokyo's economic and political expansion. World war also brought new allies, such as Italy. In 1914 it was nominally an ally of Germany, but Rome's territorial ambitions were primarily directed against Austria–Hungary, in the Alps and on the Adriatic. On 26 April 1915, in the secret Treaty of London, the British and French promised Italy considerable parcels of territory, from Turkey as well as Austria, as reward for entering the war. Italy, however, proved of dubious military value. It declared war on Austria in May 1915, but avoided war with Germany until August 1916. Lloyd George hoped for great things from the Italians, but in October 1917 they suffered a major defeat at Caporeto after which the British and French doubted whether concessions promised by the Treaty of London should be given. The country which, by then, had done most to tip the balance in the Allied favour, reversing the initial success of Germany's 1918 offensive, was the United States. From the start Grey recognised the importance of the US not only as a source of loans, but also of steel, arms and food as well as a potentially valuable military ally. British propaganda to America made use of their common language and history, and such German actions as the sinking of the liner *Lusitania* (in May 1915), to ensure Washington tilted towards the Allied side. The blockade of Germany provoked problems but the Royal Navy tried to carry out searches of American ships quickly and US businessmen were happy with growing orders for goods from the Allies. For their part, the British were upset by Wilson's continuing neutrality and his attempts to negotiate peace in 1915 and 1916. Grey tried to sound interested in the proposals and, fortuitously for London, the Germans scotched all peace efforts. In April 1917, in the wake of the Zimmermann Telegram and Germany's use of 'unrestricted submarine warfare', with its implication that all cargoes bound for the Allies would be sunk, Wilson decided to enter the war. Large numbers of American troops began to arrive in Europe, after training, the following year. But Wilson fought as an 'associate' not a full ally, continued to take actions independent of London and Paris, and portrayed the war to Americans as an idealised struggle for justice and democracy. For the UDC of course, his belief in 'new diplomacy' and the 'self-determination' of nationalities made the President a hero. The British government, however, knew he might use American power to blunt Britain's Imperialist aims. They also feared that his ideal of 'the freedom of the seas' would restrict Britain's ability to enforce a blockade in future. Indeed, in autumn 1918 the British tried to restrict the number of US troops arriving in Europe, so that America would not be able to dictate the peace. That, of course, was meant to be Britain's role.

Wilson's attempts at a negotiated peace were not the only ones to trouble the Allies. The idea of negotiations was most serious in December 1916, in the wake of the Battle of the Somme, when Berlin believed it might gain more through diplomacy than war, Wilson pressed both sides to state their aims, and some in the British Cabinet felt the burden of war had become too much. Lord Lansdowne, the former Foreign Secretary, whose son had been killed in action, argued that the military aim of a 'knock-out blow' was illusory, and that the conflict was destroying British society. Yet even with military deadlock, there were problems for any negotiated peace. Both sides wished to justify the loss of life and believed, until summer 1918, they could achieve victory. For Britain a compromise peace seemed merely to promise a return to a strong German Navy, industry and ambition. In November 1914 Asquith stated British aims as the independence of Belgium, French security and the end of German militarism. But the last was an ideological aim, implying a change in German government and society which only total defeat would induce the Kaiser to concede. The army wished to defeat Germany soundly, yet Robertson saw the need to preserve Germany after the conflict when Russia might become a menace. Early in the war, British ministers were reluctant to annex territories themselves, well aware of the costs of defending and administering them. But war aims expanded over time. When Lloyd George finally gave a detailed statement of British aims at Caxton Hall in January 1918, it included the annexation of all German colonies and a vast reduction of the Turkish Empire. Three days later Wilson made a rather more idealistic statement with his 'Fourteen Points', including open diplomacy, freedom of the seas and a League of Nations. Britain always had to consider the war aims of its allies of course and these would have to be dovetailed together in an eventual settlement. It should be noted that during the war Britain tried to detach Austria–Hungary from the German side but had no success, partly because Austrian land had been promised to Allies like Italy, Romania (which entered the war in 1916) and Serbia.

By the end of the war Britain had clear territorial ambitions designed, in the eyes of their exponents, to make the Empire secure, yet generating new commitments and potential problems. This was clearest in the Middle East, which saw the greatest wartime expansion of British power. When Turkey had entered the war in November 1914 it presented various difficulties for London: Egypt, controlling the Suez Canal, and the Persian Gulf, important to Indian defence, might be vulnerable to Turkish attacks and the religious position of the Ottoman Sultan raised the danger of an Islamic 'jihad' against British rule in India and elsewhere. But it also provided opportunities: Turkey was seen as a corrupt, decrepit regime and 'Easterners' argued it would easily fall to a determined assault, weakening the whole German and Austrian position. Such racially motivated thinking led to the Gallipoli expedition of April 1915, especially advocated by Churchill and the Admiralty. It led to 250 000 Allied lives being lost, before it was called off the following January, and rather than helping the Allies it encouraged Bulgaria to join the Central Powers. Continued underestimation of the Turks led to an invasion of Mesopotamia (Iraq) in 1916 by the ill-prepared Indian Army, which resulted in another humiliating defeat, at Kut. Eventually British efforts did win rewards. A renewed advance into Mesopotamia in March 1917 captured Baghdad. Meanwhile Egypt became the base for an advance into Palestine where Lord Allenby took Jerusalem on 9 December 1917. Britain then dominated the Middle East and Russia's exit from the war destroyed – temporarily – an old rival for influence in the region. As early as 1915, when Grey questioned the wisdom of expanding the Empire, he was told by Asquith, 'If ... because we didn't want more territory ... we were to leave other nations to scramble for Turkey ... we should not be doing our duty'.[2] However, in the process of destroying Turkey the British made fateful promises of territorial gains to others. Thus, in October 1915, the Foreign Office representative in Egypt, Henry McMahon, gave Sheikh Hussein of Hejaz (western Arabia) vague promises of a substantial Arab state, under British 'guidance', if he entered the war. But at the same time the India Office, predominantly concerned with the Persian Gulf, was giving undertakings to another Arab leader and rival of Hussein, Ibn Saud. Italy and, later, Greece (which joined the Allies in 1917) were promised Ottoman territory and, although they played little part in military campaigns in the area, so were the French. The Sykes-Picot agreement in March 1916 promised France control of a portion of the Middle East around Syria and Lebanon largely to prevent it asking for more. Finally, there was the Balfour Declaration of November 1917, which promised a 'national home' for Jews in Palestine whilst, supposedly, respecting Arab rights. The declaration was designed to impress American opinion and win Jews to the Allied cause. Even more than other promises, it would create difficulties in future.

The return to 'normalcy'

A month after the armistice, a general election was held which saw the overwhelming triumph of Lloyd George's Conservative-dominated coalition. Asquith's Liberals suffered a precipitate decline and it was Labour, with 2 million votes, who became the main Opposition party. The election was held on an extended franchise, the first to give votes to women. It brought about genuine democracy in Britain and forced politicians to give greater weight to popular views on policy. After the carnage of the western front, British people seemed less willing to defer to their leaders and the rise of Labour led many Conservatives to fear social upheaval if popular demands were not met. It has been said that Lloyd George now 'believed that foreign policy was the product less of ... traditional concepts of power and special interest, than of ... pressures for change from the electors'.[3] In fact, as already seen, public opinion had placed limits on the general shape of Britain's pre-war foreign policy; on the other hand, since 1918, it has been quite possible for governments to pursue day-to-day policy without reference to the electorate. Inevitably ministers and officials, with control of the diplomatic apparatus, an ability to act in secret and expert knowledge of world events, are better able to control most decisions; in contrast the public are often ignorant, divided or confused over policy. Yet the impact of international issues, broadly interpreted, on elections after 1918 is clear: in 1922 all three main parties felt the need to promise tranquillity abroad, the 1923 election was influenced by free trade and that of 1924 by relations with the Soviet Union. In 1918 the public was exhausted by the exertions of war and, in contradictory fashion, there was a strong desire both for 'open diplomacy' and a vengeful peace, as well as a wish to return to 'normalcy' ending conscription, high taxes and extensive state controls – except to provide some social reform such as the 1919 Housing Act and improved unemployment insurance. When it came to the business of negotiating peace, Lloyd George was forced to answer popular calls, stirred by the *Daily Mail*, to 'make Germany pay' (reparations would weaken Germany *and* help British reconstruction) and even to 'Hang the Kaiser!'. The government also had to satisfy traditional British interests, such as Imperial security and a European balance of power, whilst dealing with the menace of Bolshevism and coming to terms with the economic and naval power of Japan and America. A range of options, not necessarily mutually exclusive, presented themselves as ways to protect British interests: the Round Table pressed the benefits of reliance on the Empire which might allow Britain to survive independently in the world; 'Atlanticists' hoped cooperation with Britain's transatlantic 'cousins' might bring US resources to bolster British interests; continuing wartime alliances with France, Italy and others could preserve a favourable balance of power in Europe; and a League of Nations seemed essential as a way to please the US President, answer demands for 'open diplomacy', and provide a basis for global stability.

There was a clear difficulty in Britain seeking to enforce a tough settlement on Germany, maintain a vast Empire against internal and external threats, and play a leading role in world affairs whilst trying to 'normalise' conditions at home and cut government spending. Yet, with the war over, every country demobilised and the impact of post-war retrenchment on Britain's security was hardly disastrous. Certainly the Treasury was determined to re-establish its primacy over budgetary matters, to pay off debts to America and drive down inflation. The army, which stood at 5.5 million in November 1918, was reduced the following year at the rate of 10 000 men per day. In August 1919 the Cabinet inaugurated the 'ten-year rule', whereby the armed forces need not expect a major war for a decade, and in March 1920, in answer to popular demands and despite Conservative doubts, conscription was ended. By 1922 defence spending was below £200 million, a tenth of the amount spent in 1918. However, the process of retrenchment was not easy. Britain's armed forces remained substantial, given that there was no threat from other Great Powers. As well as possessing the world's greatest navy, Britain also had the largest air force in 1919, aircraft having become technologically more advanced during the war. Under the Chief of Air Staff, Hugh Trenchard, the Royal Air Force (RAF) developed an important role in keeping order in the Empire through 'air policing', whose effectiveness was first demonstrated by the defeat of 'Mad' Mullah Muhammed in Somaliland in 1920. The 'ten-year rule' was not as important a restraint on defence spending as it later became and the retreats forced on Britain were mostly due to taking on unrealistic, unpopular commitments as the war ended. This is not to say that mistakes were not made. More troops might have made it easier to cope with problems and it was ridiculous to believe, after the upheavals of the Great War, that there was a way back to the supposed certainties of the Edwardian era: the popular belief that Britain could cut its armed forces and rely on 'new diplomacy' to maintain peace involved a strong element of wishful thinking; whilst at home 'corporatism' had come to stay and, however much the City and the upper classes might dislike it, health, housing and insurance provision meant that spending and taxation ran at triple their 1914 levels even a decade after the war. The creation of an independent RAF meant a new competitor for defence spending and the army was especially badly hit, having to cope with its traditional garrison role in India, occupation duties in Germany and emergencies in Ireland, Russia and the Middle East. Nonetheless, the determination of conscripts to be demobilised (as witnessed by the Calais mutinies of January 1919) was irresistible and, after all, British wealth had long been supposed to rely on low-cost armed forces, low taxes and a concentration on entrepreneurial flair rather than military might.

Just as the domestic and international scenes were radically altered by war, so too was the policy-making environment in Whitehall. True, peace saw the return of the CID as one of only three permanent Cabinet committees, and to the FO's satisfaction the Ministry of Information was wound down; despite the problems caused by inter-service rivalry, the idea of a single Ministry of Defence was rejected; and in the FO the Political Intelligence Department and the Ministry of Blockade disappeared. But many changes had come to stay. Competition between the FO and Board of Trade had led to an Overseas Trade Department being set up in 1917, which took on its own importance in the important field of international commercial relations in the inter-war years. The intelligence services remained significant, with MI6 active against the Soviet Union and MI5 and Special Branch devoting much of their work to Communist subversion within Britain, but there was less sympathy among the government and public for such work in peacetime and all the intelligence services faced spending restrictions. Code-breaking too was now a permanent feature of intelligence operations, though its focus shifted from naval-military to diplomatic work and in 1922 the new Government Code and Cypher School was put under FO control. FO officials were still uncomfortable with propaganda but the News Department was preserved and press attachés became important figures in British embassies. In 1921 the FO, with 482 staff, was still much larger than in 1914 (when there had been 132), a reflection of the ever-rising volume of material: whereas 43 000 papers had been handled in 1906, 15 years later there were 147 000. And peace brought its own changes, not least in the decision to merge the FO and the Diplomatic Service, to give wider experience to officials. Hitherto, there *was* some movement between the two services, but many FO staff never worked abroad. Merger had first been proposed in 1885 and again in 1914. By 1919 there was also a need to answer criticisms that diplomats were a closed elite, deaf to public concerns. Such criticisms were easy to make when in order to enter the diplomatic service individuals nominally needed to have an independent income of at least £400 per year, were unpaid for the first few years and had to finance their own transfer between postings; and the FO tended to recruit from a narrow social group, educated at public school and Oxford or Cambridge University. One official who was closely involved in the post-war reforms still hoped that the new, combined service would recruit exclusively from public schools; furthermore, he wished to exclude all 'Jews, Coloured men and infidels who are British subjects'.[4] With such attitudes it is not surprising that the impact of the 1919–21 reforms was limited. True, the two foreign services were merged, the £400 property qualification was abolished and certain non-Oxbridge graduates entered diplomacy. One grammar school product, William Strang, went on to be Permanent Under-Secretary in 1949–53. But in practice Oxbridge domination of the FO continued and of the 16 men who held the top four posts in the FO between the wars, ten had spent their whole careers in London.

No amount of FO reform could have brought back the days when Grey had dominated foreign policy. There had always been prime ministers who took a lead in foreign policy and Lloyd George continued to play a major international role relying in peace, as he had in war, on the likes of Hankey in the Cabinet Office and Kerr in the 'garden suburb'. The Prime Minister, identified as 'the man who won the war', believed that he should both direct policy and personally represent the British people, not only at the Paris Peace Conference of 1919 but also a subsequent series of conferences, where outstanding problems of the settlement were discussed. Yet Lloyd George's time was limited and, whilst he concentrated on the general lines of policy and had a major influence on policy towards Russia and Turkey, he left a considerable number of issues for the FO to deal with, including settling the details of the European settlement. Even so, prime ministerial activity offended Lord Curzon, who became Foreign Secretary in October 1919. Though he and Lloyd George shared a common outlook on many problems, Curzon was a vain, autocratic, insecure individual, less ready to defer to Downing Street than had been the languid, philosophical Balfour. Once a majority of Conservative MPs rebelled and overthrew the 'Welsh wizard' in October 1922 there was a reaction against his policy-making methods. The ailing, gloomy Andrew Bonar Law, who served as Prime Minister until May 1923, stated in his only memorable phrase that Britain could not 'act alone as the policeman of the world';[5] and his dull successor Stanley Baldwin, though interested in defence issues, gave limited attention to foreign affairs. True, both met foreign leaders at times and Curzon still had to cope with interference from Downing Street. But neither possessed the restless enthusiasm of Lloyd George and, arguably, their lack of dynamism proved harmful to British interests: at least Lloyd George, if impulsive and inconsistent, had tried to clear up the problems left by the war. In 1924 Labour's first Prime Minister, MacDonald, combined his position with that of Foreign Secretary, but did not survive in office long. Even with less interventionist premiers international affairs were too controversial an area for one department to dominate. The Treasury was more active during the 1920s in international economic issues, such as reparations and war debts; the Admiralty, War Office and RAF had an important say in the military control of Germany and disarmament; and post-war Imperial crises gave a vital role to the Colonial Office, notably in 1921–22 under Churchill. To outsiders, London's foreign policy machine could seem as diffuse and confused as ever. Yet it has been argued that it 'was not a case of muddling through, nor was it a product of central decision-making; rather it evolved organically' into an effective apparatus which, notwithstanding many disappointments, allowed the British in 1919–23 to obtain more than most from the peace treaties.[6]

The diplomacy of peace

Everyone hoped for lasting peace after the 'war to end all wars' and one ideally based on liberalism and the rule of law, but achieving a stable settlement was never likely to be simple. The desire to punish Germany, promises made to other powers, the technical problems in defining a settlement, all added up to a daunting challenge. There was no agreement on how punitive the settlement should be, how to balance the frequently contradictory claims of the victors, or how to police a settlement. Questions of 'justice', the balance of power, economic stability and long-term self-interest were obscured by the scale of the problems. The continent faced inflation, currency instability and disrupted trade patterns and as the Ottoman and Austro-Hungarian Empires collapsed vast areas were swept into turmoil. In Eastern Europe, local politicians seized the chance to set up new states, Poland, Czechoslovakia and Yugoslavia, which tied Allied hands in making peace treaties with Austria in September 1919 and Hungary in June 1920. The Eastern European settlement made little strategic or economic sense: the new states often possessed indefensible borders and pursued territorial disputes with one another. Neither did some new states have experience of governing themselves and most soon succumbed to a form of authoritarian government. Eastern European states were also often left with substantial ethnic minorities, including large numbers of Germans in the Sudetenland of Czechoslovakia and in western Poland. British people took two decades to understand how the unstable settlement in the East could affect their interests, especially when Germany and Russia recovered and threatened to expand there. However, Lloyd George *was* concerned at the outset about the large German minority included in the 'Polish corridor' (designed to give Poland access to the Baltic). He found it impossible to resist the pressure, from the idealistic Wilson and the anti-German French premier, Georges Clemenceau, to establish a large Poland, but did succeed in turning the Baltic city of Danzig into an international port. Lloyd George also recognised the danger to Eastern Europe of Bolshevik Russia. Indeed, the threat presented by the Bolsheviks, as the leaders of a substantial power *and* a world-wide Communist movement, over-shadowed the Paris Peace Conference, even though they were not represented there.

A basic problem with the German settlement was that Berlin had sued for peace on the basis of Wilson's Fourteen Points at a time when

Germany had not been invaded by Allied armies. The British and French, who had hoped for a decisive victory, could hardly continue the war in these circumstances but they largely ignored the political transformation in Germany (which became a Republic) and, as the German military had fully expected, sought a vengeful peace. Lloyd George's performance as a peace-maker remains the centre of controversy. For some he was deceitful and unprincipled, motivated by a simple desire to retain power; others see him as genuinely ambivalent, exploiting situations as they arose in the confused world of the Paris Conference. Many Britons were disappointed at their leader's performance, even considering him 'the man who lost the peace'; they did not appreciate that the war had created new difficulties which could only be resolved gradually and painfully, in its aftermath. Yet recent historians have seen a wider vision behind Lloyd George's flexibility. While maximising British gains and answering calls (from the electorate and Conservatives) for a harsh peace, he sought to work with both America and France, limit the problems left by the settlement and create institutions which might modify its flaws in future; and he wanted to bring Germany and Russia back into European diplomacy, as part of a new balance of power. His personal views were very different to those of the public. His Fontainebleau memorandum of March 1919 showed concern over instability in Eastern Europe and fears that a revived Germany might follow a policy of revenge. A moderate settlement, in which German territorial losses were limited and her economy could expand, would be easier for the Allies to maintain than a draconian treaty, and prevent Germany being driven into the hands of the Bolsheviks. Yet such arguments were not so much enlightened as based on British interests in a cheap defence policy, anti-Communism and expanded trade with Germany. Lloyd George could afford to sound principled about the settlement in Europe when Germany's navy and colonial empire were destroyed, fulfilling Britain's own desires. And it is not surprising that other allies refused to share Lloyd George's outlook. On the 'Council of Four', the Prime Minister was joined by Wilson, Clemenceau and Italy's Vittorio Orlando. Orlando counted for little and could not secure the gains promised by the Treaty of London (a failure which alienated Italy from the peace settlement). Wilson arrived with a formidable reputation, firm principles and a belief in the League of Nations, but was weakened by his Democratic Party's losses in the 1918 congressional elections, had little detailed knowledge of European problems, and found it hard to turn principles into concrete proposals. Worst of all he had a self-righteous streak which made it difficult to strike compromises. British ministers hoped that by supporting him on the League they could win his sympathy for their aims elsewhere. But Wilson's desires had also to be balanced against the clear, simple approach of Clemenceau, who had little faith in the Fourteen Points and no interest in safeguarding either a fair balance of power or Britain's commercial prosperity. Clemenceau's main aim was to guarantee French security by measures which permanently weakened Germany such as large reparations, the destruction of the German Army, turning the Rhineland into a French military redoubt and establishing a system of pro-French states on Germany's eastern border (which further served as a *cordon sanitaire* against Bolshevik influence). But to say that Lloyd George tried to mediate between Wilson and Clemenceau is only partly true. As seen over Poland, sometimes the aims of the latter part combined to defeat British preferences. On issues like the establishment of the League, the Welshman might align himself with the President, but on others, such as reparations, might side with Clemenceau.

Inevitably the Treaty of Versailles, dictated to Germany on 28 June, was a compromise which left no one fully satisfied. The League of Nations was the first permanent international organisation designed to ensure peace, the most obvious sign of the coming-of-age of 'multilateral diplomacy' and a stronger institution than Lloyd George would have liked. Cecil and Smuts had a major influence on its structure (including a Council of major powers) and functions (including provision for arbitration in disputes and for economic sanctions – though not military action – against aggressors). The British had a unique expertise in organising international meetings, thanks to their Imperial conferences, and when the League was formally established in Geneva in January 1920 it had a British Secretary-General. The exact way the League would work remained to be seen, however. Clemenceau hoped it might behave as a 'victor's club' (which was just how the Germans saw it), designed to enforce the Versailles settlement, and Americans were disappointed to see the organisation tied to the vindictive Treaty of Versailles, whose ratification was dramatically rejected by the Senate in March 1920. This marked a major reversal for British hopes of tying the US into international peace-making. Instead, the US began to slip back into isolation. The League was still of greater significance than any previous international organisation, most of the world's states joined and it helped in resolving some territorial disputes. But hopes that it would guarantee lasting peace proved naive. Like other organisations, it was at the mercy of its members and, ultimately, individual states still had to decide whether to support 'collective security' in a crisis. American withdrawal was damaging in numerous ways. It removed the most powerful representative of international democratic principles, made League institutions less effective and less well-funded and, given America's economic importance, made the use of economic sanctions problematic. Given that the USSR, Germany and others were non-members too, the organisation even appeared unrepresentative of world opinion. The British found that they, rather than the Americans, were the leaders of the new body, expected to take special responsibility for world peace yet without the will or the reliable allies to do this. Over the following years London tried to prevent the League setting restrictions on British policy, and instead of creating a military force to back the League London feared losing independent control over its own armed services. Lacking a firm internationalist faith, British ministers were ready to use the League to discuss problems but preferred traditional tools of naval pre-eminence and Great Power diplomacy to achieve their aims. Yet, paradoxically, whilst Britain did much to deny effective power to the League, it continued to see the organisation as a barrier against future conflict. With a renewed 'continental commitment unthinkable, and America in diplomatic isolation, collective security ... [became a surrogate] for foreign policy and defence strategy'.[7] America's rejection of Versailles also had a highly detrimental effect on French self-confidence. At the Paris Conference Clemenceau successfully regained Alsace-Lorraine, created a pro-French Poland, limited the German army to 100 000 men, but could only secure a 15-year occupation of the Rhineland, the traditional springboard for German invasions of France. In place of a permanent occupation he accepted a joint American and British promise of a written guarantee against German aggression. But this promise proved worthless, for once the US Senate rejected Versailles the British were reluctant to enter into a unilateral guarantee. As a result the French continued to feel insecure and were reluctant to revise Versailles, despite the bitterness it stirred up in Germany. Probably no settlement could have been moderate enough to please Germany but Versailles both humiliated it and left it intact enough to recover, with Eastern Europe an obvious target for its future expansion. The settlement was too anti-German to be easily enforceable and required joint action by the victors if it was to last long. Yet whilst the French and some of their Eastern allies were 'satisfied' powers determined to uphold Versailles, America and Italy had been alienated from it for different reasons and the British soon concluded that it must be altered. A feeling of regret in Britain over the way Germany was treated emerged in 1920, which brought popular feeling into line with Lloyd George's attempts to improve the settlement. Many Britons came to believe that the Great War had been caused by the workings of the international system and that Germany was not alone responsible for it.

The alienation of the victors from one another, the resentment stirred in Germany, the withdrawal of America from European politics and the instability of Eastern Europe reinforced the sense of pessimism left by the war. Italy succumbed in 1922 to a new nationalist political movement, Fascism, led by Benito Mussolini, and an early indication of *his* aggressive instincts came when he temporarily seized the Greek island of Corfu, after four Italians were killed in Greece. The *entente cordiale* survived in a vague form, but the misunderstandings between London and Paris were wide-ranging. They bickered for several years about the status of the Moroccan port of Tangier (which the French wished to control but which Britain preferred to neutralise as a potential threat to Gibraltar). They argued over spheres in the Middle East. But their most important differences still centred on Europe and Germany. After years of conflict on their soil, French hatred of Germany took longer to cool than Britain's. Thus, London, faced by unemployment at home, wished to see Germany's commercial revival for the benefit of British business: in 1914 Germany had taken about 8 per cent of British trade, yet in 1920 only 2 per cent. But the French, pre-concerned with issues of security, wished to restrict German economic growth. Before long, many Britons saw France as a trouble-making, militarist state, aiming at hegemony in Europe, whilst the French saw the British as unreliable, obsessed with profits and unwilling to enforce Versailles on the Germans, who were thereby encouraged to ignore its terms. With plenty of problems outside Europe the British would ideally have liked to satisfy France's security concerns. And Lloyd George was determined to deal with Germany from a position of strength, to make it respect Allied rights and to ease, but not abandon, the burdens imposed by Versailles. Yet this was combined with a desire to revive Germany as part of a self-enforcing balance of power in Europe, removing the need for regular British involvement. The French in contrast were ready to enforce Versailles unilaterally and to the letter: in March 1920 their troops occupied Frankfurt to punish Berlin for having sent an armed force into the Ruhr; and in 1921 they insisted that half of Upper Silesia should go to Poland, even though most of its population voted to stay in Germany. For their part the Germans blatantly broke the military limits placed on them by Versailles and had no intention of paying reparations, whatever the sum. Lloyd George continued to cooperate with the French on reparations, demanding £7 billion from Germany (a large amount but one Germany was capable of paying). However, the arrival of the uncompromising Raymond Poincaré to the French premiership in January 1922 led to new difficulties. In April he refused to attend a conference organised in Genoa by Lloyd George. The Prime Minister intended Genoa to be 'the crowning achievement of his administration',[8] to discuss the resolution of Europe's economic problems and bring both German and Soviet representatives back into international talks. But the French refused to discuss certain vital issues and the Germans and Soviets, seeing there would be little gain from the conference, seized the opportunity to establish diplomatic and trade links with each other, in the Treaty of Rapallo. This confirmed the

British fear that, if they could not win readmittance into the international community, the two pariah nations were ready to work together. Rapallo also included secret Soviet military assistance to Germany.

Shortly after this, talks on an Anglo-French alliance, which had been underway for some time, fizzled out. London was interested in a guarantee to reassure the French, but Poincaré wanted a treaty to provide a safeguard, not only against a German attack on France, but also against a German threat to Eastern Europe. This the British were unwilling to do. One 'of the lowest points in Anglo-French relations since the turn of the century'[9] came at a meeting in September when Curzon accused the French of 'desertion' and Poincaré hurled abuse at the Foreign Secretary. In January 1923, furious about Rapallo and determined to force reparations payments from the recalcitrant Germans, France (supported by Belgium) occupied Germany's industrial heartland, the Ruhr. It proved a fateful error. By the following November the French were finding the occupation costly and the Germans had not backed down. The British largely stood aside from the dispute, reluctant to criticise the French government in public but reasonably satisfied at the outcome, when France agreed to establish a committee on reparations under an American, Charles Dawes. In August 1924 the 'Dawes Plan' rescheduled German payments, promised an end to the Ruhr occupation and opened the way for American loans to revive the German economy. Meanwhile Poincaré lost power, succeeded by the moderate Edouard Herriot. It was clear that France had suffered a major defeat: her ability to enforce Versailles unilaterally had failed and, helped by the Anglo-American desire to revitalise the European economy, the Germans succeeded in altering the peace settlement. For the British this, again, potentially opened the way towards a stable Europe, in which Germany was more generously treated and France accepted limits to its power. But it was apparent that, in order to achieve such an arrangement, London would still have to offer Paris some firm security guarantee. Under MacDonald there were attempts to satisfy French security concerns via the League. He and Herriot agreed on the Geneva Protocol, which committed all League members to accept compulsory, binding arbitration in disputes and would have treated any state which rejected arbitration as an aggressor, liable to sanctions. The Protocol underlined the importance of settling disputes peacefully, reassured France that German trouble-making would not be tolerated, yet was worded vaguely enough to limit British liabilities: thus states were only expected to oppose aggression so far as their geographical and military situation allowed. Even this was too much for the subsequent Conservative government, however, who threw out the Protocol. Attempts to placate France on the security issue therefore came to nothing and the European situation was depressingly unsettled.

A more hopeful situation prevailed in the Far East, despite the continuing rise of American and Japanese power. These two states were building formidable, technologically advanced fleets which now presented *the* major challenge to the Royal Navy. American policy was especially worrying because, with its huge economy and a new building programme in 1918, it was capable of becoming the world's largest navy. Despite its rejection of League membership, Washington *was* active in foreign affairs, on selective topics, especially financial matters (as seen with the Dawes Plan), in regions which directly affected US security (such as the Pacific) and where it seemed possible to achieve internationalist ideals (such as disarmament). Royal Navy hopes of outmatching the US would have been costly to fulfil and both the Treasury and FO preferred a policy of placating America, in the hope of limiting its navy by agreement. Ministers believed that, so long as Britain did not antagonise Washington, the Americans would not actually proceed with the 1918 programme. Yet such a course was complicated by US suspicion of Japan and dislike of the Anglo-Japanese alliance. The alliance, so important to Britain at the start of the century, had become tarnished by 1920, when the Foreign Office began to study its renewal. Britain and its Dominions were offended by Japan's aggressive policy towards China and Canada was opposed to renewing the Japanese alliance for fear of the US reaction. Not wishing to insult Tokyo, the FO decided the ideal solution to Britain's Far Eastern dilemma would be an Anglo-American-Japanese *entente*. The US was predictably opposed to a formal alliance but in July 1921 President Warren Harding proposed a multilateral gathering of major powers to discuss Pacific security and the global naval balance. The upshot was the Washington Conference of November 1921–February 1922, which saw a range of agreements: to Tokyo's annoyance, Britain agreed to end the Japanese alliance; but in December Britain, America, Japan and France agreed to respect each other's territorial rights in the Pacific, a move which did something to compensate Japan; and a treaty was signed which gave only vague guarantees of Chinese 'independence', whilst respecting the extra-territorial rights of other powers, such as Japan, on Chinese soil. The crowning achievement was a Five-Power Treaty which limited the number of capital ships (those over 10 000 tons) owned by the Great Powers according to a ratio – 5 each for Britain and America : 3 for Japan : 1.75 each for France and Italy. This treaty marked a success for Great Power diplomacy rather than cooperation through the League, and it omitted both smaller surface vessels and submarines. But it was an important first step towards the ideal of disarmament. The Royal Navy had to accept the principle of a 'one-power standard' (parity with America) but retained its freedom to build cruisers, which fell below the 10 000 ton limit and were vital for protecting the sea lanes of the far-flung Empire. Agreement seemed better than engaging America in a naval race which Britain, for all its shipbuilding capacity, might have lost. As before 1914, therefore, London chose compromise with a potential antagonist and, far from recognising its declining power, it can be argued that the Five-Power Treaty made no difference to the *substance* of London's naval supremacy. 'Each state continued to control precisely those areas which it had [in 1906], with Britain still dominating ... the bulk of the world's seas.'[10] As a separate issue, however, historians are critical of Britain's loss of the Japanese alliance. This arguably made it harder to restrain Tokyo's ambitions, which were all the more dangerous because of British military weakness in the Far East. In return, all Britain received was the momentary satisfaction of American wishes, which did nothing to defend British interests in the Pacific over the next two decades. Yet Japan had shown in the war that it was *not* restrained by the British alliance and in 1921–22 it can be argued that Anglo-Japanese relations 'did not suddenly deteriorate, because they had been bad before'.[11] With *realpolitik* out of fashion and no one able to predict Japan's later aggression, the Washington Treaties seemed the most sensible way to resolve British problems *vis-à-vis* Japan, America and the Far East. Then again, America and Britain continued to differ on many issues and, above all, about war debts. The British argued that they had paid for their own war effort and had only run up debts with American financiers in the common Allied cause, so that the amount demanded should be reduced. But Americans insisted that a debt was a debt. In July 1923 Britain accepted a final settlement of financial claims which necessitated a high burden on the Treasury for years to come. Although no one on either side wanted conflict, Anglo-American relations were marred by suspicion as Washington's industrial, financial and naval might increasingly called British predominance into question.

The crisis of Empire

The Great War had shown the immense value of the Empire as a source of manpower, armaments and raw materials, strengthening the Round Table's vision of a more united Empire as the prime source of British greatness. All the Dominions had become belligerents and together contributed 900 000 troops to the war effort, allowing London to deploy a vast army in Europe whilst also pursuing several smaller campaigns elsewhere. The Canadians alone contributed half a million, though New Zealand's 100 000 represented more as a percentage of their population and the Australians paid with the most lives: 60 000 men out of 330 000. Beyond the Dominions, India mobilised an army of 1.5 million, provided financial help and remained quiescent enough for the British garrison to be reduced to

20 000. Yet, simultaneously, the interests of various parts of the Empire often diverged and as a corollary to the aid given, Dominions were determined to have their views heard by London. Smuts developed ideas for a 'Commonwealth' based loosely on traditional ties rather than a centralised structure. An Imperial War Cabinet met in March–April 1917, and again in 1918, giving Dominion prime ministers a chance to state their views, which included a desire to share in the disposal of German colonies. Even though London continued to deny the Dominions independent foreign policies, their governments could have an impact on British diplomacy: it has already been noted how the Canadians helped widen British differences with Japan. The Dominions and India were also among the many non-European countries which expanded their own industries, becoming less reliant on British manufactures afterwards, even if they did continue to need the loans and financial services of the City of London. 'War Imperialism' led to greater strains on colonial societies as, in parallel to developments at home, British administrators sought to coordinate the Empire behind the war effort, directing the use of labour and commandeering produce. Food shortages, inflation and heavy-handed officialdom stoked up nationalist resentment, especially in Egypt and India, where pro-independence movements were becoming more sophisticated. Even in the Dominions the demands of war could stir unrest, notably when conscription became an issue. The Wilsonian ideal of 'self-determination', the egalitarian doctrine of Bolshevism and the advance of democracy in the 1918 election stirred up the intellectual debate over the morality of colonialism. Colonial subjects were less respectful of Europeans after the destruction of war and the years after 1918 brought a crisis in British rule which some have seen as a forewarning of the Empire's collapse. Just as the edifice reached its zenith, British leaders faced a widespread series of riots and revolts. The crisis forced the abandonment of the 'forward policy' of Imperial expansion in Persia and the Caucasus and a turn towards concessions to prop up support among local elites, usually by conceding a degree of self-government. Yet, the basic aims of preserving the Empire, safeguarding British security and protecting trade were achieved and it can be argued that, on strictly contemporary evidence, 'there is little to suggest that the management of Imperial policy was informed by novel conceptions of imperial rule, still less by any loss of confidence in the future of the British world system'.[12] Despite the Great War, the British were determined to shore up the Empire, rebuild their investments in Latin America, China and elsewhere, and outclass their Imperial competitors. They retained their ambition and, compared to all the other Great Powers, remained both strong and successful.

Unrest touched the British Isles themselves, with (as after the Napoleonic Wars) fear of social discontent and outright rebellion in

Ireland. Pressure to end the Anglo-Irish Union was well-established and Gladstone's governments had unsuccessfully introduced Home Rule bills in 1886 and 1893. Early in the century Ireland was at its quietest for decades but the 1910 election left Asquith's government reliant upon support from Irish Nationalists, who dominated the southern Irish Catholic vote and favoured home rule. Inter-marriage, the large Irish community in Britain and Irish economic weakness all suggested that some links to Britain should be preserved and the Sinn Fein movement, formed in 1905 to work for an independent republic, had little support. But the introduction of another Home Rule bill in 1912 provoked a controversy which still dominated British politics in July 1914. The Conservatives (who called themselves 'Unionists' at the time) were sympathetic to Irish Protestants, the majority population in some counties of Ulster. Led by Edward Carson, half a million Ulstermen signed a Covenant refusing to recognise any Dublin parliament. The difficulty of forcing a settlement on Protestants was highlighted by the March 1914 'Curragh Mutiny', when 58 army officers declared they would resign rather than coerce Ulster. When the Home Rule bill was passed the Unionists secured an amendment which excluded Ulster from its terms, and therefore raised the possibility of partition, but Ireland's future was still uncertain when war came and momentarily united the country. In September the Home Rule bill received royal assent, but its operation was suspended for the duration of the war. Some historians have seen in these developments a parallel to events in Germany, Russia and Austria–Hungary, where governments saw war in 1914 as a way to escape internal divisions. There is no evidence that London welcomed war specifically as a way to solve the dilemma in Ireland, however, and in fact the conflict exacerbated the Irish problem. The nationalist Irish Volunteers tried to exploit the conflict in 1916 by launching the 'Easter Rising' in Dublin. With limited support, it was put down in five days but the suppression which followed led to protests in Ireland, Britain and America. Nationalist opinion, already upset by Carson's inclusion in the British Cabinet, began to support Sinn Fein and discontent reached new heights when Lloyd George tried to introduce conscription into Ireland. In the 1918 election Sinn Fein won most seats, though less than half the vote, in Ireland and set up its own parliament. The Irish Republican Army (IRA) then began a policy of intimidating civil servants and murdering policemen, designed to cripple the administration of Ireland. There was sporadic violence throughout the South in 1920 and martial law was introduced in some areas. The British Army found it difficult to adapt to guerrilla warfare, the intelligence services were penetrated by IRA informers, and the use of counter-terror, by ex-servicemen organised into 'Black and Tan' units, simply escalated violence. For some in government it was vital to hold Ireland, which was a potential base for a foreign power. Its loss would also be an unwelcome signal to nationalists elsewhere in the Empire. But others believed Ireland to be an economic liability, of little military value, and many had already come to terms with Anglo-Irish separation during the Home Rule debate. In Britain some of the Press (not only the *Manchester Guardian* but also *The Times*), trades unions, Labour and Liberals questioned continued British involvement, which also served to alienate American opinion. By July 1921 the British Army was faring better in Ireland but at the cost of committing 80 000 troops there, and both Lloyd George and Irish leaders proved ready to compromise. By a treaty signed in December Ireland achieved its independence but as a 'Free State', a Dominion within the Empire, not as a republic. Six counties of Ulster were given their own form of 'home rule', with a parliament in Belfast. The settlement was galling enough, on one side, for Irish republicans to fight a civil war against pro-treaty elements (now aided by Britain which was anxious to stabilise its new neighbour) in 1922–23. On the British side, it contributed to Conservative dissatisfaction with Lloyd George. True, the Empire was preserved intact but only at the cost of a wide degree of self-government and the creation of a land border with another state.

There was a similar general pattern elsewhere. In India Mahatma Gandhi emerged as a leading member of the Congress Party and popularised independence among the poor masses, hitherto ignored by the educated elite. The Secretary for India, Edwin Montagu, promised Indians a gradual move to self-government in 1917 and with the support of the Viceroy, Lord Chelmsford, gave more power to provincial Indian parliaments in 1919. For nationalists, however, this was insufficient and growing unrest also led the British to use coercive measures. The worst loss of life occurred at Amritsar in April 1919 when 379 Indians died after being fired on by British troops. When Gandhi launched a campaign of peaceful disobedience the following year, however, the British responded mildly, and by 1922 discontent had subsided. In Egypt too unrest in 1919 cost about 1000 lives. In February 1922, following further unrest, the British High Commissioner, Lord Allenby, issued a declaration giving Egypt internal self-government under King Fuad. But Britain retained control over foreign policy, defence and administration of the neighbouring Sudan. The nationalist Wafd party were well aware that Allenby's action was designed to solidify British control where it mattered to London, whilst leaving Egyptians to tackle their own domestic problems. The High Commissioner still intervened in Egyptian affairs when Imperial interests were threatened, and was able to play off the autocratic tendencies of the Palace against the Wafd, who were too elitist to mobilise mass support behind their cause. Egypt had gained renewed importance with the expansion of London's influence in the Middle East. In 1919 British Imperialists dreamt of creating an arc of influence from Sinai to the North-west Frontier which would act as a barrier to Russian expansionism and – an increasingly important factor – provide access to oil resources. By the Treaty of San Remo in April 1920, the British restricted French rule to Syria–Lebanon, whilst Mesopotamia, Transjordan and Palestine became British 'mandates' and the Hejaz, ruled by Sherif Hussein, became independent (though it was soon conquered by Saudi Arabia). Iraq was especially vital to the security of the Persian Gulf, which had become a virtual British lake, but the War Office's enforcement of military rule there, and the belief that wartime promises of independence to the Arabs had been broken, led to an ill-organised revolt in 1920. Once this was suppressed, the British pursued their usual line of conciliation, setting up Sherif Hussein's son, Feisal, as King of Iraq and portraying themselves as protectors of Arab nationalism. War Office control gave way to the gentler hand of the Colonial Office and Iraq became a particularly successful example of the RAF's ability to control a large, barren territory by the inexpensive means of 'air policing'. Transjordan was placed under another of Hussein's sons, Abdullah, and, despite Jewish immigration, Palestine – seen by the British as a shield for the protection of Egypt – as yet witnessed only short-lived Arab disturbances.

In India, Egypt and the Gulf the British confirmed their ability to rule a far-flung Empire with resilience and adaptability. Only when they expanded beyond the Arab Middle East can they be said to have 'overstretched' themselves. Lloyd George and Curzon, despite the doubts of some ministers, were eager to exploit the opportunities created by the collapse of Turkey and Russia. They wished to secure control of Constantinople, strategically placed, and important to Moslems as the seat of Caliph. Lloyd George and the Foreign Office agreed that Greece was the most reliable ally in the Near East and favoured Greek expansion on the Aegean coast of Anatolia. Pursuit of these aims was quite ruthless at first. Notwithstanding the India Office's worries over reaction in the Moslem world, Treasury concern over the potential costs and War Office doubts about enforcing a harsh peace on Turkey, a joint allied force occupied Constantinople and in May 1919 the Greek Army began to seize land in Anatolia. The August 1920 Treaty of Sèvres, the last treaty of the Paris Conference, confirmed the harsh peace settlement. By then, however, the Turks, led by Kemal Ataturk, had begun to reassert themselves. The French and Italians, suspicious of British ambitions, came to terms with Ataturk whose Nationalist army drove the Greeks out of Anatolia in August 1922 and then turned towards Constantinople. A small British force was left facing the Nationalists at Chanak, and Lloyd George, widely accused of obsession with the Greek-Turkish problem, made bellicose noises but neither the British people nor the Dominions were ready to fight and the Foreign Office abandoned hopes of maintaining the Treaty of Sèvres. Ataturk was allowed into Constantinople in November and a new treaty was signed at Lausanne the following August, confirming Turkish rule over all Anatolia, with a foothold in Europe. In the treaty negotiations, Curzon secured British domination of Egypt, Cyprus and the Arab mandates and it was France, Italy and Greece who lost promised territory. Yet there can be no doubt about the blow suffered by British prestige in the Turkish episode. The subjects of the Ottoman Empire, who initially welcomed the British as liberators, now saw them in a more jaundiced light; as in the war, Turkish resilience had been woefully underestimated; and Britain and its former allies had again fallen out. Chanak had a fateful impact on Lloyd George's reputation. He fell from office within weeks of the crisis.

In Persia and the Caucasus, too, the British were unable to hold positions designed to contain Russia and provide security for India. Troops were withdrawn from Persia in 1921 and a local leader, Reza Khan, succeeded (rather like Ataturk) in establishing a stable government there. Curzon's long-standing hopes of dominating Persia were thus disappointed, even if Reza Khan's anti-Sovietism was reassuring. The equally short-lived incursion into the Caucasus in November 1918, when British troops seized control of the Baku–Batum railway, was closely linked to the wider issue of Allied intervention in Russia. The main reason for intervention at first was to keep an eastern front open against the Germans and prevent them dominating the new Russia. London was fearful that a German-Turkish combination could dominate Central Asia. In July 1918 an Anglo-Franco-American force landed in Archangel and in August Britain encouraged large-scale Japanese intervention (alongside small British and American contingents) in Siberia. By the time Germany was defeated, Allied support for 'White' opponents of Bolshevism had taken its own inertia and there were plenty of reasons to despise the Communists who, as well as betraying the Allied cause, had reneged on Russia's war debts, seized foreign-owned property and, after setting up the Communist International (Comintern) in 1919, threatened to stir up class war in the West. But once Germany was beaten popular support for the intervention was virtually non-existent, there was no guarantee that a White government would be friendly to Allied interests and the Whites were in any case divided among themselves. The Allies never sent sufficient troops to make any real impact on the Russian Civil War. The Treasury and War Office were reluctant to despatch more given the financial cost, pressures for demobilisation and commitments elsewhere. Lloyd George signalled the end of British intervention in November 1919 and the last troops left the Caucasus the following summer. The half-hearted intervention simply helped Lenin consolidate his hold on the Russian Empire. It also stirred up discontent at home as people became less willing to fight in campaigns whose purposes they did not understand: 1919 saw the 'hands off Russia' movement and in August 1920 workers organised 'Councils of Action', refusing to ship arms to the Poles, who were still fighting in Russia. Depression and rising unemployment were accompanied by numerous strikes, which threatened to encourage Bolshevik trouble-making in Britain. The Prime Minister turned in early 1920 to a policy of reconciliation, trying to draw Moscow back into normal, as opposed to revolutionary, behaviour on the international stage and wanting to forge trading links with the Soviet Union, which represented a vast potential market. Despite the doubts of Curzon and Churchill, Lloyd George secured a commercial treaty in March 1921, but hopes of using trade profits to dissolve Marxism proved illusory. War debts remained unpaid, and, as seen above, Lloyd George's attempt to draw the Soviets back into Great Power talks backfired with the Treaty of Rapallo. In February 1924 MacDonald's minority Labour government extended full diplomatic recognition to the USSR, which the Conservatives had hitherto opposed. The step was arguably an acceptance of realities, but it proved no more beneficial to MacDonald than the trade treaty had to Lloyd George. It divided the minority Labour government from Asquith's Liberals and helped bring an election in October which Baldwin won (largely because the Liberal vote collapsed). In the campaign the Conservatives accused Labour of weakness in the face of the Communist menace and the celebrated Zinoviev Letter was published, most likely with the connivance of the intelligence services, exposing Soviet-directed subversion in Britain. Anglo-Russian relations were therefore even less satisfactory than relations with France, America and Japan, and fear of Communism had become deeply ingrained in British government and society, even though the British Communist Party, founded in 1921, numbered only about 5000 members. Communism after all was opposed to much that Britons held dear: capitalism, colonialism, liberal democracy, individualism and monarchy. In the USSR, furthermore, this terrifying doctrine became linked to the ambitions of a country long seen as a menace to the British Empire in Europe, Central Asia and the Far East.

Notes

1 Quoted in Rothwell V., *British War Aims and Peace Diplomacy, 1914–18* (Oxford, 1971), 9.
2 Lowe C.J. and Dockrill M., *The Mirage of Power, Vol. III, Documents* (London, 1972), 524–7.

3 Morgan K., *Consensus and Disunity: The Lloyd George Coalition, 1918–22* (Oxford, 1979), 147.
4 Steiner Z. and Dockrill M., 'The Foreign Office reforms of 1919–21', *Historical Journal*, **17**(1), 1974, 140.
5 *The Times*, 7 October 1922.
6 Goldstein W., *Winning the Peace: British Diplomatic Strategy, Peace Planning and the Paris Peace Conference* (Oxford, 1991), 286.
7 Egerton G., *Great Britain and the Creation of the League of Nations* (London, 1979), 205.
8 Morgan K., *Consensus and Disunity*, 269.
9 Dockrill M. and Goold J., *Peace without Promise: Britain and the Peace Conferences, 1919–23* (London, 1981), 232.
10 Ferris J., 'The Symbol of the Substance of Seapower'. In McKercher B. (ed.), *Anglo-American Relations in the 1920s* (London, 1991), 75.
11 Nish I., *Alliance in Decline: A Study of Anglo-Japanese Relations* (London, 1972), 392.
12 Darwin J., *Britain, Egypt and the Middle East* (London, 1981), 212.

4
The Locarno era, 1925–1936

The years since victory in the First World War had been ones of frustration. In 1918 it seemed that Britain might dictate a settlement which secured Imperial interests for the foreseeable future. Instead, by 1924 the German peace treaty was regretted and that with Turkey had been redrawn; in Europe, Britain and France had become disenchanted with one another, the Bolsheviks triumphed in the Russian Civil War, Italy had become Fascist, Germany had been neither placated nor fatally weakened, and there was no stable balance of power; in the Far East Japanese power had grown as China slipped further into turmoil. The 'war to end all wars' had simply generated new uncertainties and fears. London's ability to shape world events was still great, but undermined by the demise, or souring, of those alliances and *ententes* which had been built up between 1902 and 1917 – with Japan, France, Russia, Italy and America. And as the government wrestled with a wide range of problems, popular distrust of politicians deepened, so that a national reluctance to run risks abroad became a vital factor restricting external behaviour. Lloyd George's attempt at a dynamic policy, seeking compromise with Germany and Russia whilst vigorously defending the Empire, ran into the ground with Rapallo and Chanak, and British policy had since assumed a certain aimlessness. War-weariness, and a desire to tackle social problems at home sapped the country's desire to play an active international role. Yet while social spending did increase, it was not sufficient to create the 'land fit for heroes' promised during the war. The Conservative Party, the growing middle class and the financial-industrial community wished to preserve free enterprise, reduce state activity and keep taxation low, whilst doing a little by way of social reform to neutralise the appeal of socialism and trade union militancy. Understandably the Great War has been seen as a watershed, dividing the supposed confidence of the Edwardian era from the onset of British decline. Yet actually Britain remained, in the inter-war period, the world's pre-eminent Imperial and naval power. The growth of Asian and Middle Eastern nationalism, the country's declining share of world trade (from 14 per cent in 1910 to less than 10 per cent in 1928), the reduction of 'invisible' earnings, the increasing pressures on Sterling, the declining competitiveness of industries like textiles, steel and shipbuilding, and the relentless advance of technology – not least the advent of airborne weapons – would prove detrimental to Britain in the long term. But their full impact would not be felt until 1945 after another long war sapped national strength. In the short term the First World War had mixed results. All the continental Great Powers had suffered and by 1924 the British emerged better off than most. The post-war Imperial crisis had been overcome, the Empire had been extended, the Dawes Plan gave hopes of stability in Germany, French policy had become more moderate after Poincaré, neither Mussolini nor the Japanese had yet embarked on a determined policy of aggression, America had retreated from Europe and the Soviets were preconcerned with their internal problems. Although unemployment stuck at about one million, manufacturing output was back to pre-war levels. Britain had preserved its political stability (outside Ireland), the Dominions were loyal enough and, in *absolute* terms, British trade in the mid-1920s was above the levels of 1910. The shipping, insurance and financial services controlled by London were enormous. Even if Germany, Italy, Russia and Japan were all potentially revisionist powers there was no strong combination of foes yet who could threaten British security, the country could plan on the basis that war was unlikely for at least a decade and, by the mid-1920s, defence spending was again below 3 per cent. The League of Nations, on which so many hopes were placed, had some early successes and the Washington Conference had made the first steps towards the ideal of disarmament.

It is fair to conclude that, compared with the two decades before the war, 'Great Britain was slightly more powerful in relation to every other European state, while somewhat weaker in relation to Japan and particularly the United States'.[1] Even in the 1890s America had had a larger population and industrial capacity than Britain and by 1918 it had greater financial power, with the potential, if it wished, to be the greatest power on earth in military terms too. However, the US was still no actual security threat to the British, being a neo-isolationist, liberal-democratic and status quo power; nor did it yet seek to outstrip Britain as a naval force. London and Washington were commercial and financial, rather than ideological and military rivals and for the moment the British could avoid signs of subservience to America. In this way too the full effect of the factors which eventually contributed to Britain's relative decline was masked. Yet in a sense this was the country's problem. Britain was far from all-powerful but possessed the prestige, wealth and territory which made other states treat it as a leader. International opinion sometimes expected the Royal Navy to enforce the wishes of the League world-wide. But British leaders wished to protect their own interests rather than to play the world's 'policeman', they designed the Royal Navy for the purposes of Imperial defence and, so far as Europe was concerned, they once again lacked the necessary land army and the sense of involvement to play a consistently constructive role. It has been said that 'The role of producer of security is necessarily expensive and she did not even spend enough to ensure the security of her own territory and interests',[2] yet the gap between the expectations placed on Britain and its ability to wield military power was only really exposed after 1931 and it was not only a lack of material power which was the problem. The desire to avoid another world war, the belief that the pre-war *ententes* were a mistake, the reluctance to rearm or to build close alliances with other Great Powers, and the lack of an imaginative, vigorous leadership combined to give British policy a dangerous sense of drift in the early 1930s.

Austen Chamberlain and the 'spirit of Locarno'

Policy-makers in the 1920s did not see another war as inevitable and, especially in 1925, it seemed that a new European order might emerge, based on the Locarno Pact which Britain's Foreign Secretary, Austen Chamberlain (the son of Joseph Chamberlain), did much to secure. The middle years of the inter-war era should be seen, not as just 'the aftermath' of one war or 'the origins' of another, but as a period of hope and uncertainty, in which governments tried to apply the old means of trade, low-cost defence and pragmatism to achieve equally traditionally aims of global peace, a European balance of power and British freedom to act in its own interests. The objective was to build a stable world on the basis of the Paris settlement, and to guarantee material prosperity, not prepare for another destructive conflict: Nazism and Stalinism did not yet exist. There was still an intense debate in London over exactly which international policies to pursue. Despite America's retreat from the world, individuals like the Labour leader Ramsay MacDonald remained convinced 'Atlanticists'. Among Conservative ministers internationalism and disarmament were championed by Robert Cecil and could never be ignored because the 'new diplomacy' held a strong sway over educated opinion. More numerous were those who wished to distance Britain from European concerns, preserve the Royal Navy as a source of strength and consolidate the Empire. Leading 'Imperialist-Navalists' included Hankey, still Secretary to the Cabinet throughout this period, and Leo Amery, who in 1925 was able to combine control of the Colonial Office with that of a newly independent Dominions Office. Most of those in government could not fit neatly into such categories, however. There was a mixture of 'new' and traditional diplomacy in the outlook of the Cabinet and most simply wished to preserve Britain's pre-eminence in world affairs at minimum cost. The Conservative Prime Minister, Stanley Baldwin, is often accused of showing little interest in foreign policy, and, in contrast to Lloyd George, was ready to give his foreign secretaries a great deal of leeway. But Baldwin continued to chair the CID and understood 'We can't afford to let Europe go to pieces'.[3] His administration saw some important innovations in policy-making, including a regular slot in the Cabinet agenda for the Foreign Secretary to report on foreign affairs. Although it did not prevent 'inner cabinets' forming to discuss international questions, this did reduce complaints that the Cabinet was effectively excluded from such matters. Another development was the Chiefs of Staff (COS) subcommittee, first formed in 1924 as a way to induce the armed services to adopt common policies. It did not, by any means, end inter-service rivalry and it might have been better to have created a single Ministry of Defence, but in 1926 it began to produce annual reports on the overall defence position.

That same year, despite doubts from Amery and others, the government began to restrict military spending ruthlessly. Winston Churchill, back in the Conservative fold as Chancellor of the Exchequer, wished to put emphasis on financial stability, economic development and the repayment of war debts, rather than arms expenditure. He was further restricted by the decision, taken in April 1925, to return Sterling to the Gold Standard. Much criticised in retrospect, at the time the Treasury, the City and industry all supported this step as a way to restore Britain's reputation for stable, sound money, and give greater certainty to investors and traders (thereby aiding exports and reducing unemployment) whilst reducing prices of imported food and raw materials (which in turn would reduce trade union pressures for higher salaries and keep industrial costs down). Other countries took the same decision. It was soon clear, however, that the return to the pre-war Gold Standard made Sterling overvalued. Not only did government spending have to be restricted to deflate the economy, bringing unemployment, but export trade was harmed as well. Instead of re-asserting London's financial prestige in the face of the dollar, the experience revealed that Britain lacked the necessary capital to prop up a stable, liberal system of trade and payments in the pre-1914 style. Another reason to restrict military spending was the need to maintain reasonable levels of social welfare in order to minimise the appeal of the Labour Party, especially when the dangers of discontent were revealed by the General Strike of 1926. Thus, in July 1928 Churchill decided that the so-called 'ten-year rule' of 1919 should be annually renewed, rather than letting it expire in 1929, and all three services had to abandon their expansion plans. Ironically, for a former

First Lord of the Admiralty, Churchill found his toughest opponents in the navy. They succeeded in persuading ministers to maintain the 'one-power standard' against America, but had to trim their hopes of building a 70-cruiser navy and were unable to complete quickly the Singapore base in the Far East. Churchill's attitude to defence spending had a certain logic: he argued that it was sensible to restrict spending and improve the wider economy at a time when Britain lacked strong enemies; if danger re-emerged the armed forces could both be expanded and take advantage of the latest technology. Such an approach, however, depended on a perceptive leadership reacting swiftly to any changed circumstances. As it was, when international dangers did re-emerge after 1931, British forces were at a low level of preparedness and the government was slow to react. British policy in the late 1920s was summarised in an April 1926 Foreign Office memorandum, which shows a striking resemblance to Victorian outlooks: 'We ... have no territorial ambitions nor desire for aggrandizement. We have got all we want – perhaps more. Our sole object is to keep what we have and live in peace.' The way to achieve this was 'to keep our hands free in order to throw our weight into the scale on behalf of peace'. British policy was certainly not altruistic, whatever its people might believe: 'The fact is that wars and rumours of war ... in any corner of the world spell ... harm to British commercial and financial interests', so that 'whatever else may be the outcome of the disturbance of the peace, we shall be losers' and therefore Britain was interested 'in almost every dispute that arises', a fact which itself could breed quarrels and commitments.[4] There was a need for Britain, as the world's pre-eminent state, to build a balance of power at both the global and European levels. A well-worn retrospective judgement on this period is that Britain should have played a more active role in Europe and chosen one of two courses: either she should have worked closely with France in enforcing Versailles against Germany; or she should have made a determined effort to persuade France to accept Germany as an equal. The first option could have prevented any German revival in the 1930s. But at the time the government believed the danger of war to be remote and the 1914 experience had led to a strong aversion against 'taking sides' in Europe: a general security framework was preferable to 'bloc' politics. The restrictions bred by the Empire, low defence spending, 'new diplomacy' and a pacific public could not be wished away. And there were other possible dangers in ministers' minds, not least that posed by the Bolsheviks who, building on Rapallo, might forge a closer relationship with Germany if that country was not won over to a more 'Western' outlook.

Austen Chamberlain had an early warning of his countrymen's aversion to a close relationship with Paris when, in March 1925, his Cabinet colleagues rejected his preferred policy of Anglo-French alliance which he saw as a step towards negotiating with Germany from strength about a new security framework. Again remembering 1914, ministers were loath to make commitments which tied Britain closely to European problems, neither did they wish to harden the divide between 'victors' and 'vanquished'. It was widely believed that France was treating Germany unjustly and that Britain must act as a kind of umpire between them. But the exact way to do this was unclear and the Conservatives had already rejected the Geneva Protocol, favoured by MacDonald and Herriot. It was in these circumstances that the Cabinet decided to adopt a suggestion from the German Foreign Minister, Gustav Stresemann, for a mutual security pact and territorial guarantees which might satisfy all the European powers. In October Stresemann's basic idea became the Locarno Pact, negotiated over 11 days in Switzerland by Chamberlain, Stresemann and France's Aristide Briand. There were guarantees of western German borders, as defined in 1919 (including the demilitarisation of the Rhineland), by France, Germany and Belgium, with a commitment by Britain and Italy to go to war with any country who breached this agreement in a 'flagrant', 'unprovoked' way. In the event of a dispute over any of Germany's borders a system of arbitration was agreed which included Germany's eastern neighbours, Poland and Czechoslovakia. But, in what has been seen as the major flaw in Locarno, Germany's eastern borders were *not* guaranteed. As a firm nationalist, Stresemann refused to do so, and the British, never having much interest in East-Central Europe (beyond wishing to trade there), had no desire to argue. Chamberlain had famously written in February 1925 that the 'Polish corridor', created at Versailles, was not worth 'the bones of a British grenadier'.[5] Instead the French alone made bilateral alliances to reassure the Poles and Czechs. Thereby the impression was created that Eastern European borders were less sacrosanct than those in the West and that Britain would not fight to preserve them. Other weaknesses may be seen in Locarno. By treating Germany and France as equals, it suggested not only that the latter was as likely to threaten war as the former – something which many Britons did believe – but also that Britain was ready to fight France in defence of Germany, which was never likely. The Pact did not lead Germany to abandon cooperation with the USSR: instead Rapallo was renewed by Stresemann in June 1926. Another criticism was that Locarno, as a multilateral agreement among certain powers, undermined the position of the League. It also provided Britain with an excuse to avoid military talks with France (since such a step would mean the end of London's even-handed treatment of Germany), so that the reassurance given to Paris about security was minimal. Britain of course lacked a large army for action on the continent anyway, and some doubt whether she had any intention of fulfilling the Locarno guarantee. Arguably Britain had patched up Franco-German differences so as to concentrate on Imperial concerns. Chamberlain himself talked of a policy of 'semi-detachment' from Europe. Yet semi-detachment is not detachment and it would be wrong to see him as behaving cynically. Compared to London's previous reluctance to commit itself on European matters, Locarno was a dramatic step, which *could* have led to British involvement in a future war. No firmer guarantee was made by Britain in Europe before March 1939. Whether ministers liked it or not, Britain had to be concerned with European security and it gained as much as any power from Locarno. The security of France and Belgium had always been more vital than that of Eastern Europe and the General Staff considered that the 'true strategic frontier of Great Britain is the Rhine'.[6] Locarno promised to stabilise an area of vital concern at minimum cost and the settlement helped pave the way for a firmer economic recovery in Europe, which was of importance to British exporters. At the time Locarno was seen as bringing real peace to Europe and heralded continuing signs of an improved atmosphere: in January 1926 Allied forces ended their occupation of Cologne; in September Germany joined the League of Nations, even controversially becoming a member of the League Council; and the trio of Chamberlain, Briand and Stresemann held a number of subsequent meetings. It was a marked improvement from the days of Poincaré, Curzon and the Ruhr crisis.

Nonetheless, Chamberlain essentially failed to build on the 'spirit of Locarno' over the following years. It seems reasonable to conclude that his policy 'was directed towards the calming of French fears, in order to produce a negotiated application of ... Versailles, rather than its one sided enforcement by France'.[7] But Locarno gave sufficient succour to neither France nor Germany. The former still felt too insecure to make major concessions, the latter still felt harshly treated in 1919, and Britain was unwilling to go further in pleasing either. There was a certain complacency in the late 1920s, when the fragile nature of the 'spirit of Locarno' was not understood, and international idealism reached absurd heights. In 1927 the inter-allied Military Control Commission was withdrawn from Germany, removing the last means of enforcing the military clauses of Versailles, and in August 1928 15 foreign ministers, including a sceptical Chamberlain, put their signatures to the utopian Briand-Kellogg Pact, dreamt up by the French Foreign Minister and US Secretary of State, which supposedly outlawed war as a policy. Then again, no one could foresee the impact of the slump which suddenly struck in 1929, and the desire for a quiet interlude was understandable after the turmoil of the early 1920s. In any case Chamberlain was limited in his achievements by French and German policy. Thus, in July 1928, when it was revealed that he and Briand had been having secret talks on disarmament, there was an outcry from Germany, America, Italy and supporters of the 'new diplomacy' at home. Two months later the French were concerned when a new international committee was set up, under the American Owen Young, to take another look at German reparations. By 1929 Chamberlain was dogged by ill-health and his reputation was tarnished. In some ways the diplomatic situation was worse than that he had inherited, notably in relations with Russia and America. He had tried initially to maintain diplomatic relations with the Soviets, but key Cabinet ministers (notably Amery and Churchill), Conservative backbenchers, the intelligence services and the *Daily Mail* were all opposed to such a policy. In May 1927 the Home Secretary, William Joynson-Hicks, used the fear of Communist agents to organise a search of the All-Russian Cooperative Society in London. The hasty, much-publicised raid, directed by Special Branch, actually uncovered little but was followed by the mutual withdrawal of Anglo-Soviet ambassadors. More surprisingly perhaps, during 1927–29 Anglo-US relations declined to what has been called 'their lowest point in this century'.[8] The Americans persisted in claiming compensation for the Royal Navy's interference with neutral shipping in 1914–17, but the British insisted on their right to blockade an enemy. In summer 1927 the two countries also failed to agree, in talks at Geneva, on further limits to their naval strength. President Calvin Coolidge hoped the conference would build on the 1922 Washington Agreements, but a key difference arose over the number of cruisers each should have. The Americans wished to secure an equal number of 40 but the Royal Navy, faced by the defensive demands of a global Empire, already had 48 such vessels and hoped to build more.

The Baldwin government has been blamed for its failure to secure international disarmament. 'The potential vulnerability of Britain's position in the world ... meant that it was in [its] interests' to secure 'an effective and verifiable disarmament convention.'[9] The First World War was seen, in the 1920s, as being caused in part by the arms race and the mutual fears it generated. Disarmament, it was argued, would prevent states from immediately launching war with one another and allow a period for second thoughts before conflict was entered. Germany had been disarmed in 1919 partly in the hope that other states would disarm to her level. But pro-armament views still affected many in government: the Admiralty, under William Bridgeman, predictably argued the need to preserve naval power and had support from Imperialists like Amery. It was argued that arms were the result, rather than the cause, of tension and there was a belief that armed forces helped preserve peace by deterring aggression. Disarmament also faced practical problems, including the verification of any agreement and the technical difficulty of deciding how to 'equalise' the arms of countries with vastly different populations, territorial size and security concerns. Also, most people agreed that disarmament only made sense in the context of stable relations between states, but this pointed governments back to the vexed questions of reforming Versailles and making the League effective. The problems did not just lie with Britain: the League's 'Preparatory Commission' on disarmament, which met in 1927, made little progress. But the only British Cabinet minister with a sincere interest in the issue, Cecil, resigned in August 1927 over the failure of the Coolidge naval conference. Baldwin and Chamberlain were indifferent to disarmament, which was rarely discussed in Cabinet, and even Churchill, busy restraining arms spending, believed that Britain must retain its freedom to rearm when necessary. This led to a dangerous situation where Britain effectively disarmed unilaterally in the late 1920s, vainly hoping others would follow. It may have been better, whatever the difficulties, to have attempted an international agreement which put clear legal obligations on other states. Yet when the subsequent government did secure a naval agreement, it was at the price of solidifying Britain's vulnerability in the Far East.

MacDonald and Henderson

Following their election victory in July 1929, Labour leaders were reluctant to have MacDonald combine the premiership with the Foreign Office once more. He was widely respected in the Labour movement, not least for his opposition to war in 1914, but during the 1924 government he had been ambiguous over the role of the League and his close relations with Paris had upset those like E.D. Morel, the leader of the UDC, who saw France as the main danger to peace. Morel had died in 1924 and the UDC had gone into decline, but its internationalist ideals remained strong in the Labour movement. Unable to hold the FO himself, MacDonald hoped to place it in the hands of a pliant colleague, but instead was forced to accept Arthur Henderson, who had led Labour during the war. Criticised by the Conservatives for his lack of international experience, 'Uncle Arthur' was popular in the party and, though he spoke no foreign languages and had no formal education, had learned the art of negotiation from his trades union days. A Socialist internationalist, who supported the League and was suspicious of Locarno as a return to traditional diplomacy, Henderson combined belief in disarmament with a conviction that sanctions must be used against aggressors. He was convinced that unilateral British disarmament, favoured by some on the Labour Left, made no sense and in 1931 persuaded the League Council to call a World Disarmament Conference the following year. He also supported the so-called Optional Clause, which bound any League members in dispute to accept arbitration by the International Court in the Hague: the FO, COS, the Conservatives and the Dominions all feared that such a step could force Britain itself into unwelcome arbitration on certain matters. Henderson also stood up to his FO officials, Conservative opinion and even the monarch, George V, by agreeing to exchange ambassadors with the USSR again in November 1929. The existence of such a popular, forthright and, as many saw it, successful Foreign Secretary, led to a difficult relationship with Downing Street. MacDonald sometimes took initiatives on foreign policy without reference to Henderson, and even maintained links, behind Henderson's back, with the latter's Permanent Under-Secretary, Ronald Lindsay (1928–30). Henderson was equally capable of acting without reference to Downing Street as when he accepted the chairmanship of the forthcoming Disarmament Conference. He was also able to move Lindsay to the Washington Embassy, replacing him with Robert Vansittant (1930–38), a refined, witty but stubborn man who, trained in the Crowe school and regardless of current opinion, was suspicious of Germany and sympathetic to France.

One way MacDonald and Henderson managed to continue working together was to concentrate on different issues. The former was predictably interested in improving cooperation with America. Building on ideas from the previous government, he favoured another attempt at naval limitation which would please the Treasury by keeping British defence costs low, contribute to wider disarmament and avoid a destructive naval race. In October 1929 he became the first serving Prime Minister to visit Washington and found a ready audience in President Herbert Hoover. From January to April a conference met in London, which resulted in an agreement by the five principal naval powers – Britain, the US, Japan, France and Italy – to have a 'holiday' in battleship building until 1936. More remarkably the British, Americans and Japanese agreed to complex limits on the numbers and sizes of cruisers, destroyers and submarines. Britain accepted naval 'parity' with the US here, rightly believing that the Americans would not build many ships once they ceased to see the Royal Navy as engaging them in a 'race'. Besides, the navy was able to build a larger number of *small* cruisers than the Americans, fulfilling the needs of Imperial defence. The Japanese, able to build to 60 per cent of British strength, were left with considerable local superiority in the Far East, however. Although it was held outside the auspices of the League, the London conference seemed a success and gave further evidence that, in 1930 at least, the US was far from fully isolationist. Yet, once again, the hopes of British Atlanticists for a close relationship were thwarted. The slump turned Americans ever more inward and in June 1930 they adopted the highly protectionist Smoot-Hawley Tariff, which contributed to a general rise in 'economic nationalism', as each country looked after its own interests. True, in June 1931 Hoover agreed to a moratorium on intergovernment debt payments, removing an important element of Anglo-US tension, but by then European economies were in a terrible state. When Labour came into office there were still hopes of building on Locarno to secure a Franco-German settlement. In particular, at the August 1929 Hague Conference, tough negotiations between Henderson, Briand and Stresemann led to the acceptance of the Young Plan (which limited the size and timespan of German reparations) and an Allied withdrawal from the Rhineland in June 1930, five years ahead of the Versailles deadline. In September 1929 Briand put forward a dramatic proposal for a European Union. A precursor of post-1945 ideas for European unity, this aimed to replace France's vindictive policy towards Germany with one based on cooperation, while limiting German independence by forcing it to work through European institutions. But Briand, who also hoped his plan for a 'common market' might enable Europe to match the economic power of America, did not produce a detailed scheme until May 1930. By then slump-hit America no longer seemed an economic menace, Stresemann was dead and a more virulent form of nationalism was on the rise in Germany. In September Hitler's Nazi Party became the second largest in the Reichstag. The Briand Plan rapidly faded from view, which suited the British: Henderson had not wished to sound negative about the proposal, and the government did see the need for joint international action to tackle economic problems, but the Board of Trade, under William Graham, wished to work on a global basis, ideally with US cooperation, and to concentrate on free trade agreements, from which British exporters traditionally gained. By March 1931, the impact of the Depression in Europe, with its rising unemployment, already had a detrimental political effect. That month the German government, attempting to satisfy nationalist sentiment and protect its economy, proposed a customs union with Austria, a country populated by Germans. But the Treaty of Versailles ruled out any *Anschluss* (union) of Germany and Austria, and the French were totally opposed to the customs union. Henderson persuaded the Germans to put their proposal before the International Court, and the delay which followed allowed Paris to kill it, alongside any hope of a Franco-German rapprochement. This was the last time, however, that France felt confident enough to enforce, unaided, its interpretation of the 1919 settlement.

France was seen in Britain as the villain of the piece in 1931, not only because of the Austro-German controversy but also because Paris did little to help Britain and Germany (where British financiers had substantial investments) out of their economic difficulties at a time when the Depression had barely hit France. Her gold reserves stood at a remarkably high £3000 million, compared to Britain's £600 million. In July

1931 the financial crisis in Europe reached a new height with the collapse of the Kreditanstalt bank in Vienna which provoked instability in Germany and Central Europe. The ensuing turmoil claimed MacDonald's government as a victim because many European banks sold Sterling in order to seek security in Gold. Britain had already found itself unable to escape the profound upset to trade which followed the collapse of business confidence in the US. The financial-industrial might of America, and the interdependence of global commerce, ensured that unemployment rose everywhere, though Britain was not hit as badly as the US, Germany and Japan. Faced by the need to stabilise the Pound, the Labour Cabinet split in August over the question of spending cuts. But rather than resign, as the government collapsed MacDonald agreed, to the dismay of most of the party, to remain as Prime Minister of a National Government including Conservatives and some Liberals. Within two months an election confirmed this coalition in office with a massive 554 seats to Labour's 56. Meanwhile steps were afoot to adopt a British form of economic nationalism in the face of Depression. Joseph Chamberlain's dream of Imperial trade preferences was about to be fulfilled.

Trade preferences and the inter-war Empire

The August 1931 financial crisis stunned the British government and made politicians determined it must not be repeated. The Treasury's desire to maintain low taxes, low public spending and low inflation was solidified. Even when recovery began after 1932 governments were reluctant to spend money on additional social reform or armaments. The crisis came as unexpected succour to the Conservatives. They had been deeply divided in Opposition, especially over the 'Empire Crusade' launched by the Press magnates, Lords Beaverbrook and Rothermere, in favour of Imperial preferences. Between 1910 and 1929 coal exports had fallen by about a fifth in volume, and cotton exports halved, and there was a growing recognition that British industrial problems were not just due to the dislocations of the First World War: other countries were developing textile industries and demand for oil had led to a stagnation of the market for coal. The Conservatives' success in the 1931 election opened the way to a protectionist policy, justified by the need to shore up liberal capitalism in the face of a virtual halving in the volume of world trade since 1928. Even the City – whose invisible earnings helped offset a substantial visible trade deficit – favoured an element of protectionism by now, proving ready to abandon free trade in order to preserve loans from, and exports to, the Empire and Commonwealth. In September the coalition had already left the Gold Standard, leading the Pound to fall by a third in value by the year's end. Thereafter London sought to prop up the value of the Pound on the basis of an Empire-centred currency zone. The basis of the 'Sterling Area' was that most Dominions (but not Canada, which relied on the Dollar) and colonies, and a few other states, pegged the value of their currency against the Pound and held their currency and gold reserves in London, where they earned a low rate of interest. In November, despite the need to boost exports globally, the government also introduced limited import duties. At first these were designed to deal with the problem of 'dumping' by unscrupulous competitors. But the policy was extended in February to a general 10 per cent tariff. The Import Duties Act proved so controversial that the Cabinet broke with the principle of collective responsibility and agreed that ministers might vote on opposite sides in the Commons. The following summer saw an Imperial Economic Conference in Ottawa, where a system of preferential trade was agreed, discriminating against outsiders. The scale of tariffs was not high compared, for example, to the US, and actually disappointed the Dominions, who had hoped largely to monopolise the British market. Britain was still basically a low tariff, liberal trading power. Then again, it could afford to be, since its manufacturing output fared better in the Depression than producers of food and raw materials. But the end of free trade – even if other powers had taken the decision earlier – was undoubtedly a significant step, too much for some Liberal ministers who quit the National Government along with one of the few Labour coalitionists, Philip Snowden. Privileged access to the British market for Commonwealth producers also benefited the City (who were reassured that the Dominions would be able to repay their debts to British banks) more than manufacturers (who had to cope with the competition). Tariffs surprisingly had little impact on popular opinion, however, because food prices were falling due to the Depression. It should be noted that Britain *did* try to secure a global approach to currency, credit and trade problems at this time by calling a World Economic Conference, with the hope of breaking down trade barriers and recreating an 'open' system in which exports could thrive. But this only met in June 1933 and was doomed by American indifference. Trade preferences were unable to prevent a continuing deterioration in British exports in 1933, after which there was a limited recovery, but the country did become increasingly dependent on Imperial markets. By 1939 nearly half her exports went to, and a third of her imports came from, the Empire, compared to 36 per cent and 25 per cent respectively in 1914. Arguably, the concentration on such a 'soft' market helped reduce the competitiveness of British industry, even if the policy helped to shore up investment and trade in a difficult period.

The Sterling Area and Ottawa Agreements suggested an abiding British commitment to Empire, and were not the only signs of Imperial enthusiasm in the inter-war years. Rivalries with other powers in this period were as intense as ever, not in scrambles for land perhaps, but in competition for trade, investment, shipping and insurance, as well as in new areas like radio and air transport. In 1922 the Empire Settlement Act had given financial support to emigrants to the Dominions and in 1924–25 the first Empire Games had been held in the new Wembley Stadium. An Empire Marketing Board had been established in 1926 to promote trade and carry out commercially linked research in the Empire. (This early, limited attempt at trade preference was not well-funded by the Treasury, however, and came to an end in 1933, superseded by the Ottawa Agreements.) The Cable and Wireless Company was formed in 1928 to improve Imperial communications and 1929 saw a Colonial Development Act. But the latter provided only small sums for such purposes as health and education, and the beneficial impact on poor colonies in Africa and the West Indies was negligible. Another noteworthy step, in 1932, was the inauguration of BBC radio's Empire Service and the monarch's first Christmas broadcast as a way to bolster mutual Imperial identity. Alongside such developments, however, there were signs that the Dominions were becoming more independent. Already, at the Paris Peace Conference, they had had their own representatives and Chanak had seen them distinctly lukewarm about backing Britain. Pressures from the Irish Free State, South Africa and Canada led to a clearer definition of Dominions rights during the Imperial Conference of 1926. They were 'autonomous communities ... equal in status ... though united by a common allegiance to the Crown'. The Statute of Westminster, which regularised this state of affairs in 1931, even allowed Dominions to leave the Commonwealth. This ended any dreams that the Empire might somehow function as a single state and undermined the FO's insistence that the Empire possessed 'diplomatic unity' (a doctrine which led Britain to sign the Locarno Pact for the Empire as a whole). In 1924 the Irish sent an independent representative to Washington and Canada followed in 1927. The Irish were at the forefront of pressures for even greater independence, particularly when Eamonn de Valera became premier in 1932. His government pursued a trade war with Britain for most of the 1930s, ceased to attend Imperial conferences and introduced a constitution which laid claim to Northern Ireland. In the mid-1920s Amery had believed that a looser 'Commonwealth' would nonetheless remain united. But a decade later it seemed doubtful whether, in the event of war, the Dominions would loyally follow Britain as they had in 1914. No Imperial conference was held between 1930 and 1937, and it was impossible to persuade the Dominions to contribute more money to Imperial defence. Thus in the late 1930s Australia devoted only 1 per cent of its GNP to armaments, despite its vulnerability to Japanese expansion, and in 1938, as part of a general settlement of differences with

Ireland, Britain even gave up the three 'treaty ports' which had been preserved in 1921 for use by the Royal Navy. This was just one year before war began and control of the seas around Ireland proved vital to British survival.

Although problems with internal Imperial security eased after the crisis of 1919–22, there were still difficulties in several areas. In Egypt the assassination of Sir Lee Stack in 1924 was met with harsh action by the High Commissioner, Allenby, who demanded a £500 000 fine from the Egyptian parliament. Indications that London preferred a gentler touch led Allenby to resign but he was succeeded by an equally strong-minded Imperialist, Lord Lloyd, who was eventually sacked by the Labour government in 1929. In order to blunt local opposition, the British were able to play off the constitutionalist Wafd party against the more autocratic views of Egypt's King Fuad. But relations with both were bad, and for years it proved impossible to negotiate a treaty to formalise Egypt's internal independence whilst legalising British control of the Suez Canal, defence and foreign policy. A treaty, to last 20 years, was finally signed in 1936 but only because the Egyptians were worried about Italian ambitions in the Mediterranean. Egypt was allowed to enter the League, but Britain retained extensive military powers (in an arrangement similar to that reached with Iraq in 1930). Anglo-Egyptian differences were thereby patched up, but once the Italian threat was removed the divisions were likely to return. Meanwhile another Middle Eastern country, Palestine, presented serious difficulties, again because a contradictory British policy could find no convenient solution. There was growing tension between the Arab inhabitants and Jewish immigrants who had been promised a 'homeland' by the Balfour Declaration and who arrived in greater numbers from Germany after Hitler's rise. In summer 1936 an Arab revolt forced Britain to despatch 10 000 troops to the Mandate. The following year the Peel Commission, with Colonial Office approval, recommended that Palestine be partitioned between Arabs and Jews. However, the Arabs opposed this, the FO feared growing ill-feeling throughout the Middle East, and in 1939 Britain adopted a policy of limiting Jewish immigration, desperate not to drive the Arabs into the arms of Italy (which now posed as a defender of Moslem rights) and Germany. It was hoped to achieve independence for Palestine under an Arab majority in ten years without partition.

An equally unsatisfactory situation developed in India. In 1927 the British established a commission under Sir John Simon to review the future of Indian government. But since, in the paternalist tradition, it included no Indian representatives it merely added to unrest on the subcontinent, a situation which led the Viceroy, Lord Irwin (later Lord Halifax), to issue a declaration in 1929 promising eventual Dominion status to India. The declaration, issued without reference to Simon, offended many Conservatives, notably Churchill who resigned from the Opposition front bench (a move which put him on the backbenches for almost a decade). The Simon Report, issued in June 1930, then fell short of the Irwin Declaration by recommending self-government only at a provincial level. By now Gandhi had emerged as the most formidable opponent of British rule. His 'march to the sea' to collect salt, on which he then refused to pay tax, won widespread sympathy and led to his imprisonment. Even this mild form of coercion ensured that Congress Party politicians refused to attend a 'round table conference' in London on India's future, and so the British again put the emphasis on conciliation: Gandhi was released, having agreed to attend another 'round table' in September 1931. But this conference still failed to reach agreement and the National Government, faced by deadlock, reluctantly concluded that the impetus towards Dominion status was irresistible. In August 1935 the Government of India Act promised not only stronger, elected regional governments, but also a national parliament. Notwithstanding the doubts of Churchill and a few other 'die-hards', Britain had come to terms with the fact that, even if it was unclear when, India would some day have an autonomous government. The Act was not as generous as it seemed, however. As during the various crises of 1919–22 the British purpose was to grant timely concessions to ensure low cost, orderly rule in the Empire while protecting Britain's political and economic interests. The Act was designed to moderate, and perhaps divide, the Congress Party, by exposing it to the responsibilities of office; it included an important undemocratic element by providing a continuing role for the Indian princes in government; and it retained emergency powers, as well as control of foreign and defence policy, in the hands of the Viceroy – who declared war without reference to Indian opinion in 1939. In any case the Act proved difficult to execute, being opposed by the princes despite its safeguard of their power, and whilst the Congress did win control of many local parliaments, a national legislature was not formed before war broke out.

Manchuria and the advent of Hitler

The Labour government left behind an uncertain international scene. Relations with the USSR were poor, America was preconcerned with its own problems, Franco-German relations had returned to their antagonistic state and Germany had clandestinely begun to rearm. The spirit of Locarno had evaporated even if the Pact itself remained in force. Yet the most serious crisis to meet the incoming National Government was not in Europe, but the Far East. In September the seizure of Mukden by the Kwangtung Army, though not officially sanctioned by Tokyo, began the Japanese conquest of Manchuria. Despite the demise of the Anglo-Japanese alliance a decade before, relations between the two had remained good. Japan inaugurated its own 'ten-year rule' in 1925 and the lack of threat to British interests from that quarter was one reason Churchill felt able to reduce naval spending. In the mid-1920s relations had been worse with the Chinese Nationalist government of Chiang Kai-Shek: in 1925 ill-feeling against British extra-territorial rights led to a Chinese boycott of British goods and in 1927 20 000 troops were sent to Shanghai to prevent the Nationalists seizing the British concession there. Thereafter, however, Anglo-Chinese relations improved. London had a vested interest in seeing the Nationalists end the political turmoil in the country, thus creating stable conditions for commerce. The Japanese in contrast wished to keep their giant neighbour weak and divided, and the effect of the Depression on Japan was to foster expansionist ambitions. In 1932 it was the Japanese, rather than Chiang Kai-Shek, who threatened Shanghai, exposing the fact that, despite substantial economic interests in the Far East, Britain had few forces with which to defend them. It would be erroneous to see this as 'proof' of British decline: even in the 1890s, when faced primarily by Russian expansion, London lacked the capacity to act forcefully in the Far East on its own. That was the reason why the Japanese alliance had been made in 1902. Thirty years later only the USSR or US had the capacity to join in action against Japan, but cooperation with the former was anathema, and the latter showed only a fitful willingness to condemn Tokyo's behaviour. Once again Britain's inability (or failure) to find strong allies stands revealed as a major reason for its difficulties. The Manchurian crisis was widely seen as a test case for collective security and Britain was the only League member with sufficient naval power to challenge Japan. But the Royal Navy had little desire to fight a strong opponent on the other side of the world, whilst economic sanctions would damage British trade and perhaps lead Japan to repudiate its debts to Britain. Everyone was morally repelled by aggression but few wished to pay the price of opposing it. The British public viewed the far-off events with indifference and their leaders were at first too concerned with resolving the August political crisis and election. In December 1931, in response to anguished Chinese protests, the League set up a Commission under Britain's Lord Lytton to investigate events in Manchuria but it took until the following October to report and only urged a partial Japanese withdrawal. Caught between the desire to uphold the League's authority and reluctance to antagonise Tokyo, the new Foreign Secretary, John Simon, then made a speech in Geneva which was even-handed in its criticism of Japan and China. Such weakness did nothing to end Japanese extremism: in early 1933 Japan walked out of the League and seized more Chinese territory. Perhaps Simon had no alternative. Even the pugnacious Vansittant gloomily concluded that, in the absence of US support, Britain must accept humiliation in the Far East. However, the failure to adopt a moral stance upset liberal, educated opinion at home and weakened the League. The Manchurian crisis led to the abandonment of the 'ten-year rule' in March 1932. But the Treasury, having got spending under control in the 1920s, and having faced the nightmare monetary crisis of 1931, had no desire to see defence costs rise much. Of vital importance to British foreign policy in the 1930s was the primacy given by the government to internal financial stability, making it almost impossible to run risks abroad. Indeed the new Chancellor of the Exchequer, Neville Chamberlain (half brother of Austen), was determined to have an influence on Far Eastern policy, favouring conciliation rather than coercion. In 1934 he advocated a non-aggression pact to moderate Japan. The suggestion made some sense, since by then Germany too was a potential aggressor, and a war against both Germany and Japan would be enormously costly. But the FO feared that a policy of friendship towards Tokyo would offend America, Russia and China, and it was soon clear that Japan was not susceptible to negotiation. Instead, in December 1934 it renounced the Washington treaties, thereby ending the system of peace in the Pacific created in 1921–22 and hopes of another conference on naval disarmament. In 1937 Japan went on to launch full-scale war against China, unrestrained by any fear of what Britain might do in response.

Events in East Asia served to highlight factors in British foreign policy which militated against a firm response to aggressors. The need to defend a scattered Empire, the desire for peace and trade, a preference for pragmatism over principle and a readiness to buy off potential trouble-makers with concessions were long-standing features of British policy. And the Depression, with its 20 per cent unemployment, merely reinforced the desire of most Britons to avoid another experience like 1914–18. The public was not widely favourable to pacifism as a moral principle, in the way some Christian and Socialist groups were: ultimately most believed the use of force was legitimate. But they would now go a long way before using it. The February 1933 Oxford Union debate, which passed the motion 'That this house will in no circumstances fight for its King and Country', was moral self-indulgence by a privileged elite, but it attracted world-wide Press interest. The October Fulham by-election, which the Conservatives lost to a pacifist Labour candidate on a swing of 19 000 votes, was not simply fought on the peace issue, but it shook Conservative leaders and pointed out the need for a popular education campaign before rearmament was undertaken. Most powerfully of all, in 1934 the League of Nations Union, which on paper numbered one million members, took up Cecil's idea for a 'Peace Ballot', a kind of public opinion survey. The questions were hardly framed in a neutral manner and the ballot showed a majority in favour of military sanctions against aggressors, but it supported the view that the public wanted peace and a strong League, rather than balance of power politics. The ballot had a great impact on the National Government ahead of the November 1935 election and helped secure the appointment of the young, popular Anthony Eden as Minister for League of Nations Affairs in the FO. This step at least brought a more energetic (if vain and shortsighted) figure to foreign policy making than was otherwise the case. The former socialist, MacDonald, presiding over a Conservative-dominated government, was an increasingly forlorn figure, weakened by insomnia and failing eyesight before his belated resignation in June 1935. His successor, Baldwin, still took only a limited interest in foreign affairs and Simon, the Foreign Secretary, was the very embodiment of 'drift', as seen in his Manchurian policy. Having resigned as Home Secretary in 1916 in opposition to conscription, he could safely be counted among the 'pro-peace' lobby. He owed his high position to being leader of the Liberals who supported the National Government and had few close allies in Cabinet. Simon certainly worked hard, being out of the country at international meetings for about six months of his first two years in office – a great contrast to the single overseas visit Grey made as Foreign Secretary before 1914, and testament to the growing importance of multilateral meetings, such as those of the League. Simon was not lacking in intellect, yet too often his understanding of all sides of a question bred self-doubt. A more decisive, imaginative individual may at least have *appeared* to be in control of events.

In this situation it was unsurprising that the strong-minded Neville Chamberlain emerged as a powerful figure in foreign policy. Along with the Permanent Secretary of the Treasury, Warren Fisher, Chamberlain had a vital role in shaping Britain's reaction, not only to the Japanese, but to the frightening revival of German power. In 1931 the FO still hoped to reassure the French sufficiently about their security to allow a peaceful revision of Versailles. The fate of the Austro-German Customs Union suggested France was in a powerful position, whilst the apparent economic weakness of Germany led to the suspension of reparations payments in July 1932. When Adolf Hitler became Chancellor in January 1933, it was clear they would never be revived. Hitler had set out his racial theories and hopes of eastward expansion in his book, *Mein Kampf*, and his rise to power provoked concern in London. There was a tendency, however, to equate him with the conservatism of the Kaiser rather than to see Nazism as a radical, totalitarian ideology; and there was a belief, too, that office would moderate him. It seemed incredible that any leader would want war only 15 years after the last. FO officials were suspicious of Germany but persisted in their belief that compromise would secure results and were encouraged by Hitler's insistence that he wanted peace, or even an alliance, with Britain. In October 1933, however, he walked out of the League and out of the World Disarmament Conference, which had been meeting in Geneva for the previous 18 months and was now effectively doomed. Hitler excused his exit by arguing that other powers wished to enforce limits on Germany while preserving their own arms. The British now faced a situation where Germany might rearm openly, France would feel even less able to revise Versailles and pressure for greater defence spending would grow. Thus, in November, the government established a Defence Requirements Committee (DRC) which included the service chiefs and three other top officials, Hankey, Vansittant and Fisher. There were obvious potential differences between these three: Hankey, with his concern for Imperial defence; Vansittant, who recognised the violent, irrational nature of Nazism, and favoured a continental commitment; and Fisher, anxious to avoid high arms production which could lead to increased raw material imports, worsening the trade situation and weakening the Pound. But Hankey knew the importance of Western Europe to British defence, Vansittant recognised the need to rearm gradually and concentrate British resources on one enemy, ideally Germany, and Fisher was not opposed to rearmament outright, but wished to be selective about spending, to avoid unpopular tax increases and cuts in social provision. The first DRC report in February 1934 identified Germany as 'the ultimate potential enemy' whilst confirming the Japanese threat and the needs of Imperial defence. Italy at this time was seen as no more of a threat than America or France. The DRC recommended an additional £71 million be spent before 1939 particularly in three areas: to bolster the navy, which would bear the burden of any Pacific war; to create a small British Expeditionary Force for use in Europe, where it would reassure the French; and to build up the RAF's bomber force, seen as a potent *deterrent* to Germany, given the widespread expectation that aerial bombardment would have a devastating effect. (Historians see, in British thinking at this time, the origins of post-war nuclear deterrence.) Against the background of the DRC report it is easy to understand why Neville Chamberlain hoped to placate Japan. But at the same time he sought to reduce the proposed spending programme by setting a priority in favour of the RAF as a (hopefully) cheap but effective way to dissuade Hitler from aggression. The Treasury's domination of expenditure policy, bolstered by the 1931 crisis, ensured his success. In July the Cabinet agreed an arms programme of only £60 million, a third of which was for the air force. It was the army which suffered most, despite past evidence that inability to intervene on land in Europe weakened Britain's diplomatic hand there.

Baldwin actually told the Commons at this time that – as the COS had asserted in 1925 – Britain's first line of defence was on the Rhine, and Simon had already reasserted the importance of Belgium to British defence. But in the mid-1930s there was no substantial BEF and no staff talks with France. Financial constraints, Imperial commitments and the fear of aerial bombardment were understandable reasons leading to Chamberlain's choice, and there was a strong belief that the country was better suited to a 'maritime strategy' than trench warfare in Europe. But the British seemed to achieve the worst of several worlds. Their rearmament started at a slow pace, two years after Germany's, undermining any real hopes of 'deterring' Hitler. They inspired no confidence in France, which was the only firm ally against Germany. And neither did they moderate Hitler, whose nationalist ambitions were given further encouragement in January 1935 when the people of the Saarland (separated from Germany in 1919) voted to rejoin the Reich. When British rearmament was announced in March the German leader simply seized the opportunity to reintroduce conscription, a flagrant breach of Versailles. The policy-making machinery in London at this time, for all its complexity, expertise and comprehensive discussion, and despite Chamberlain's strong-mindedness, was poorly directed from the top, confused as to its purpose and indecisive.

The turning point: Abyssinia and the Rhineland

Even in the 1920s, when Germany was represented by a sane nationalist like Stresemann, when there was no Japanese threat and US policy was less than fully isolationist, Britain had not made much progress in satisfying German discontent over Versailles. By 1935 the situation was far bleaker but there was a sense of growing danger which ought to have given urgency to British policy-makers. Vansittant especially pressed the case for cooperation with Italy as well as France, to restrain Hitler. Mussolini was a volatile character but a vain one and, it seemed, could be placated by a little flattery. Furthermore, he was himself fearful of German ambition, not least because of the danger of an *Anschluss* between Germany and Austria, which bordered on Italy: in 1934, when the Nazis threatened a coup in Austria, Mussolini was quick to move troops to the border. In April 1935 therefore it seemed logical for Britain, France and Italy to meet at Stresa, condemn German conscription and insist on the continuing validity of Versailles and Locarno. MacDonald himself led the British delegation in this attempt at diplomatic deterrence, which again showed a preference for Great Power cooperation over action by the League. Yet the 'Stresa Front' had many internal fissures. Although the French Foreign Minister, Pierre Laval, was anxious to cooperate with

Italy, the two countries were rivals in the Balkans. Although Britain was opposed to any *Anschluss*, Mussolini knew the British would provide little help if he chose to fight Hitler over Austria. Anglo-French differences too were well known: the one a global trading power, with deep concern over the Japanese threat; the other a continental protectionist state, obsessed with the German problem. The British were upset in May when the French made an alliance with the USSR. The alliance made sense in terms of France's desire for an 'eastern Locarno' (to prevent changes in Germany's eastern borders) which the British said they favoured, and London itself was not above using hints of Anglo-Russian cooperation to intimidate Hitler: Eden had recently visited Moscow. But British fear of Soviet Communism was unabated and a leading FO official, Orme Sargent, pointed out that the alliance of Paris and Moscow must 're-awaken memories of 1914, when we were dragged into war ... because France was involved through her alliance with Russia'.[10] In fact, largely due to French doubts, the Franco-Soviet alliance never amounted to much and, in any case, in June Britain itself breached the Stresa Front by grasping at Hitler's willingness to sign a naval agreement, limiting the size of Germany's surface navy, but not submarines, to 35 per cent of the British. Since 1930 (before Hitler came to power) Germany had been building 'pocket battleships' which were fast and powerful but did not breach the Versailles naval limits. The agreement reflected, once more, Britain's concern with naval matters and her strong desire to work with Hitler on a legal, written basis. There was some hope it might lead to other agreements, such as an Air Pact to prevent sudden aerial attacks, the fear of which was now intensified by exaggerated estimates of the size of the German air force. It reassured the Admiralty that there would be no 'naval race' with Germany to contend with, and offered the Treasury a chance to avoid greater naval expenditure. But the agreement added to the sense of dismay about British policy in France, where the Depression was now wreaking its full effect and political divisions were growing.

The Stresa Front was finally torn apart by Italian action against Abyssinia. Tension in East Africa had been growing for years as the Italians, who already controlled Eritrea and Somaliland, prepared to avenge a defeat at Abyssinian hands in 1896. Despite warnings that London would condemn any attack on Abyssinia, Mussolini launched war in October. This was one month before the general election when Baldwin's government portrayed itself as both peace-loving and sympathetic to the League. In fact, as the Abyssinian crisis revealed, these two principles were not completely compatible, for the League had little choice but to condemn Italian aggression and introduce economic sanctions, raising the danger of war. The future of collective security was again at stake, but so too was British cooperation with Italy and France against Germany. As over Manchuria, British policy became confused and indecisive, but once again not without good reason. Abyssinia created awful policy choices. Laval was unwilling to fall out with Mussolini, so Britain could not count on help from Paris. The Dominions were generally indifferent and lack of US support made it pointless to enforce the one economic measure which might have troubled Mussolini: oil sanctions. It is simplistic to claim that if a tough sanctions policy had been adopted by Britain it might have deterred the aggressors once and for all, for America could have given Mussolini all the oil he needed. To prevent Italian troops reaching East Africa, Britain might have closed the Suez Canal to them, but this would have been illegal under the 1888 Convention and Mussolini, now described by the British as a 'mad dog', warned he would treat it as an act of war. With Germany and Japan already recognised as threats, the COS had little desire to add to the list, and the Royal Navy, which had been concentrating in the Mediterranean since July, was increasingly concerned at the prospect of fighting Italy. The claim that 'in the 1930s ... buttressed by the Royal Navy ... British foreign policy was hardly to be challenged' is an exaggeration.[11] Vulnerable to submarine and air attack in the restricted Mediterranean waters, the navy was forced to pull back its main force from Malta to Alexandria, a smaller port with inadequate facilities. Furthermore, the army in Egypt could hardly be confident, in its neglected state, of defeating the Italian forces in neighbouring Libya, who were on war standing. The COS were soon confirmed in their belief that collective security embroiled Britain in problems it should have avoided. The result of these pressures was that the new Foreign Secretary, Samuel Hoare, praised the League before the general election but, once it was won, returned to cooperation with France and Italy. Vansittant encouraged the Foreign Secretary to travel to Paris in December and agree to the Hoare–Laval Pact, which would have given Italy a third of Abyssinia if hostilities ended. But this shift in policy, made without any attempt to prepare public opinion, led to an outcry in the Press and parliament which rapidly brought Hoare's replacement by the 38-year-old Eden. The Pact may have made sense to Vansittant (and Laval) as a way to keep Italy in an anti-German front, but to the public it marked a return to the old diplomacy of secrecy, power politics and the cynical disposal of small nations. True, there was a minority who saw Italian expansion as preferable to the inefficient Abyssinian monarchy and no different to British Imperial aspirations, but generally there was less sympathy for Mussolini's behaviour than there was for Hitler: the latter at least was felt to have justification in wishing to revise Versailles and had not yet used blatant aggression against his neighbours. Such moral outrage did little good. By

May 1936 Mussolini had conquered Abyssinia, the League was finished as a force for peace and Chamberlain led the way in calling for sanctions to end. This came too late, however, to prevent Mussolini's alienation from Britain and increasing closeness to Hitler, who had cynically declared his sympathy for the Abyssinian campaign. The Abyssinian crisis had virtually eliminated two means for Britain to resist aggression in unison with other states: collective security had failed utterly; and Italy's behaviour removed the chance to resist Hitler through an Anglo-Franco-Italian alliance.

The arrival of Italy as a third potential menace to British interests in the hitherto safe Mediterranean deepened the gloom about British defences, although Eden doubted Italy would ally closely with Germany. The March 1936 Defence White Paper increased defence spending further but was still behind German levels and did not deter Hitler. Meanwhile Eden, despite his reputation as an 'anti-appeaser', still hoped to win Hitler over to a security agreement which might include an Air Pact, disarmament, economic assistance and even recognition of German 'special interests' in Eastern Europe. But on 7 March 1936 the German leader again demonstrated his preference for unilateral action when he marched troops into the Rhineland, arguing that the Franco-Soviet Treaty (which had just been ratified) breached Locarno. By ending the demilitarisation of the west bank of the Rhine he simultaneously breached Versailles and Locarno, removed an important element in French security policy, made nonsense of British talk of basing their defence on the Rhine, and demoralised the Belgians who declared their neutrality in October. Locarno had effectively disintegrated, yet beyond trying to win some guarantees from Hitler that he would not fortify the Rhineland, the British government did nothing. There was little understanding, even in government, of the strategic advantage Germany received from the re-occupation. The public, still anxious for peace, critical of the French for failing to make concessions earlier and still believing Versailles to be unjust, saw the remilitarisation of the Rhineland merely as Germany taking control of its own borders. Labour, critical of power politics and keen to see money spent on social problems, had already attacked the government's modest rearmament programme. Hitler, talking in moderate tones, hinted that he might return to the League and sign a series of non-aggression pacts – an offer which tempted those wishing for a new, stable European system. The League criticised his actions and the French, to some British concern, called for sanctions, but in contrast to 1923 Paris felt unable to enforce Versailles unilaterally. France was increasingly divided and demoralised, and its army would have taken weeks to mobilise. Italy predictably had no complaints about Germany's actions. Again, the Rhineland crisis is one of those instances where it is thought that aggression should have been halted and such arguments are not merely retrospective. At the time Austen Chamberlain asked the Commons, 'Was there any international law or had we returned to the rule of force?'.[12] However, in a clear reflection of Britain's unenviable position, his solution to the Rhineland problem was not to fight – after all, Britain lacked an army to do that – but to reconstruct the Stresa Front. Hardly anyone advocated the use of force in March 1936. After all Britain had learnt after 1914 that 'even if she were victorious in a war it might do her ... as much harm' as being beaten.[13] Some FO officials, dismayed by the uselessness of negotiation, believed the best policy was somehow to contain future German expansion whilst rearming quickly in the expectation of future war; but most in government still favoured only moderate rearmament and continuing attempts to arbitrate a European settlement. The scale of problems facing Britain had grown enormously, even since the summer of 1935, when 'Looking around Europe ... it seemed that, whatever the danger ... Germany might present, there were ample means to cope with it'.[14] The Stresa Front had collapsed, the League had been humiliated, Versailles was in tatters, Locarno was a dead letter, Hitler was more confident, France demoralised and Britain faced a triple danger, from Japan in the Far East, Italy in the Mediterranean and Germany in Europe. Britain was still a strong power, stronger than Italy or Japan in isolation certainly, and perhaps the match of Germany too. But even at the height of Victorian predominance the challenge of three aggressive Great Powers would have created daunting problems. In November 1936 the terrifying prospect arose of a link between the Far Eastern and European threats when Germany and Japan signed the Anti-Comintern Pact (though again Eden was unconvinced that these two would unite against London). Britain was obsessed at that time with the Abdication crisis, but the following spring finally saw the end of the policy of drift which marked the end of the Baldwin–MacDonald era.

Notes

1 Ferris J.R., 'The Greatest Power on Earth; Great Britain in the 1920s', *International History Review*, **13**(4), 1991, 739.
2 Orde A., *Great Britain and International Security, 1920–26* (London, 1978), 212.
3 Middlemass K. and Barnes J., *Baldwin: A Biography* (London, 1970), 180.
4 *Documents on British Foreign Policy, 1919–39*, Series 1a, Vol. I (1966), 846–7.
5 Self R. (ed.), *The Austen Chamberlain Diary Letters* (London, 1995), 270.
6 Quoted in Bond B., *British Military Policy Between the Two World Wars* (Oxford, 1980), 77.
7 McGhee F., '"Limited Liability"? Britain and the Treaty of Locarno', *Twentieth Century British History*, **6**(1), 1995, 6.
8 McKercher B., *The Second Baldwin Government and the United States, 1924–9* (Cambridge, 1984), 1.

9 Richardson D., *The Evolution of British Disarmament Policy in the 1920s* (London, 1989), 203.
10 *Documents on British Foreign Policy, 1919–39*, Series 2, Vol. XII (1972), 793–5.
11 McKercher B., 'Great Britain Pre-eminent in the 1930s', *International History Review*, **13**(4), 1991, 751.
12 Dutton P., *Austen Chamberlain: Gentleman in Politics* (London, 1985), 320.
13 Porter B., *Britain, Europe and the World, 1850–1986*, 2nd edn (London, 1986), 102.
14 Gooch G.P., *Studies in Diplomacy and Statecraft* (London, 1942), 197.

5
Appeasement and global conflict, 1937–1945

Chamberlain and appeasement

Neville Chamberlain, who became Prime Minister in May 1937, has often been portrayed as parochial in viewpoint, inexperienced in foreign affairs, and cowardly in his response to the dictators. In 1940 he and his advisers were condemned as 'guilty men' who betrayed small nations to the evils of Nazism, brought their country's reputation low and refused to rearm sufficiently before having to fight anyway. Their failure heralded precipitate national decline. Yet in 1937–38 Chamberlain was seen as an energetic, resolute, self-confident, even – in the terms of liberal democracy – ruthless politician, who dominated his Cabinet and the Commons. Since the 1970s historians have tried to reach a better-informed view of his policies, analysing a range of factors from economics and rearmament, through the party-political battle and government structure, to the British national character and diplomatic tradition. Many have become sympathetic to him and, at the very least, it is agreed that he gave a sense of direction to policy after years of drift, when the government could not agree which enemy to conciliate most determinedly or what military strategy to adopt. 'Intolerant of muddling through, Chamberlain planned to make action, efficiency and decisiveness the bywords of his regime'.[1] As Chancellor of the Exchequer he already had clear views about the choices Britain must make. These were based on the need to preserve a strong economy and gave primacy to the needs of British internal prosperity over foreign adventures. He was well aware of the vulnerable nature of Britain's commitments, its military deficiencies and the desire of its people for peace. The last point was especially important for a Prime Minister who expected to face an election in 1940. Memories of the Great War and the 'lost generation' who died in it loomed large in his own mind and he had a craving for peace, which he knew to be in the interests of British Imperial, commercial and financial security. He believed in taking a forthright role, using personal diplomacy to negotiate with the dictators, especially Hitler, who he correctly identified as the most formidable adversary. But in private he frequently spoke of his distrust of the German and accompanied the strategy of conciliation with a gradual build-up of British forces, hoping to create a position of strength in due course. This is not to say that Appeasement was an attempt only to 'buy time' for rearmament: Chamberlain really hoped he could avoid war. Nonetheless, his policy may be described as working for peace while preparing for conflict. Some historians have even seen him as a far-sighted arch-realist, with a cohesive strategy for maintaining British greatness. They argue that he foresaw not only rapid British decline if another war broke out, but also the rise of the US and Soviet Communism.

It is often claimed that there was no cohesive alternative to Chamberlain's 'Appeasement'. That emotive term has been avoided earlier in this study because of its connotations with the supposed treachery and surrender of the 1930s. Yet if the logic of Appeasement was to buy off one's rivals by acknowledging their grievances and negotiating timely concessions rather than risking war, it was an art at which the British were past masters, even at the height of their power. The *ententes* in the Edwardian period can be seen in the same light and Appeasement can be linked to other, diverse traditions such as that of the radical dissenters, who urged the benefits of a pro-peace policy over the balance of power, or isolationists who wished to preserve the 'free hand' and low cost defence. (One view is that inter-war Appeasement had firm roots in the Victorian era, that it was a moral, optimistic tradition based on the principle of negotiation from strength and that Chamberlain's craven policy was 'a distortion of all that appeasement [really] stood for'.[2]) Yet a major point of recent studies is that the only choice British leaders had abroad after 1937 was a choice of evils, all of which would result in decline, and some of these interpretations are quite deterministic and mechanical. Structural problems in British policy were such, it can be argued, that Chamberlain's character did not have much importance in deciding Britain's course. It is possible to draw up a list of factors which would have pointed any leader on the road to Munich. Many have already been touched upon. One bedrock factor, certainly, was the British approach to world affairs, a pragmatic, moralistic outlook which believed in rationalism and compromise, saw peace as 'normal' and thought others would see the wisdom of such an approach. Despite a deep-seated fear of Communism, British foreign policy was traditionally 'non-ideological' and ready to deal with the most distasteful of regimes to maintain peace. Of course, there was considerable hypocrisy in this outlook, which was driven by an interest in tranquillity as a way to guarantee commercial wealth and preserve the world's largest Empire, but it was far removed from the self-seeking of the fanatical, aggressive Hitler, whose revolutionary, expansionist aims were underestimated in London for too long.

Onto this outlook the years 1914–20 grafted a horror of modern conflict, a realisation that even victorious wars could sap national power and a willingness to make concessions to Germany because it was unjustly treated at Versailles. Until 1939 it was hoped that Hitler's ambitions could be confined to absorbing German-populated territories, and that Appeasement could create a more just settlement in Europe which Germany would respect. The Great War had also brought renewed dislike of involvement in European affairs and a reluctance to stand close to France. A similar war was only to be entered after everything was done to avoid it. Then again, it is possible the British might have emerged with an alternative to Appeasement if three vital factors had not combined. One, perhaps most potent, was the threat posed by three aggressor powers – Japan, Italy, Germany – to different parts of a vulnerable Empire. Again Britain's reluctance to tackle all three need not be read as a sign of inevitable national decline: a combination of three aggressive Great Powers would have been formidable at any time. But this particular combination gathered at a time when Britain lacked major allies, had little taste for the prospect of war and *was* becoming concerned about its financial position and declining share of world trade.

The most potent menace was Germany, whose rearmament was three years ahead of Britain's, which produced 50 per cent more steel and had a population of almost 70 million compared to Britain's 48 million. The Chiefs of Staff (COS) repeatedly warned of the dangers of fighting all three opponents at once, and reinforced the idea that diplomacy must be used to divide the dictators, keeping one or more well-disposed to Britain. In 1937 the Royal Navy wanted to adopt a 'new power standard' to match Germany and Japan, but this ran contrary to the second vital factor, the limits of economy and finance. In 1937 Simon, now Chancellor of the Exchequer, told the Cabinet that the maximum available for rearmament over the next five years was £1500 million, not a vast sum. In February 1938 a review was completed by Thomas Inskip, who had been appointed to a new position, Minister for the Coordination of Defence. The Inskip Report, influenced by Treasury preferences, confirmed the first priority of rearmament as air defence and stated that a land campaign in Europe was less important than the protection of Imperial sea lanes. The Treasury, overshadowed by memories of 1931, wished to preserve the value of Sterling, minimise raw material imports and keep inflation low. Importantly, Britain's pace of rearmament was also restricted by lack of industrial capacity and skilled labour.

The third vital factor, in contrast to the Edwardian period and partly due to Britain's own reluctance to run diplomatic risks, was the lack of allies who could compensate for British deficiencies. The US under Franklin Roosevelt was unwilling to play a strong role in Europe or the

Pacific, the USSR was viewed by Conservatives with as much distaste as the aggressors and France was still distrusted in spring 1937, though it became a close ally over the following years. Other, less important factors which reinforced Appeasement included the attitude of the Dominions, who were keenly in favour of peace; the strain placed on resources by Imperial troublespots, especially in 1936–39 Palestine; and specific problems associated with Eastern Europe, an area of limited British interest and impossible for London to defend, yet which was the focus of Hitler's ambition in 1938–39. If Eastern Europe were to be stabilised without risk of war, there *must* be an agreement with Germany. The region could not simply be conceded to Hitler without a frightening increase in German power.

In addition to pursuing gradual rearmament, the government boosted Britain's intelligence and propaganda agencies as a safeguard against war. Spending on MI6 and the Government Code and Cypher School (GC&CS) grew from £180 000 in 1935 to £500 000 in 1939 – though this was insufficient to provide sufficient wireless sets to MI6 agents. Another development was the highly secret Industrial Intelligence Centre, set up around 1929 to gather information on the economic potential and vulnerabilities of countries. British intelligence had mixed success in the late 1930s. On the negative side, a Soviet agent was uncovered in the FO Communications Department in 1939, an event which led to the (long-overdue) appointment of an FO Security Officer. The German air threat was generally exaggerated until 1938; counter-intelligence work was undervalued; and both the Berlin and Rome embassies were guilty of lackadaisical security. Information was harder to collect in the dictatorships than in liberal democracies. But intelligence did improve. By 1939 information on German military capabilities was interpreted with greater accuracy; GC&CS was able to read Italian and Japanese codes at times; and, encouraged by Vansittant, MI6 began to reveal the ideological, expansionist nature of Nazi policy. German spies found it hard to operate in Britain, Oswald Mosley's British Union of Fascists was never a serious threat and MI5 (which, around 1931, had won out decisively over Special Branch in this field) could still devote most of its counter-subversion activities to Communist sympathisers. Importantly, spring 1939 also saw important advances in the coordination of intelligence between the FO (with responsibility for MI6 and GC&CS) and the intelligence services of the armed forces, culminating in the formation of a Joint Intelligence Committee, under FO chairmanship. Propaganda work had also begun to receive more resources in 1934 when the British Council was founded to publicise British values and achievements, and to influence 'elite' opinion abroad. This development was long overdue: France had had such a cultural propaganda agency since 1880. As well as arranging lecture tours, disseminating literature and encouraging overseas students, the Council helped set up the Joint Committee on Films in 1936 to distribute newsreels. The need to counter German and Italian propaganda was obvious and in 1938–39 a committee met under Vansittant to improve British efforts whilst the BBC began foreign language broadcasts over the radio, the most important, rising form of mass media. Despite the BBC's reputation for independence, its foreign news programmes by 1939 were largely controlled by the FO, which separated its own propaganda work from the News Department into a Foreign Publicity Department. Plans for 'black' – covert, unattributable – propaganda were made by MI6's 'Section D' (which looked at all non-military means of attacking an enemy) and another FO department, known as Electra House. In a remarkable operation, MI6 secured the 'pirate' radio station Radio Luxembourg as a source for broadcasts into Germany during the Munich crisis. A subcommittee of the CID also drew up blueprints for a Ministry of Information, on 1918 lines, should war come. Nonetheless 'Britain entered the war of words in September 1939 not speechless, as ... in ... 1914, but certainly inarticulate'.[3] Most ministers and officials were still uncomfortable with propaganda, and the structure of work was clearly very confused. Furthermore, Chamberlain was offended by the anti-Appeasement attitudes of the FO News Department under Rex Leeper. This made the Prime Minister anxious to disguise divisions in Whitehall and disseminate news via his Downing Street Press Officer (a post first created in 1929). This officer, George Steward, had a close relationship with newspapers, providing stories to journalists, who in return backed Appeasement even when the general public had begun to question it. The relationship, underpinned by personal links between politicians and newspaper barons, compromised the supposed independence of the Press, undermined the discussion of alternative policies and led Chamberlain to believe his policy was widely approved.

It may have made no difference if Britain had chosen an alternative policy to Appeasement, for it seems Hitler was bent on expansion regardless. He certainly would have liked an agreement with Britain, which he recognised as a strong enemy, but only on the basis that he could dominate Eastern Europe completely. Alternative policies to Appeasement were not easy to define. The time for European integration, or even collective security, had passed. Britain could not withdraw into isolation because its extensive possessions were potential targets of aggression. Chamberlain had support from most MPs, the Press and, it seemed, public opinion. The public still tended to be 'pro-peace' in the sense of a general aspiration, rather than pacifist on moral or religious grounds, although there was a fracturing of 'pro-peace' opinion around 1936. Some Labour internationalists became ready to fight Fascism, even if the bulk of the party still hoped for a resuscitation of the League; but other people moved in the opposite direction, joining Canon Dick Sheppard's pacifist 'Peace Pledge Union', which reached a peak membership of 136 000 in April 1940. Chamberlain's political opponents were a disparate group, ranging from Labour anti-Fascists to Tory Imperialists, but they included some able figures and their growth reflected increasing doubts about how to deal with Germany. In 1937–38 Churchill was less forthright in his condemnation of Appeasement than he later claimed, had few sympathisers in the Commons and was generally viewed as an ageing, outdated maverick. But he did make early, if exaggerated, warnings about German rearmament, was ready to work closely with France and also favoured cooperation with the Soviets to deter German aggression. In February 1938 Eden, who had not worked well with Chamberlain, resigned as Foreign Secretary. Eden was not close to Churchill, tempered his criticisms of government because of hopes of a return to office, and was not enthusiastic about a Soviet alliance. But he may have run more risks than Chamberlain, saw the value of working with America and was keen to stand up to Mussolini. The FO Permanent Under-Secretary, Vansittant, was prepared to stand close to France, to work with Russia and use a psychological policy of 'bluff', turning against Hitler his own tactic of intimidation. It may be true that crude differentiation between 'appeasers' and 'anti-appeasers' is unhelpful; that Vansittant, Churchill and Eden differed more in *method* than substance from Chamberlain. They all hoped to preserve peace, protect British security interests and achieve European stability by negotiating with Britain's enemies whilst rearming. But *method* might have made all the difference in dealing with an irrational bully like Hitler and a more vigorous attempt to find allies could have strengthened Britain's hand. The dictators had their weaknesses, there was a strong desire for peace in Germany and, at Munich, Hitler *was* moved by the threat of war to moderate his demands. Fear of conflict, a desire for material prosperity and an abhorration of high taxes and state intervention were hardly the best combination of attitudes to hold when faced by a determined megalomaniac – and the fact that many other Britons held such views is not an entirely adequate excuse for Chamberlain: leaders must sometimes point their people in a new direction. It certainly seems that, with a campaign of 'moral rearmament', the people would have accepted a tougher policy at an earlier date. The few opinion polls taken in the 1930s actually suggest little faith in Appeasement: one poll in February 1938 showed that 58 per cent disliked the policy, with only 26 per cent in favour.

Whatever claims are made about a 'lack of alternatives', Chamberlain's policy had serious flaws: it *did* fail to account for psychology in dealing with Hitler and was based on a belief that aggressors were susceptible to rational negotiation; it tolerated violent breaches in international agreements; and it tried to combine elements of both deterrence and Appeasement, which undermined each other. Some elements of Appeasement were little more than wishful thinking. In 1937–38 for example, before Hitler focused attention on Eastern Europe, Chamberlain became convinced that colonial concessions would help secure a comprehensive settlement. A Whitehall study made in 1936, after Hitler raised the subject in a speech and when Eden was interested in such concessions, had shown that the Dominions (who controlled several ex-German colonies) and the armed forces disliked the idea of abandoning areas where the Germans might build military bases. Yet in January 1938 Chamberlain presented ministers with ideas for German participation in a consortium to exploit colonies in Africa. Then in 1938–39 attention focused on 'economic appeasement'. The idea of relieving the Depression by the joint use of economic resources was a well-established, even sensible one which, again, Eden had explored. Historically, Germany was a major trading partner and area for British investment. The Nazis' move to an autarchic economic policy in Central Europe was almost as worrying as their political aggression, and just as threatening to the trade-dependent British economy. Appeasement has been described as an ambitious plan to settle differences with Germany on the political *and* economic levels; rather like Lloyd George's hopes of neutralising the Bolshevik threat in 1921, 'Commerce would expand and ... prosperity would guarantee ... the status quo ... at home and abroad'.[4] But, as with 'colonial appeasement', the British interpreted Hitler too much in terms of their own experience when they believed he would be satisfied with guaranteed access to raw materials and finance rather than the physical conquest of Eastern Europe. It is also significant that when, in January 1938, Roosevelt suggested a conference of major powers on disarmament and economic problems, Chamberlain was indifferent to the idea. His distrust of the US was such that (though he recognised the desirability of US sympathy) he preferred to deal with the dictators alone, a policy which offered no encouragement to the few signs that America *might* awaken from its isolationist slumbers. Nevertheless, whatever the flaws of Appeasement, grave difficulties would have surrounded a more aggressive line. A consistent policy of bluff would have taken strong nerves, and alliances with France and Soviet Communism would have recreated the fateful 'Triple Entente' which was blamed for war in 1914. The danger of driving Hitler (and Mussolini) into war by aggressive policy was a constant fear.

Chamberlain's personal diplomacy was accompanied by reliance on non-FO advice. His closest confidant was Horace Wilson, an expert on labour disputes. More experienced in international affairs was Neville

Henderson, the Ambassador to Berlin from April 1937. A professional diplomat, Henderson shared Chamberlain's dislike of the Soviets, distrust of France and certainty that toughness would push Hitler into war. The Ambassador believed German predominance in Eastern Europe was inevitable, that this need not affect British vital interests and that a comprehensive settlement was possible. Henderson was able to bypass the FO and secure a direct link to Chamberlain who also had a 'secret channel' to Mussolini, via Major Joseph Ball, a Conservative Party official and ex-MI5 officer (who in 1927 had founded a Conservative 'intelligence service' to infiltrate spies into the Labour Party). In December 1937 the Prime Minister was able to have one dangerous critic, Vansittant, replaced as Permanent Under-Secretary. But Vansittant was kept in government in the unusual position of Chief Diplomatic Advisor, which allowed him to continue urging resistance to Hitler. And there were other groups within government who gradually turned against Appeasement. Junior ministers in particular became disenchanted and one, Duff Cooper, resigned over Munich. More important was Eden's successor as Foreign Secretary, Lord Halifax. Halifax had that serious flaw of intellectuals, a desire to see all sides of a question, and in 1937 he agreed that 'Diplomacy must bear the burden of diminishing Britain's enemies'.[5] But his Anglo-Catholic faith ensured his distaste for Nazism, he was strong-willed enough to argue with the Prime Minister and, after Munich, guided the government towards anti-German resistance.

Munich and the road to war

It has been seen that Britain was desperate to prevent a combination between Germany, Italy and Japan. Thus, London took no firm action against Mussolini when in 1937 his submarines began to sink British-registered vessels sailing to Spanish ports. The previous July civil war had broken out in Spain between supporters of the Second Republic and their right-wing, Nationalist opponents led by General Franco. In London there was deep suspicion of Communist influence among Spanish Republicans and the British government, which escaped the bitter ideological divisions of continental Europe in the 1930s, had no desire to see the struggle spread beyond Spain's borders. In August 1936 Britain backed a French proposal for 'non-intervention' which led to an agreement by 27 states, including Italy, Germany and Russia, to prevent arms being imported into Spain. But non-intervention did not stop Mussolini sending 50 000 'volunteers', and Hitler the 'Condor Legion', to help the Nationalists; nor did it deter the Soviets from organising 'International Brigades' to help the Republicans. Spain thereby became the cockpit for an ideological conflict between Communism and Fascism and a number of Britons went to fight there, mostly in the International Brigades. The use of Italian submarines against merchant ships reflected the growing violence of the war. Italy's involvement in the sinkings was well known, but Chamberlain's government preferred to accept the fiction that attacks were made by 'pirates'. It was an argument over how exactly to deal with Italy which led to Eden's resignation in February 1938. The increasingly tired Foreign Secretary was ready to talk to Mussolini despite a bitter personal dislike for him, but believed the Italian leader could be pressed hard by Britain: after all Italy was anxious to win recognition of the conquest of Abyssinia and was still concerned over German ambitions in Austria. Eden encouraged the FO and BBC to counteract Italian radio propaganda against British Imperialism in the Middle East with British broadcasts in Arabic, thus beginning Britain's first 'radio war' with a rival power. But Chamberlain refused to take a hard line with Mussolini and in April recognised Italy's Abyssinian gains. It is easy to underestimate the impact of the Spanish Civil War, which ended in March 1939, on British policy. True, the war was restricted to Spain and direct links between the conflict and the outbreak of wider war in September are difficult to draw. Nonetheless, events in Spain had strategic and psychological importance. France was left with a potentially unfriendly state on its Pyrenean border, the Soviets and British remained far apart, and the war provided a terrifying reminder of the destructiveness of modern weaponry, and thus the desirability of Appeasement. Most importantly, it showed Hitler and Mussolini that aggression could succeed and brought them closer together.

A sign of their improved relations was that Hitler felt able to renew pressure on Austria. In March 1938 the Austrian Chancellor, Kurt von Schuschnigg – who had done nothing to win British and French support – tried to outwit Hitler by calling a referendum on the country's independence, but before it was held the German army invaded. Once again, Hitler had broken the terms of Versailles while the other powers looked on. Mussolini made no complaint about this strengthening of German power in Central Europe, which marked Hitler's first challenge to the territorial order in Europe. Chamberlain, appalled by the use of force, issued a protest but still believed Hitler's ambitions were limited to the absorption of German-populated areas. It was well-known that the Sudetenland in Czechoslovakia was likely to be the next target and ministers quickly decided *not* to give assurances of support to France if she fulfilled her treaty obligations to Czechoslovakia. French commitments in Eastern Europe were viewed as embarrassing and there was a deep aversion to being pulled into war, 1914-style, in the wake of them. The COS reported that the Germans could easily overrun Czechoslovakia and that a war to liberate it would be lengthy, perhaps allowing Italy and

Japan to menace British interests. Britain's relations with Czechoslovakia were not close and it was believed that the Czechs *did* oppress their German subjects. The local German leader, Konrad Henlein, began to campaign for an autonomous Sudetenland and during the 'May Crisis' which followed there were even rumours that Hitler would attack Czechoslovakia. Over summer, the British encouraged Henlein and the Czechoslovakian leader Edvard Benes to find a peaceful solution to their differences, without success. In public France declared its intention to defend Czechoslovakia and Chamberlain decided to send Lord Runciman, an expert in labour disputes, to find a settlement. His mission, which recommended the separation of the Sudetenland from Czechoslovakia, was drawing to a close when the decisive crisis broke: on 12 September several days of rioting began in the Sudetenland after an inflammatory speech by Hitler; and on the 14th the Cabinet agreed Chamberlain should meet Hitler at Berchtesgarden in a dramatic attempt to resolve matters. The shift from a passive British policy to a highly active role reflected the danger that Czechoslovakia *could* have led to war. But the Prime Minister's aim was still to work for peace, offering Germany limited concessions, whilst restraining bellicose elements elsewhere. At Berchtesgarden, Chamberlain offered self-determination of the Sudetenland and over the following week joint pressure from Britain and France forced a reluctant Benes to accept this. The French, it transpired, had no intention of defending Czechoslovakia, though they preferred to see Britain take the lead in humiliating Prague. Whether the Soviets would have fought for Czechoslovakia if others did, was not clear. It was at this point, with a settlement in sight, that Hitler demonstrated his preference for violence. When Chamberlain returned to see him, at Godesberg on 22–23 September, the Nazi dictator declared self-determination was no longer enough: the German army must occupy the Sudetenland immediately. Halifax was stunned and Britain, like Czechoslovakia and France, prepared for war. Chamberlain, however, argued that the Godesberg demands were not much more than those offered at Berchtesgarden and, over the radio, spoke of Czechoslovakia as 'a far-away country of which we know nothing'. Little attention was paid to the value of Czechoslovakia as an ally (with a large arms industry and an army of 34 divisions). Significantly, Hitler too, when threatened by a war his people did not want, was willing to talk and Mussolini was ready to act as mediator, helping bring about the Munich Conference on 29–30 September. There Chamberlain, Hitler, Mussolini and France's Edouard Daladier (without consulting the Czechs) effectively agreed to the Godesberg demands, except that the Sudetenland was detached peacefully without a German invasion. The four powers guaranteed the territory remaining to Czechoslovakia. Chamberlain also extracted the famous note in which the German leader stated his readiness to solve future problems by consultation. The note, ridiculed as it later was, had a clear purpose: 'If Hitler ... kept the bargain, well and good; alternatively, if he broke it, he would demonstrate to all the world that he was totally untrustworthy.'[6] Britain, in the event of war, could more easily claim to be morally right. Even Hitler acknowledged he had retreated at Munich. But this made him determined to prepare the German people for war, to avenge himself on the Czechs and, despite Chamberlain's note, to avoid any future consultations about German expansion. In Britain, the Munich agreement was initially greeted with relief and Chamberlain had a rapturous reception. Yet almost immediately doubts and a feeling of guilt began to grow among politicians, the military and the public. A small country had been browbeaten into concessions, and Hitler had again extended his borders using the threat of force.

Although the Munich agreement easily passed the House of Commons, 22 Conservatives joined Labour in voting against it. Left-wing and liberal newspapers like the *Daily Herald* and *Manchester Guardian* were also critical. Moral revulsion over Munich was fuelled in November by *Kristallnacht*, the night of terror against Germany's Jewish community. Thereafter, intelligence reports suggested that German armed forces were being actively prepared for war, even perhaps for a strike westwards, against the Netherlands, rather than to the East. Vansittant's interpretation of Hitler as a violent expansionist was more widely accepted in Whitehall, undermining Downing Street's belief that moderation might yet triumph in Berlin, and Chamberlain's hopes of dividing Mussolini from Hitler also seemed less realistic. Instead the Italian pressed claims for French territory which made Paris even more anxious for some assurance of British support in war. The British had no wish to encourage France to think of war, but neither could they afford to see it, in fear, seek a bilateral deal with Hitler or Mussolini. Chamberlain therefore gave way, and on 8 February told the Commons that Britain would protect French interests wherever they were attacked. The next month new army estimates prepared seriously for a British Expeditionary Force of four divisions. The Prime Minister's policy by then was poorly articulated. Even if one believes that, down to Munich, Chamberlain's Appeasement was a defensible policy, by early 1939 he seemed to lag behind elements in his own government, and public opinion, when he failed to take a more vigorous stance. If he had pursued it with determination 'a close Franco-British alliance ... might have dealt firmly with Mussolini's pretensions, and ... acted as a nucleus around which those states with reason to fear the Third Reich could assemble'.[7] But staff talks with France only began in May. Then again, erratic and uncertain behaviour was not limited to Chamberlain. On 20 February the COS produced a strategic appreciation which was more accurate than past reports about German military and economic failings but had little to say on Eastern Europe and remained pessimistic about fighting a German-Italian-Japanese combination. Yet confidence about defeating Italy alone led some defence planners to advocate a quick war against Mussolini which would deny Hitler an ally and, once won, would free the Royal Navy to concentrate in Far Eastern waters against Japan. Before long, however, the CID concluded it was better to hope for Italian neutrality rather than risk a war which would absorb scarce resources and perhaps spark a general conflict.

Whatever the confusion, by March 1939 many in government were prepared to resist German expansion on the continent. But London was again caught unprepared by Hitler's occupation of the rump of Czechoslovakia that month. It was a vital psychological moment. Nazi extremism was confirmed, the Munich agreement had been flagrantly breached and it was clear that Hitler's ambition stretched beyond ethnic German territories. On 15 March Chamberlain tried to minimise the importance of events but more Conservative MPs began to question Appeasement and leading right-wing newspapers, such as the *Daily Telegraph* and *Daily Express*, also expressed dissatisfaction. The prime ministerial tone changed at Birmingham on the 17th, declaring that Hitler was bent on global conquest and that war might be necessary. Five days later Hitler forced Lithuania to surrender German-populated Memelland, and the FO became concerned that Poland was the most likely next target of Nazi ambition. Hitler demanded the return of Danzig at this time but the Poles were ready, unlike the Czechs, to fight. As fear and moral indignation combined, Alexander Cadogan, who had succeeded Vansittant as Permanent Under-Secretary, wished to build 'a dam in the East ... as a deterrent to avert war'; even if this scheme failed, it was 'the right thing to do'.[8] For several days, the government even toyed with the idea of working with the Soviets, before Britain and France decided to provide a guarantee of Polish independence on 31 March. The guarantee did not rule out changes in Polish *borders* and the British still recognised the 'Polish Corridor' as an unjust element of the Versailles treaty. But the need to deter further German advances meant a stand had to be made somewhere, and there was no doubt about the significance of the guarantee. It marked a revolution in British diplomacy, ending the policy of 'limited liability' in Eastern Europe for good and increasing the risk of war by antagonising Hitler. The guarantee, however unrealistic in military terms, gave reassurance to the Poles, making it less likely they would negotiate a settlement of the Danzig problem for which Chamberlain still hoped. Arguably Britain had compromised its diplomatic independence and in defence of a poor case. Appeasement could hardly flourish when policy became based openly on a strategy of deterrence and there was even hope, especially in Paris, of binding together Poland, Romania, Greece and Turkey into a strong military group on Germany's eastern border. Anglo-French guarantees were given to Greece and oil-rich Romania on 13 April and over the summer the French would have liked to plan the despatch of Anglo-French forces to the Balkans. But the British were never enthusiastic about this and a viable eastern front never actually emerged: Poland was recognised by Western military experts to be virtually indefensible and Britain lacked economic and military resources to send there; Eastern European states bickered among themselves and were unwilling to guarantee each others' borders; and German diplomacy was able to prevent most of them from allying with the Western powers. Nor did Britain's sudden readiness to defend France, her alliance with Poland or the reintroduction of conscription on 23 April have any impact on Hitler. Instead, British preparation for a land war in Europe probably – as Chamberlain feared – made him more anxious to provoke war.

The Polish guarantee impeded links to a more formidable, potential ally in Eastern Europe, the Soviet Union – an ally which might also have been useful against Japan. An alliance with the Soviets would have been difficult to negotiate anyway, given British and French distaste for Communism and the belief that the Red Army would be little use in war (especially after its officer corps was decimated by Stalin's Purges of 1937). The British had rejected repeated attempts by the Soviet Foreign Minister, Maxim Litvinov, to forge a closer relationship and in April Stalin replaced him with the more anti-Western Vyacheslav Molotov. However, retrospective Soviet claims that Chamberlain was trying to bring about a Russo-German war (to exhaust these two powers whilst keeping Britain at peace) have no foundation and in May the Prime Minister grudgingly accepted that conversations with the Soviets must begin. There was some hope that the very act of talking to Russia might deter Hitler and at first the British hoped they could avoid real commitments to the Soviets, inducing the latter simply to guarantee Poland and Romania. But it was soon clear that a mutual security pact was the only way forward and on 12 August negotiations on this began in Moscow. Then, however, the whole idea of a Soviet link ran up against Polish and Romanian suspicion. Neither wished to see the Red Army march across their territory. Yet, since Germany and Russia lacked a common border, Soviet forces insisted they must be able to cross into neighbouring countries to come to grips with the Germans. When the British and French were unable to persuade Poland and Romania to accept this, the Soviets turned to an alternative policy: on 23 August Molotov signed a pact with the Germans. Few believed that a cynical marriage between

Communism and Fascism could last but the agreement made sense to both signatories: whilst Stalin was able to secure both short-term peace and territorial gains, Hitler was able to avoid a two-front war. Chamberlain of course had feared an Anglo-Russian alliance would bring war: instead a German-Russian alliance heralded conflict. British intelligence knew Hitler was already preparing to invade Poland. Even Neville Henderson made it clear at this point that Britain would fight, but, given past experience, and despite a formal Anglo-Polish alliance on 25 August, it is not surprising that Hitler expected Chamberlain to back down. In late August the British supported the idea of renewed German-Polish talks on Danzig and the Corridor, Mussolini was ready as late as 31 August to organise another Munich-style conference, and the French were even less enthusiastic than Britain to fight. Nonetheless on 1 September Hitler proceeded with the invasion of Poland. The following day Chamberlain tried to avoid an ultimatum to Germany, but Cabinet opinion moved against him, MPs were aghast and there was even talk of his being replaced. War was finally declared at 11.00 a.m. on the 3rd. The French, who always knew they would bear the brunt of any land war, followed suit several hours later.

Policy-making in the Second World War

The attempt to contain German expansion had utterly failed, and the commitments given to Poland had carried Britain into war. In trying to avoid the bloc politics, naval race and bellicosity of pre-1914 Britain found itself in a worse position when conflict came. Poland was doomed, France was the only significant ally and the Treasury did not believe Britain could afford to fight for long. Italy was too weak to consider war immediately but gave economic assistance to Germany, undermining the Royal Navy's blockade policy. A greater breach in the blockade was caused by the USSR, which provided vast amounts of materials to the Third Reich. The Soviets also seized half of Poland, before launching the 'Winter War' against Finland, and Britain and France even considered going to war with Russia. British people entered the struggle with a sense of resignation but also a conviction that their government had done everything to avoid violence, a point which instilled a readiness to fight despite memories of the 1914 conflict. The experience of the Great War meant the population was better prepared for the higher taxes, central direction of industry and conscription which war demanded. Chamberlain's Cabinet had at least made practical preparations for war, albeit grudgingly and with some serious flaws. Conscription in April had boosted French morale, but was mainly intended to help cope with pressures of home defence. A Ministry of Supply had been created in

May 1939 to deal with defence orders from industry, but there remained a strong aversion among Conservatives to state intervention in the economy or cooperation with trades unions. Preparation of the BEF meant 150 000 troops were in France by the end of September, but the French were disappointed that by spring 1940 there were only ten British divisions in place, less than one-tenth the size of the French Army. As in 1914 Britain hoped to rely on the French early in the conflict and slowly build up their own contribution; but there was no wish to repeat the carnage of the western front. Chamberlain hoped peace would be secured by a defensive strategy, holding any initial German assault before relying on economic blockade and an appeal to 'moderate' opinion in Germany. There was an obvious continuation of elements of Appeasement here: the Prime Minister pursued a low-risk policy, designed to husband British resources whilst hoping, somehow, that all-out war could be avoided. The idea was not so much to defeat Hitler as convince him he could not win. Chamberlain almost wished to insist on 'business as usual' as Asquith had in 1914 and, although a War Cabinet was set up, a coalition government was avoided. Over winter a situation known as 'phoney war' prevailed: neither side launched campaigns and the RAF dropped millions of propaganda leaflets, rather than bombs, on Germany. The intelligence and propaganda services also avoided 'offensive' activities and it was only in March 1940 that the Ministry of Economic Warfare (set up to direct the blockade) began to seize German coal exports at sea. In Britain a sizeable peace lobby still existed, of pacifists, churchmen and certain politicians, businessmen and aristocrats (the last three groups fearful of the social and economic upheaval war might provoke). Yet, despite German peace-feelers, Chamberlain's readiness to establish links to German anti-Nazis and attempts at mediation by Roosevelt and other neutrals, there was no sign of a settlement.

It was to enforce the blockade that in March 1940 the British and French conceived an operation to prevent the supply of Swedish iron ore via the Norwegian port of Narvik to Germany. But as so often before, Hitler took his enemies by surprise, invading Norway and Denmark in early April. Churchill had been recalled to office as First Lord of the Admiralty in September but failed to exploit British naval supremacy to keep the Germans out of Norwegian harbours. Troops were landed at certain points but, to public disappointment, quickly withdrawn. The result was not Churchill's demotion, however, but his succession to the premiership. For, when the Commons debated the Norwegian campaign on 7–8 May 100 Conservative MPs refused to support the government. Chamberlain could not survive and Churchill's only rival for Downing Street was Halifax, who failed to fight hard for the position. Labour leaders were ready to serve under the new Prime Minister, thereby creating an image of national unity, but there was potential tension between Labour and Conservative ministers. Chamberlain remained leader of the Conservative Party until his death in November, and Halifax was a potential rival until Churchill sent him to Washington as Ambassador in December, replacing him at the FO with Eden. Churchill's succession might easily have divided the Conservatives, for he represented the adventurist, patriotic wing of the party very different to the pro-peace, low-spending, anti-interventionist elements who had held sway under his predecessor. Churchill had many faults: frequently eccentric, self-obsessed and inconsistent, he constantly interfered in issues of military strategy and diplomacy, and made many errors of judgement. Yet he had formidable experience, was brave and energetic, injected dynamism into government and proved an inspiring leader. His warning to the country on 10 May to expect 'blood, toil, tears and sweat' proved prescient. For that same day Hitler launched his *blitzkrieg* against the West, coordinating paratroops, dive-bombers, armoured divisions and mechanised infantry in a way few Anglo-French experts had believed possible. Striking north of French fortifications on the 'Maginot line', the Germans cut off British and French armies which had advanced into Belgium. The seaborne rescue of 300 000, mainly British troops, from the beaches of Dunkirk was a morale booster but the surrender of France on 22 June was a stunning blow. So desperate was Churchill to keep the French fighting that he offered a political union to Paris with a single parliament and Cabinet. But French leaders saw this as an attempt to take over their colonial empire and did not think Britain could escape defeat. Several thousand French troops decided to fight on under General Charles de Gaulle, but in France itself a collaborationist regime was established at Vichy.

In the wake of France's fall, some in London did favour peace. For decades Britain had relied on France to supply a land army in Europe; now there seemed no way to liberate the continent. Furthermore, Italy entered the war on 10 June, sharing in the defeat of France and threatening Britain in the Mediterranean and Near East. As in the Great War, the Royal Navy hunted down German surface ships but found it difficult to deal with U-boats. The Admiralty had believed that convoys (as used in 1917–18) and a new invention, sonar (for locating submarines), would defeat the U-boats, but instead during 1940–41 the Germans sank an average of 250 000 tons of allied shipping per month and the Battle of the Atlantic was only finally won, with American help, in 1943. The fall of France also opened up dangers further afield, allowing Japanese forces to occupy French Indochina. Yet the navy was too stretched in the Atlantic and Mediterranean to send a large fleet to the Pacific. To win the war Britain clearly needed allies, but the Soviets were aligned with Germany and America was still isolationist. Indeed, Roosevelt doubted Britain could survive. Even if America and Russia entered the war, they were likely to pursue their own interests and outmatch British power. For the country had already lost one-third of its export trade and foreign debts had tripled. The leading advocate of exploring peace terms in mid-1940 was Halifax, backed by Chamberlain. It is certainly true that in continuing the war Britain was being 'more heroic than many of her people appreciated at the time'.[9] But Churchill advocated negotiations only from a position of strength and, whilst not ruling out talks in future, argued that Britain was unlikely to receive generous terms at present. He was committed to maintaining the Empire and believed that America and Russia *would* eventually join the conflict. Public support for continuing the struggle was reflected in the collapse of the Peace Pledge Union. Indeed, under Churchill, popular unity in the face of war, though marred after 1942 by strikes and by-election votes for the Common Wealth Party (a new grouping, outside the government coalition), was better than in 1914–18. There are still those who believe Britain should have sought peace in order to preserve her power, and that by 1945 'it was hard to argue that Britain had won in any sense save that of avoiding defeat'.[10] Yet peace at this point would have drained British confidence and marked a terrifying increase in German power. If Germany had then attacked the USSR, the result would have been the domination of Europe by one of these states on 'Napoleonic' lines and meanwhile British power would have been sapped by rising nationalism in the Empire. It is perverse to argue that Britain should both have sought a preservation of national strength whilst fleeing before the moral challenge of Nazism. In any case Britain was not quite 'alone'. Except for Ireland, all the Dominions had entered the conflict (though, in Canada's case, only after a parliamentary debate) and Britain had the psychological reassurance that most countries conquered by Germany remained nominally at war, with governments-in-exile in London.

The RAF proved that the British had the capacity to *survive*, when it prevented the Germans seizing control of the air as a preliminary to invasion. One major feature of the 1937 Inskip Report had been a decision to build fighter aircraft in preference to bombers. This marked a shift from the emphasis on a deterrent bomber force, popular in the mid-1930s, but made sense in a number of ways. Small, short-range fighters cost a quarter the average price of a four-engined bomber, so the Treasury was happy. The growth of the German air force to one-and-a-half times the size of the RAF meant that, in order to survive the much feared 'knock-out blow' against the vulnerable British capital, more fighters must be built. At the same time other air defences – searchlights, anti-aircraft guns and a new discovery, radar – were developed. The decisions paid off in July–September 1940 when the technically superior *Spitfires* and *Hurricanes* were able to outmatch enemy aircraft. Some 45 000 civilians were killed in the 'Blitz' on London and, for a time, there was considerable disaffection among the population. This, however, was disguised in British propaganda which assured American audiences that 'Britain can take it.' September also saw successes for British arms in Libya against the Italians. Italy, as predicted, had serious military weaknesses, failed in an attack on Greece and provided Britain with further victories in East Africa, where Abyssinia was liberated in April 1941. Another British success was the conquest of Vichy-controlled Syria–Lebanon in June 1941, after the Germans threatened to use it as a base to help an anti-British revolt which had recently broken out in Iraq. During these campaigns the Middle East (and Egypt especially) assumed a key importance in the mind of Churchill and other Britons which would linger after the war. Its loss would have been a decisive blow. Fortunately Hitler did not even recognise the opportunity to strike at the Middle East in 1941. The few divisions of Irwin Rommel's *Afrika Korps*, which were sent to North Africa, caused grave difficulties and German military superiority was proven again in March–May when they overran Yugoslavia, then bundled the British out of Greece and Crete. However, these campaigns proved the precursors not to more attacks on the British but the invasion of Russia on 22 June.

With Churchill in power a much greater sense of vigour was instilled in government. Given the life-or-death battle in which the country was engaged, the defensive-minded attitudes of the phoney war had to be replaced. As well as forming a coalition, Churchill himself took the title Minister of Defence and replaced the CID with a Defence Committee of key ministers and the COS. There was a continued reliance on blockade as a way to weaken Germany but to this was added a large-scale bombing campaign. Some RAF figures believed this might prove a decisive weapon, but accurate bombing of German industry proved difficult and German morale was as resilient as Britain's under air attack. An early innovation of Churchill's, in July 1940, was the Special Operations Executive (SOE), which combined MI6 and War Office experts in 'unconventional' warfare. The aim was to use terrorist-style tactics to spread discontent and disrupt the German hold on occupied Europe. Labour's Hugh Dalton, who as Minister for Economic Warfare had general charge of SOE, was told to 'set Europe ablaze' by Churchill.[11] With links to continental resistance movements SOE encouraged sabotage, black propaganda, assassination and (in Yugoslavia after 1941) full-scale guerrilla warfare. However, there were serious clashes of responsibility between SOE and other agencies such as the Ministry of Information (MOI) and MI6. The MOI found a strong-minded, successful head in Brendan Bracken in 1941 and partly because of this the SOE lost its propaganda work to a new body, the Political Warfare Executive (PWE). Using all kinds of propaganda, the PWE was intended to demoralise and confuse the enemy by, for example, spreading rumours, discrediting Nazism and encouraging potential opponents of Hitler, such as religious groups. It also had a role in military operations and developed 'psychological warfare' techniques which have been important – if highly secret – in diplomacy and warfare ever since. MI6 lost influence to SOE in Europe, but maintained its own agents abroad and had important links to intelligence agencies in other governments. These included the American Office of Strategic Services, created in 1942, which was heavily influenced by British practice, leading to a close 'intelligence alliance' after the war. The counter-intelligence service, MI5, was blamed in 1940 for a 'failure' to expose German spies in Britain and in the months of panic after May, when invasion was feared, 25 000 enemy aliens were interned. But, as in the First World War, most internees were innocent: German spies found it virtually impossible to operate in Britain and those that did were quickly discovered, many being 'turned' by MI5 and used to send inaccurate reports to Germany. Another vital 'covert' agency was GC&CS (renamed Government Communication Headquarters in 1942) which, helped by a pre-war breakthrough by Polish intelligence, began to crack Germany's 'enigma' code systems. The success of this operation, known as 'Ultra', is now understood to have had a major effect on the war. Victory in North Africa, the defeat of the U-boats and the eventual Anglo-American invasion of Europe all depended in part on Ultra.

The amateurishness of the early months of war – when two MI6 agents had naively walked into a German trap on the Dutch border – was thus replaced by a sophisticated professionalism and under Churchill, himself a great enthusiast for intelligence work, a real 'intelligence community' came into being in Whitehall. There were moves to improve the professionalism of the FO too. It was not blamed for war in the way it had been in 1914, but it was still criticised as an exclusive, elitist 'club', not least by Labour politicians. Reforms announced in June 1941 merged the Consular and Commercial Services (hitherto seen as second-class groups) with the Foreign and Diplomatic Service, created a proper personnel department and gave better training to diplomats in the fields of economic and commercial work. Yet, as in 1919, the reforms did not achieve all they intended. Few high-level FO staff had commercial experience, renewed attempts to broaden the field of entry beyond 'Oxbridge' had a limited effect and few women were employed. Churchill, like Lloyd George, took a caustic view of diplomats as long-winded time-wasters and, to the annoyance of Eden, frequently interfered in diplomacy. But Downing Street did not pursue a policy independent of the FO on the scale of 1916–18 and relations between

Churchill and Eden were close enough for the former to designate the latter as his successor.

The 'Big Three'

When strong allies emerged to fight alongside Britain the country was already bankrupt but the idea of a negotiated peace had become impossible. It was the Americans who, by providing goods (effectively) free of charge under the March 1941 'Lend-Lease' programme, kept Britain in the war. The drain on resources had actually begun *before* war broke out. The increased pace of rearmament and pressures on the Pound as war approached meant Britain entered the war with only £700 million in reserves, and in contrast to the Great War (and earlier conflicts) Britain could no longer act as paymaster to a coalition. This was a major indication of the country's relative decline. The Treasury initially forecast that reserves would dry up after three years, but this was on the basis that France would carry the burden of land campaigning. In fact, with France defeated, reserves hit dangerously low levels in December 1940. Yet Britain had to continue importing food and raw materials, it mobilised 6 million personnel and had to produce a vast quantity of armaments. There was considerable help from the Dominions and Empire, however, who provided 5 million military personnel, half of them from India. At first it was impossible to predict whether US assistance would be given, but it was in American interests that the British should hold back the expansionist, totalitarian German regime, and 'Lend-Lease' was the culmination of a belief that Washington should become the 'arsenal of democracy', aiding Britain by all means short of war. What Churchill called a 'most unsordid act' did not end the strain on British resources, however. Congress insisted that Britain should still contribute all available resources to the war, which meant that its reserves and export trade must be kept low. Even more than the First World War, the Second saw tight government control of the economy, strict rationing and high taxes which helped generate popular demands for extensive social reform programmes afterwards. Factories and houses were bombed, the merchant fleet was decimated and the national debt grew to about £3500 million making Britain the world's largest debtor. Exports eventually shrank by about two-thirds producing a trade deficit in 1945 of £1000 million, and it has been concluded that 'Britain had probably lost about one quarter ... of its pre-war wealth' thanks to the war.[12] Some £1300 million was owed to India because of a 1935 agreement that Britain would cover the increased costs of the Indian Army in wartime. The situation was much worse than 1919, therefore, and left Britain very much the third partner among the victorious Grand Alliance.

America was brought into the struggle by events in the Pacific, where tension had been rising since 1937, when Japan attacked China. Roosevelt ideally wanted to work with Britain against Japanese expansionism in the 1930s but Congress prevented him going far. Neither could the British expect much help, in peacetime at least, from the Empire: the 1937 Imperial Conference avoided any commitment to joint defence arrangements. Britain had extensive commercial, investment and (in Hong Kong and Malaya) territorial interests in the Far East but could spare few resources to defend them. The Singapore base, seen as the key to Far Eastern defence strategy, had repeatedly been subject to spending cuts. London was well aware of its predicament, but could see no solution. The weakness of the Royal Navy in the area made it impossible to deter Japan, and although Britain ideally wished to preserve Chinese independence, a forthright policy on these lines might antagonise Tokyo, driving it into alliance with Berlin. Yet a policy of appeasing Japan risked alienating America, whose support in any future war could prove decisive. In June 1939 London *was* forced into appeasement when the Japanese blockaded the British concession of Tientsin: in an agreement the following month London said it would not interfere in Japanese-dominated areas of China. However, attempts to win over US opinion were also intensified with a transatlantic visit by George VI. There was always a danger that war in Europe would encourage the Japanese armed forces to run risks in the Far East and in August 1940 the Japanese army began to occupy French Indochina, from where it could launch an amphibious landing in Malaya. Yet Churchill preferred to concentrate British resources on defending Egypt, refused to give Australia a promise of naval reinforcements and effectively relied on the US to protect Imperial interests in the Pacific. In July 1941 the Japanese seized full control of Indochina and the Americans, British and Dutch governments (the last in control of the East Indies) froze Japanese assets. The Americans still refused to give a firm promise to support British possessions, however, just as Britain refused to give guarantees to the Dutch. In the end a US oil embargo forced the Japanese to choose between retreat and war. Having decided on war they launched their first, surprise assault on 7 December against the only force which could effectively oppose them, the American fleet at Pearl Harbor in Hawaii.

In the 1930s British leaders had been terrified by the prospect of simultaneous conflict against Germany, Italy and Japan, yet paradoxically when this situation came about it was welcomed because it brought America into the war, promising eventual victory even if the short term saw further retreats. Hitler, whose armies were already at the gates of Moscow, felt confident enough to declare war on America on 11 December. The previous day Britain's vulnerability in the Far East was underlined when Japanese aircraft sank the newly arrived battleships *Prince of Wales* and *Repulse*. Hong Kong, indefensible, fell after a brave defence on Christmas Day and worse was to follow. On 15 February 1942 Singapore, with 130 000 troops, fell to the Japanese Army, whose abilities the COS had vastly underestimated. Churchill acknowledged it as the worst ever humiliation for British arms. Such a decisive setback for a European army at Asian hands could only destroy respect for colonial rule in future. Soon, after advancing through Burma, the Japanese were at the gates of India. They also, for a time, threatened an invasion of Australia, which increasingly looked to America as a protector. Meanwhile, in North Africa, the fall of Tobruk in June 1942 completed a catalogue of disasters and led to questioning of Churchill's leadership. Already, however, the tide was beginning to turn: the US Navy defeated the Japanese in the Battles of the Coral Sea and Midway; General Bernard Montgomery decisively beat Rommel at El Alamein in November, just as an Anglo-American force successfully landed in North-west Africa; and in January 1943, most remarkable of all, the Russians forced a whole German Army to surrender at Stalingrad. British influence over the course of the war was now being eclipsed. It was the Russians who continued to fight the bulk of the *Wehrmacht*, accounting for 90 per cent of German troop losses in the war. In the West Churchill and his generals still preferred to pursue a 'peripheral', low-risk strategy designed, alongside the bombing campaign, to wear down the Nazis. As with Gallipoli in 1915, Churchill also believed an attack on the 'soft underbelly' of Europe might defeat Germany at a lower cost than a frontal assault in Western Europe which the Americans preferred. Such a strategy also served to safeguard Britain's Imperial position in the Mediterranean, and it had some success: North Africa was liberated in May 1943, Italy was invaded in September, Mussolini was overthrown and the new Italian government joined the allies as a 'co-belligerent'. But the slow advance up the Italian peninsula underlined the fact that this was not a proper 'second front', and, with Churchill increasingly tired and ill the US began to dictate military policy. In November 1943, when Churchill, Roosevelt and Stalin held their first 'Big Three' conference in Tehran, it was confirmed that Anglo-American forces would invade France. They landed in Normandy in June and their successful advance, bringing Victory in Europe in 11 months, suggested an earlier successful invasion might have been possible. As British attentions focused on Europe, the remarkable success of William Slim's 'Forgotten Army' in liberating Burma was hardly noticed and it was the Americans who took the credit for defeating Japan in August 1945 with atomic bombs.

The Anglo-American operations in North Africa, Italy and France showed a remarkable level of cooperation between two sovereign and, at the outset, equal states. A Combined COS was created to direct the war; their intelligence services formed a close bond; joint strategic planning began even before December 1941; and the US sent much of its air force and half a million troops to Britain. Churchill visited the US on several occasions and put great emphasis on his 'special relationship' with the White House. Like the Atlanticists of the First World War, he had a rather romantic and racially motivated view of 'Anglo-Saxon' brotherhood and hoped American resources could be used to underpin the Empire. In August 1941 he joined with Roosevelt to issue the 'Atlantic Charter', a statement of war aims which included the disarmament of aggressors, freer trade and a new global security system. The last, vague promise eventually led to an improved version of the League, known as the United Nations. Yet, however close the Anglo-Americans were in values, aims and military organisation, there were many differences between them and both pursued their own ambitions. Thus in August 1940 Roosevelt only gave Britain 50 ageing destroyers in return for the lease of various naval bases. It has already been seen how Washington kept British trade and reserves at a low level, even as the US expanded its own commercial, shipping and investment activities. The Americans persisted in overestimating British power and failed to grasp what problems British decline might cause after the war. Commercial rivalry was also seen in the American attempts, which Churchill resisted, to dismantle the Imperial trade preferences system, despite the low level of tariff barriers involved. The Secretary of State, Cordell Hull, was a keen advocate of 'multilateralism', the drive for a system of freer, expanding world trade. This would not only provide openings for American exports but would avoid a return to the economic depression and extreme nationalism of the 1930s. Actually, whilst safeguarding Imperial preferences, Britain was ready to take part in such a system, which suited the old Victorian ideal of a *laissez-faire* global economy. The two countries both had an interest in reaching agreement: the Treasury knew it might need US financial assistance to continue after the war and, for the sake of world trade recovery, wanted the US to use its wealth to improve international liquidity; Americans recognised that London was enormously important as a financial and trading centre, even if it was the Dollar which became the linchpin of the Bretton Woods trading system established in 1944. There was a similar story of competition and eventual compromise in the colonial sphere. The US disliked formal Imperialism, criticised British rule in India and developed ideas for liquidating the French Empire. In the Far East in particular there were grave differences. American power there was overwhelming, Britain's contribution to the defeat of Japan was little valued in America, and Roosevelt tried to build up China's Chiang Kai-Shek as the post-war 'policeman' in the region. The British not only had to give up extra-territorial rights in China, but also found themselves effectively excluded from the occupation of Japan in 1945. Yet, once again, the British were not powerless. They proved determined in resisting Roosevelt's inconsistent anti-colonialism. They argued that theirs was a non-oppressive form of Imperialism, vital to world stability, and that progress to self-rule would take time. In 1945 the British Empire was fully restored, as were those of France and Holland. Ultimately the US threat to the Empire was most important in the realm of ideas, encouraging nationalists to believe that independence was inevitable. There were other differences in British and American attitudes. Churchill's attempts to build an alliance around his personal relationship with Roosevelt could not disguise the failure of each country to comprehend the other. To Americans, the British could seem unadventurous, class-ridden and self-obsessed; to the British, Americans seemed brash, uncultured and inexperienced in world affairs. Eden in particular was concerned about Churchill's growing reliance on Washington. US merchant ships and destroyers were essential to keep Britain fed during the Battle of the Atlantic and by 1944 the US was spending four times as much as Britain on arms, yet at the end of the war Britain had no firm promise of US support in future, the Americans kept the atomic bomb to themselves (even though Britain had contributed to its development) and Lend-Lease was abruptly terminated. Then again, whatever their differences, Britain was far closer in sympathy and outlook to America than it was to the other member of the Big Three, the USSR.

When the Soviets entered the war in June 1941 there was of course no love lost between them and the British. Throughout the inter-war years, relations had been poor, and since September 1939 the Russians had both seized territory in Eastern Europe and provided Germany with vast amounts of materials. Eden and many Conservatives were reluctant to give help to Stalin, but Churchill, who had predicted a Soviet-German struggle all along, saw it as vital to keep the USSR in the war. In August, there was a joint Anglo-Soviet operation to occupy Iran. This shut out German influence, opened a route for Western supplies to Russia and, like the 1907 convention, showed the two countries could agree on zones of influence in Central Asia. The Americans too saw the logic of assisting the Russians, extending Lend-Lease to them in November. There were massive retreats by the Red Army in 1941–42, but the important thing was that Russia survived, absorbing the bulk of the German Army and eventually turning the course of the conflict in 1943. Churchill and Roosevelt hoped that a policy of friendship and assistance would guarantee cooperation with Russia into peacetime. Churchill, who again placed emphasis on personal diplomacy, was fascinated by Stalin's powerful if crude character and confident that ideological differences could be toned down. The myth of 'Uncle Joe' Stalin was fostered in British propaganda and there were demands from the public and Press for the early opening of a 'second front' in Western Europe to ease the burden on the Red Army. But the Soviets – secretive, arrogant, suspicious – were never easy to deal with; their government system remained fully totalitarian; and although the Comintern was nominally disbanded in 1943, in effect Moscow continued to foster the spread of Communism world-wide. Apart from ideological differences, Soviet suspicions were aroused by the delays in the Second Front until 1944: this was seen as a deliberate Western policy designed to weaken the USSR. Secret Soviet contacts carried on with Germany and from the start Stalin made it clear to London and Washington that he wished to retain those territorial gains made from working with Hitler in 1939–40. As early as October 1943, in a remarkable parallel to arguments used in the First World War, Churchill told the Cabinet that Germany might have to be built up after the war as a barrier to Soviet expansionism.

The Prime Minister himself was increasingly fitful and uncertain about Soviet intentions. He has alternatively been criticised either for antagonising Moscow, particularly through delays to the Second Front, or for 'appeasing' it, especially when he encouraged the Poles to make territorial concessions to Russia. In October 1944, as the Red Army began to 'liberate' Eastern Europe, Churchill met Stalin in Moscow and agreed to the extraordinary 'percentage deal' on spheres of influence in the Balkans, whereby Britain would have predominance in Greece (vital to Britain's position in the Mediterranean), whilst the Soviets could dominate Romania and Bulgaria. By then Churchill was playing a weak hand and trying to make up with diplomacy what he lacked in military strength. By pursuing a 'peripheral strategy' until 1944 he had helped create a position where the Red Army's domination of Eastern Europe was impossible to prevent. The COS recognised the USSR in 1944 as the greatest potential menace to Britain after the war, but the FO had to deal with current realities and still hoped to cooperate with Stalin. A forthright policy of opposition to him would have been difficult to sell to the public, would not have saved Eastern Europe but would have divided the Grand Alliance even before Germany was defeated. Besides, Roosevelt was also determined to court Stalin and at Tehran tried to outbid Churchill for the dictator's friendship, posing almost as a mediator in Anglo-Soviet quarrels. Ever-weakening, Britain could hardly antagonise Moscow without any promise of American sympathy. But during the second Big Three conference, at Yalta in February 1945, Roosevelt told Stalin that US forces would leave Europe once the war ended, which could only encourage the Russian's expansionist ambitions. Yalta later became a byword for the betrayal of Eastern Europe to Communism: there was no overt deal on 'spheres of influence' but Polish territory was conceded to the Soviet Union and the Polish Communists, with little local support, became the nucleus of a new Polish government. There was still a great deal of confusion about Stalin's precise aims. He was brutal, clearly wished to expand and was determined to secure 'friendly' governments in the East. Yet he was also opportunistic in his method and his policy could still be interpreted as designed primarily to create a defensive barrier in Eastern Europe against German revival. In the months following, Churchill's fear of the Soviets nonetheless intensified and in April, when Roosevelt died, the Prime Minister tried to persuade the new President, Harry Truman, to adopt a tougher line. In particular Churchill suggested retaining areas in Germany which had been designated for Soviet occupation but liberated by the Americans. Truman refused and during the last Big Three conference, at Potsdam in July, Churchill again seemed friendly with the Soviet leader. By then Poland, for which Britain had gone to war, was under Russian control. The safest conclusion to draw about Churchill's policy is that he 'was neither a wanton antagonist of the Soviet Union, nor did he mindlessly appease them',[13] and he left the door open to post-war cooperation. But, contrary to popular belief, he was not much more perceptive about Stalin's intentions than was Roosevelt. At Potsdam the Prime Minister was exhausted, confused by Stalin's policies and leading a much-weakened country. It was perhaps fortuitous that at that moment the British electorate voted him out of office.

Notes

1 Post G., *Dilemmas of Appeasement* (Ithaca, 1993), 21.
2 Gilbert M., *The Roots of Appeasement* (London, 1966), 186.
3 Taylor P.M., *The Projection of Britain* (London, 1981), 291.
4 Newton S., *Profits of Peace: The Political Economy of Anglo-German Appeasement* (Oxford, 1996), 6.
5 Middlemas K., *Diplomacy of Illusion: The British Government and Germany, 1937–39* (London, 1971), 2.
6 Chamberlain quoted in Taylor T., *Munich: The Price of Peace* (London, 1979), 60.
7 Parker R.A.C., *Chamberlain and Appeasement* (London, 1993), 347.
8 Dilks D. (ed.), *The Diaries of Sir Alexander Cadogan* (London, 1971), 26 March 1939.
9 Bartlett C.J., *British Foreign Policy in the Twentieth Century* (London, 1989), 60.
10 Charmley J., *Churchill: The End of Glory* (London, 1993), 649.
11 Andrew C., *Secret Service: The Making of the British Intelligence Community* (London, 1985), 476.

12 Kennedy P., *The Realities Behind Diplomacy: Background Influences on British External Policy, 1865–1980* (London, 1985), 318.
13 Kitchen M., 'Winston Churchill and the Soviet Union During the Second World War', *Historical Journal*, **30**(2), 1987, 436.

6
Third power, 1945–1956

The legacy of war and post-war decline

Britain was the only major power to fight the Second World War continuously from September 1939 to its conclusion. Except for the US, it was also the only Great Power to escape defeat in either world war. National survival was an enormous achievement which left the country with great prestige, yet it also, in the view of many, spelt the ruin of Britain's Great Power status. Its decline relative to the US and USSR in wartime has already been seen. It was hardly novel for Britain to pursue a 'peripheral strategy' and rely at critical moments on allies for her survival: a similar strategy had been followed in the Napoleonic Wars (another war largely won due to Russian endeavours). The country's situation after 1940 was grave but it would have been so if France had collapsed 25 years before, in the early stages of the Great War. Yet clear signs of declining power there undoubtedly were. In the past London had managed to remain on roughly equal terms with its allies, especially as a naval and financial power. In 1945 the Soviets, still loyal to their totalitarian creed, dominated more of Eastern Europe than Hitler had in 1939 and British policy was soon focused on preventing further Communist expansion. The US shared similar interests to Britain and remained a close ally, but its power was daunting: it emerged from war with an atomic monopoly, huge armed forces (12 million compared to Britain's 4.5 million) and formidable economic-financial strength, establishing a hegemonic position in much of the world. By 1948 Britain's gross domestic product (GDP) per capita was half America's, whereas it had been 90 per cent a decade before; and the US navy outnumbered the Royal Navy in all classes of vessel by 1945, whereas it only outnumbered them in submarines six years earlier – figures which highlight just how important the Second World War was as a turning point in the relative power of the two Anglo-Saxon powers. The US now had 99 aircraft carriers – the new backbone of any fleet – to Britain's 52. And the British emerged from war facing two other daunting challenges. Although the Empire was fully restored, pressures for decolonisation after the Second World War proved far more determined than those after the First and there was a rapid decline too in the 'informal' Imperial machinery of financial dependency, tariff preferences and the Sterling Area. For some critics, the 'end of Empire' was generally well handled given the scale of the problem and the speed of the process (less than a generation), especially when compared to the Dutch in Indonesia, the Belgians in the Congo or the Portuguese in their African colonies. Certainly the independence of India, the bulk of Africa and the West Indies was achieved remarkably smoothly and, in Malaya between 1948 and 1960, the army successfully defeated a Communist insurgency. But in Palestine, Egypt, Cyprus and Aden Imperial retreat could prove bloody and humiliating, and overall the process was marked by uncertainty, second thoughts and persistent hopes of maintaining a global presence. The dismantlement of Empire was neither a botched affair nor a flawless triumph, but a mixture of orderly withdrawal and confused retreat. Just as Britain had particularly gained from European predominance in the eighteenth and nineteenth centuries, so it particularly suffered from the loss of European hegemony in the twentieth. Demands for independence had of course been strong in India and Egypt between the wars, 'dedominionisation' had already advanced in Ireland in particular, and there was a strong group in the Labour Party (succeeding the Liberal radicals) who had long been critical of the privilege, racism and exploitation of colonial rule. Even so, most British officials in 1945 expected to be faced, not by the end of Empire, but with another period of adjustment like that after 1918, when limited concessions kept the edifice intact. A second 'European civil war', however, proved destructive of all the colonial powers' prestige. Initial Japanese victories in Asia led Australia and New Zealand to look to the US for defence (the three formed the ANZUS Pact without Britain in 1951) and encouraged nationalists in South-east Asia and India. Both Superpowers were anti-colonial for ideological reasons and colonial peoples were encouraged to aspire to national independence by the creation of the United Nations. Colonialism as an ideal had gone out of fashion, and even seemed immoral, especially for a state which claimed to stand for freedom and social progress. Yet the end of Empire was a major threat to the country's identity, to its image of 'greatness', as well as to trade and investment, and decolonisation was not achieved without heart-searching and reluctance, especially on the Right. Even in Africa the old native elites were giving way to an educated middle class who, despite Colonial Office hopes, could not be co-opted into working with their British masters. In 1960 it was a Conservative premier who spoke of a 'wind of change' sweeping Africa and thereafter Whitehall did little to resist the inexorable move to independence. The idea that the British suffered a loss of will-power, or were unfit to hold onto an Empire in times of adversity, seems ridiculous. They had been ready to face difficult years after 1918 and the 'wind of change' affected all European Empires. The experience of the French in Indochina (1946–54) and Algeria (1954–62) stood as a chilling reminder of the costs of resisting this particular wind. Arguably, too, it became easier to make money from the developing world by ending the formal Empire and making profits through less obviously exploitative arrangements.

The third important challenge was a further shift at home from the low tax, non-interventionist policies favoured by Victorian governments to the nationalisation of industry by the post-war Labour government, Keynesian intervention in the economy and the creation of the 'welfare state', presaged by the 1942 Beveridge Report. Having failed to create a 'land fit for heroes' after the First World War, most people were determined to build a 'New Jerusalem' after the Second. When the Conservatives returned to office in 1951, with a low majority, they did little to alter this system, and the commitments to universal social benefits, full employment and the 'mixed economy' became part of the so-called 'post-war consensus'. Yet the attempt to create a more caring, egalitarian social order led to high taxes and a government spending deficit. 'Economic growth' became a more important measure of success than Imperial possessions or substantial defence forces, the population became pre-concerned with salaries and consumer goods rather than endeavour abroad, and the proportion of government spending on defence (though not the absolute amounts) fell. This shift occurred when the economy was still insolvent after the war, national wealth was little higher than in 1914, markets and investments had been lost, and the merchant fleet had been decimated. The Sterling Crisis of 1947, devaluation in 1949 and the continuation of rationing into the mid-1950s showed an economy in difficulties, even if Labour achieved a remarkable recovery of exports and industrial output. The British may have felt themselves to be a successful, efficient power but in reality their economy was marred by declining traditional industries, poor quality goods, inadequate technical education and an ageing infrastructure. In the 1980s one school of thought believed Britain's precipitate post-war decline could primarily be blamed on this attempt to erect a 'New Jerusalem'. Rather than pursuing 'dreams and illusions', Thatcherites argued, Britain should have preserved its sense of enterprise and individualism, and concentrated on investing in infrastructure and new technologies.[1]

There is inadequate space here to discuss fully the reasons for *economic* decline, especially when one survey has concluded that 'The intellectual debates on Britain's decline have produced no agreement on either causes or remedies'.[2] A proper analysis would require an investigation into

British government, social structure, industrial organisation and labour attitudes, as well as the international environment. Apart from the Thatcherite attack on the 'post-war consensus', the reasons for economic underperformance have variously been said to lie in Britain's class system, confrontational industrial relations, the strength of 'financial capitalism' compared to manufacturing industry, the failure to abandon 'soft' Imperial markets and enter the European Community at an early date, or the refusal to reduce Britain's Imperial role at sufficient pace. Some of these reasons focus on *internally* generated problems, others on *external* factors. But it is possible to combine them in different measures and to argue, for example, that post-1945 problems were brought about because Britain tried both to create social justice at home while maintaining a Great Power role abroad. There is disagreement too, of course, over when decline relative to major competitors began. As seen earlier in this study, some date it to the Victorian period, when growth rates fell to about 2 per cent per annum, Britain already seemed unable to develop new industries on a large enough scale and its share of world manufacturing exports was already tumbling. Britain's share of world shipbuilding, for example, consistently declined from over half in 1914, to about a third in 1939 and a tenth in 1960. Yet it has also been argued that 'The faults of the decline after 1945 are not to be shuffled off to earlier generations'.[3] In 1914, even if other states were catching up, Britain had the ability to remain one of a leading group in terms of wealth, as it did between the wars. Some see the world wars as having a profound effect on Britain's position; others see them merely as accentuating problems which already existed – although how long it would have taken Britain to fall so far behind America, in commercial and naval terms, if the Second World War had not occurred, is very difficult to say. It is important not to overemphasise the implications of decline – in the 1990s British people on average were wealthier than ever before – or to concentrate solely on *economic* decline: decolonisation, as discussed above, which did much to reduce Britain's world role and prestige, would have been irresistible even if the country had been wealthier. Britain had long had a smaller population than some of its main competitors – most obviously America, Russia and Germany – and it had less natural resources too. It is certainly ridiculous to lay the whole cause of Britain's post-1945 failures at the doors of the 'New Jerusalem'. After the exertions of 1940–45 the demand for social reform was well-nigh inescapable. At the time, many genuinely believed that state intervention and economic management would produce a more efficient Britain and for a time the system did deliver growth, full employment and low inflation. Demands from the electorate for social reform were hardly new and state spending grew steadily across the century and under governments of all main parties, from 12 per cent of GDP in 1914 to 25 per cent in the 1930s, a third around 1960 and almost a half in 1975. Besides, the expansion of social security was a general factor in the post-war world, pushing up taxes and deficits in Germany, France, Italy and elsewhere, sometimes to higher levels than Britain.

The case argued in this book is that the British economy *was* outperformed by leading competitors from the nineteenth century onwards and long-term problems with the British economy were certainly recognised in the 1930s. But economic strength is not the only constituent of power and the British preserved their naval predominance, the largest Empire and only genuine 'global' presence until 1941. In a sense Britain was doomed to lose its Victorian predominance whatever it did in the twentieth century because once other powers industrialised, expanded their trade and developed credit, shipping and insurance services, Britain's share of global wealth was bound to decline and it was vulnerable because of its dependence on imports. Part of the reason why Britain seemed to decline so precipitately was that before 1939 the factors operating to expose such weaknesses were masked. Technological developments, shifting patterns of industrial production and increasing Asian nationalism were all 'in train' but it took the Second World War to act as a catalyst, leaving Britain vulnerable in many areas in the post-war decade. America had lacked the will and motives to outbuild the Royal Navy, Germany had taken time to recover from the Great War, Italy and France had not yet modernised their industry or become major trading powers. But British growth rates were already lower than all these countries between the wars. A second reason for the precipitate appearance of decline in the 20 or 30 years after the war was that in 1945 Britain did still *seem* so powerful. Its Empire was as large as ever, the British constitution and liberal political system had again survived the test of war, victory had restored national pride after the shame of Appeasement, and the British economy was still the strongest in Europe. Indeed, in the 1940s its GDP was second only to the US, whilst half the world's commercial and financial transactions were in Sterling. With France, Italy, Germany and Japan having all suffered defeat it was unsurprising that the British felt able to rest on their laurels and enjoy the benefits of peace. There was little appreciation of the scale of material losses or Britain's effective reliance on American aid, and the conflict probably only emphasised Britain's sense of separateness from the continent. A decade after the war Britons still felt secure as the world's third power, and it is too easy from hindsight to say that they should have recognised their declining position and adjusted to the role of a European nation. The rate of decline was more rapid than anyone expected and habits of Great Powerhood died hard, especially among an insular people known for its pragmatism and gradual political evolution. Furthermore the country still maintained commercial and financial interests on a truly global scale which, it seemed, must be defended; and new sources of power, especially the atomic bomb exploded in 1952, gave hope of stabilising its position. There was no doubt a certain inertia in London's desire to maintain the Empire but there were numerous reasons why British leaders could not abandon the world role more quickly. During the Cold War, fear of Communism and a desire to please the US led the British to retain positions of strength in the Persian Gulf and Far East until the 1970s. There was a need to prepare colonies for independence, rather than simply abandoning them to anarchy (as the Belgians did in the Congo in 1960). With half Britain's trade focused on the Sterling Area in 1950, there was also inevitably a desire to retain close economic relations with colonies. Whatever the reasons for Britain's poor economic performance, the result by the mid-1990s was that Britain was still fifth among the top industrialised states (but only marginally ahead of Italy) with 4.9 per cent of world manufacturing exports, compared to America's 12.3 per cent, Germany's 10.1 per cent, Japan's 9.5 per cent and France's 5.7 per cent. Britain's performance was poorer than the major defeated powers of 1945 and in tables of countries' wealth per capita it had fallen from the Top Twenty. This worsening economic position now undoubtedly did take on a key importance in narrowing international options: it soon meant that Britain was unable to sustain a global system of military bases or large-sale development programmes in the developing world and its influence was reduced accordingly. Furthermore the process of retreat gradually undermined prestige and made political leaders less confident about their own policies and less able to offset material problems with the use of confident, successful diplomacy. Yet even in the 1990s Britain could hope to 'punch above its weight' thanks to its diplomatic experience, membership of numerous international organisations and continuing importance as a commercial nation.

Policy-making in the Cold War

Foreign policy has been seen as part of the 'post-war consensus' from 1945 to the 1970s, when 'disagreement [was] generally ... over a single issue rather than over fundamentals', at least between the political elites of both main parties.[4] True, in the 1930s Labour had been critical of Chamberlain. But a foreign policy consensus among party leaderships had generally been the rule in the early twentieth century and the wartime coalition bound Labour's front bench to a pragmatic, non-ideological policy which sought to maintain the country's Great Power status. A 'Socialist' foreign policy – which might have included anti-capitalism, international working-class solidarity, an aversion to power politics and democratic control over policy-making – was never pursued by any Labour government. Labour was wedded to a moderate, evolutionary form of socialism and dependent on voters who would be alienated by such an unpatriotic policy. By 1951 the Labour Foreign Secretary, Ernest Bevin, a former trades union leader of lowly background but forceful personality, had abandoned all idea of isolationism and led Britain into a peacetime, permanent alliance, the North Atlantic Treaty Organisation (NATO). The government also decided to develop the atomic bomb, preferred a global role to involvement in European integration and began a fitful process of Imperial withdrawal, policies which were maintained under subsequent Conservative governments. Each party had its fringe groups. In 1946 Labour's 'Keep Left' movement was critical of US capitalism and hoped to maintain the wartime alliance with the USSR, but Stalin's crushing of freedom in Eastern Europe convinced most of them in 1947–50 about Bevin's line and left-wing criticism of British links to America, nuclear arms and colonial policy only revived after 1951, led by Aneurin Bevan. Among Conservatives, in 1954 the 'Suez Group' mobilised those die-hards who were upset by the retreat from Empire. But the 1956 Suez crisis was the only important point at which the front benches differed bitterly and the only time that the public was aroused much over foreign policy. True, there were arguments about Labour's response to the nationalisation of British oil interests in Iran in 1951 and the Conservatives' pro-American line in the Korean War in 1952–53. But when in office, the Conservatives chose to undermine the Iranian government by subversion rather than war and the Labour Cabinet was generally as pro-American as Churchill. In 1945 there was some concern about how Labour would handle world affairs, and doubts in America about the reliability of Socialists as allies. George VI was said to have intervened to secure Bevin's appointment as a patriotic minister well-versed in power politics, who had already defended British intervention in Greece to maintain the Royal government against Communists. But the Prime Minister, Clement Attlee, was also experienced in international issues, having acted as Churchill's deputy since 1940. Attlee on the whole let Bevin dominate foreign policy but was capable of taking firm action himself, as in December 1950 when he flew to Washington amid rumours that the Americans might use atomic bombs in Korea. Bevin has been described as 'among the most successful [Foreign Secretaries] in the history of British external policy'[5] who coped well with the outbreak of the Cold War and a plethora of Imperial problems, against a background of limited resources. By becoming America's most important and loyal ally many believe he took the best course for defending British interests. In early 1947 especially the international situation seemed terrible: Indian independence, violence in

Palestine and renewed conflict in Greece, combined with food and fuel shortages at home, and there was still no guarantee of US support against the Soviets. Yet two years later US economic assistance, NATO and the apparently successful move to a multiracial Commonwealth provided the basis for the 'three circles' policy (actually enunciated in a speech by Churchill): London supposedly stood at the centre of the Western world, linking North America, Europe and the Empire–Commonwealth in the face of Soviet Communism. Nonetheless Bevin has his critics who insist that, far from winning influence in Washington, he made Britain over-dependent on America, and had inflated dreams of holding onto the Empire despite the loss of India. It can be argued that America did not need British encouragement to adopt a forthright anti-Soviet policy and that NATO was not Bevin's original intention: instead in 1945–48, 'while forced to rely on the US in the short-term, in the long-term [he] hoped to build a "third force" independent of, and equal to, America ... in the wider framework of an anti-Soviet alliance'.[6] This 'third force' was to be a British-led group embracing Western Europe, colonies in Africa and a British-dominated Middle East. But Britain proved incapable of paying to revive Western Europe, match the military threat from the East and develop colonial regions, and Bevin's vision of a 'Western Union' evaporated.

By mid-1950 Bevin was committed to Atlanticism, the Commonwealth proved an ever-looser organisation and certain European states had turned to cooperation via supranational structures, which Bevin held in contempt. His remaining months in office were marred by the Korean War, inter-allied differences over German rearmament, Cabinet divisions over British rearmament costs and his own ill-health, the last leading to his replacement by the luckless Herbert Morrison. The Foreign Office returned in October 1951 to a more congenial Foreign Secretary, Anthony Eden, whose vast experience, alongside the prestige of premier Churchill, helped maintain the image of British greatness. To one colleague Eden's domination of international issues 'was in a sense an abrogation of the role of the Cabinet'.[7] But in fact Eden *was* challenged in Cabinet at times, most notably by Housing Minister Harold Macmillan, who vainly called for a more imaginative policy on European integration. And the Foreign Secretary was permanently troubled by the ageing Churchill who, despite a stroke in 1953, clung tenaciously to power and regularly interfered in foreign policy. Churchill was critical of Eden's efforts to resolve relations with Egypt and was keen to establish a reputation as a peace-maker by holding a summit meeting with the Soviets. The Prime Minister's tendency to live in the past was revealed in his attempts to maintain the Empire intact and act as an equal partner of the Americans. With a great expenditure of nervous energy Eden, himself plagued by ill-health, was able to avoid a summit until Churchill retired and, in 1954, to achieve some remarkable diplomatic successes: resolving the oil dispute with Iran, making a settlement with Egypt, producing a solution to the nine-year Italian-Yugoslav dispute over the border town of Trieste, playing conciliator in the settlement of France's colonial war in Indochina and finding a way forward for NATO on German rearmament. Eden thereby proved that Britain could, for a few years at least, offset the effect of its declining economic power with the use of diplomatic skill, even (over Indochina) in the face of US criticism. He also took part in new regional alliances, the South-East Asian Treaty Organisation (SEATO) of 1954 and the Baghdad Pact in the Middle East of the following year. Yet neither of these structures was as reliable or important as NATO, Eden's policies in Iran, Egypt and Indochina can be seen as no more than exercises in orderly retreat and he has frequently been criticised as intuitive but undynamic, lacking any long-term vision of Britain's role. When he became Prime Minister in April 1955 he proved ready to seek *détente* with the Soviets, doing much to bring about the Geneva Conference with US, Soviet and French heads of government that July. But in 1956 his vanity, suspicion of American power and failure to see the implications of Imperial retreat helped bring the Suez débâcle. Neither Bevin nor Eden faced proper oversight by a Cabinet subcommittee in this crucial period. Bevin's character and reputation were such that, despite some compromises with the Treasury (keen to reduce costs in Greece, Palestine and elsewhere), he was rarely challenged in Cabinet and, despite a sophisticated system of ministerial and official committees under Attlee, there was no single specialist committee on foreign policy. The nearest equivalent was the Defence Committee, retained from wartime, but as its title suggests it mainly dealt with defence issues and its meetings became less frequent after 1951. The Cabinet itself can hardly be said to have had a comprehensive overview of foreign policy. Although it did receive reports on major policy items, there was a great deal it did not discuss, not least the 1947 decision to build an atomic bomb which was taken by Attlee, Bevin and a few others. When Eden became premier he put a lot of policy in the hands of small Cabinet committees under his own chairmanship, such as the Egypt Committee which handled the Suez crisis.

As after the First World War the policy-making machinery in Whitehall saw certain continuities from wartime practice, some reversions to pre-war behaviour and further evolutionary development. One impact of Imperial retreat was the merger of the Dominions and India Offices, the latter redundant after Indian independence, to form the Commonwealth Relations Office in 1947. But the need to fight the Cold War was another vital factor, especially in the field of covert operations.

The Joint Intelligence Committee (JIC) was now an important actor in international policy-making, reflecting the continued rise of the British 'intelligence community'. Indeed, after its wartime successes, JIC's advice was, perhaps, over-relied upon in the early post-war period. A century earlier secret intelligence was primarily aimed at the military-naval capabilities of potential enemies and had little impact on general diplomatic questions. By 1920 there were agencies outside the armed forces concerned with industrial intelligence, counter-subversion (MI5), intelligence gathering abroad (MI6) and signals interception (GC&CS), but they were poorly financed and coordinated. 'Total war' after 1940 demanded a comprehensive, well-resourced machine and this was true of the Cold War too when the wartime shape of the intelligence community was largely retained, although SOE was effectively swallowed by MI6. It was in the nature of the Cold War that international tension became permanent, a 'surprise attack' was always possible (if unlikely) and gathering information in Communist states through normal diplomatic channels very difficult. Covert intelligence gathering became vital, as did the use of propaganda offensives against the enemy. Although Western policy during the Cold War is usually described in defensive terms, as 'containment' of Communist expansion, it is clear that by 1948 there were important 'offensive' elements, first in US, then British strategy. The Cold War was fought using not just alliances, rearmament and the economic strengthening of the West, but also covert action (the use of sabotage, subversion and assassination), propaganda (or psychological warfare) and strategic trade controls (designed to prevent the Soviets obtaining vital materials and akin to Britain's traditional policy of blockading an enemy). MI6 had a well-established anti-Communist pedigree and particularly relished the challenge of stirring unrest in Albania after 1949. But Albania, a Communist state on the fringes of Soviet influence, did not prove as easy a target as expected and the penetration of British agents ended in 1952. One major weakness was the existence of the Burgess–Maclean–Philby spy ring, exposed in 1951, which not only leaked information to Moscow but, on being discovered, harmed Anglo-American nuclear cooperation, FO morale and faith in the intelligence services. The exposure of two atomic spies in Britain, Alan Nunn May (1946) and Klaus Fuchs (1950), had already damaged Britain's chances of obtaining atomic information from the US. Then again, the MI6–CIA relationship, forged in war, was too valuable to disappear. The two agencies often competed, and often differed in their interpretation of intelligence, but they also worked together closely. From 1950 Britain provided bases for American U-2 spy-planes, which overflew Eastern Europe and the USSR; and in 1953 both agencies helped topple the Iranian government. Among numerous other joint operations they also cooperated against nationalist leaders in Syria and Egypt in the mid-1950s before the Suez operation soured relations once more.

Britain's possession of a global system of military bases and intelligence-gathering posts (one of the assets which accompanied Empire) was very useful to the US and the most important evidence of an 'intelligence alliance' was the UKUSA agreements of 1948 concerned with signals intelligence interception and sharing, and linked to the efforts of Commonwealth countries, part of a wider 'Western intelligence community', especially Australia and New Zealand. This gave a network for intelligence gathering not only from the Communist bloc (with Hong Kong, for example, a valuable base for spying on China), but from allies and neutral states. Signals intelligence was still handled by Government Communications Headquarters (GCHQ), based at Cheltenham after 1952 and greatly expanded after the war. GCHQ was evidently not as good at breaking Soviet codes as it had been those of the Nazis but it was ahead of US practice in providing Britain with a single communications intelligence body: the US National Security Agency was only formed in 1952. At home MI5's role was profoundly affected by the Cold War, directing its energies against pro-Soviet 'front' organisations, Communists in the trades unions and suspected 'fellow travellers' among Labour MPs. MI5 also had responsibility for guarding against internal subversion in the colonies and had its own links to the American intelligence services, the CIA (Central Intelligence Agency) and FBI (Federal Bureau of Investigation). With such a complex, expanding intelligence community, the JIC's role as a coordinating body was highly important. Still under FO chairmanship, JIC had to process intelligence from covert, diplomatic and public sources to help policy decisions on a wide range of areas from defence and international trade to alliance diplomacy and Cold War strategy. Imperial problems meant that a Colonial Office member joined in 1948. But clashes between parts of the intelligence-gathering machine, duplication of work and mis-reading of information were inevitable and, although the intelligence services became an important part of the British state, with their own international links and a larger budget than the FO, they could not prevent crises and humiliation abroad. Indeed with such events as the defection of Burgess and Maclean (Soviet agents since before the war) to Moscow in 1951, or the death of Commander 'Buster' Crabb while spying on Soviet warships in 1956, the intelligence services created their own embarrassing problems for governments.

The FO itself was much-altered by the Cold War. For all his forthrightness, Bevin was sceptical about an offensive 'liberation' strategy at first. But in 1946 a 'Russia Committee' was founded, of leading officials, to educate the FO about the Soviet menace, review Communist policies and discuss the British response. In 1948 it obtained a COS representative and acted as a kind of Cold War 'planning staff', but its weekly meetings became only fortnightly in the early 1950s and it was then run down. Meanwhile in February 1949 a small, elite Permanent Under-Secretary's Committee (PUSC) was created. Like the American Policy Planning Staff, formed two years before, it answered the need for a long-term planning body in the FO and the papers it produced included PUSC (51)16, finalised in January 1952, which defined a broad three-stage strategy for fighting the Cold War: first to build up military and economic strength, then to survive a period of coexistence before finally some kind of *modus vivendi* was reached with the Soviets. In the 1950s the department built around PUSC took on a greater role in coordinating Cold War strategy and impinged on the work of JIC. Another important development was the creation in 1948 of an FO propaganda and psychological warfare agency, a successor to the wartime PWE, given the euphemistic title of Information Research Department (IRD). The establishment of IRD was encouraged by Bevin's junior minister, Christopher Mayhew, who saw the need to counter-attack Soviet propaganda and build a sense of Western identity. IRD was also active against nationalists within the Empire, especially in such troublespots as Malaya and Palestine. It produced publications, targeted at elite groups in Britain and abroad, becoming the central 'political warfare' body in Whitehall and the largest department in the FO. Yet even more than the intelligence services, its work was largely kept secret from public and parliament. Like the intelligence services IRD had its own international links, not least to the covert propaganda branches of the CIA. Its work also had to be coordinated with other information agencies such as the British Council and the BBC. Like the intelligence services it began to have an important impact on foreign policy. Indeed, whereas in the 1930s Chamberlain had shown a very poor psychological appreciation of the aggressors, by the late 1940s the need to be seen 'standing up' to Stalin whilst portraying the West as strong, united and ready to fight, was well appreciated. Psychological operations had a real impact on diplomatic exchanges: at the Geneva Summit in 1955 the Western and Soviet positions were constructed, not with the intention of real negotiation, but with the aim of avoiding concessions and, whilst appearing reasonable to one side, exposing the insincerity of the other. Thus the Western powers called for disarmament in conventional weapons, where the Soviets were superior, whilst the Soviets concentrated on nuclear disarmament, where the Americans had an advantage; and whilst the West called for freedom of information, which might disrupt the Communist bloc, the Russians called for freer trade – but only so as to end the strategic trade controls enforced by the Western alliance.

Another change in Whitehall was the creation in 1946 of a single Ministry of Defence. The hope was that such a ministry, which had long been suggested, would create a better-coordinated policy and reduce inter-service rivalries. But in actual fact, since separate service ministries continued to exist these rivalries were as intense as ever. The army was increasingly ready, especially after the loss of India, to find a *raison d'être* in a European commitment but the navy and RAF preferred to concentrate on the world role and wanted to defend Britain from invasion without continental involvement. In March 1948 the COS agreed to join other European allies in the defence of Europe 'as far East as possible' but this ambiguous undertaking was only backed up with reinforcements two years later, and a written guarantee of British force levels on the continent was only provided in 1954. Then again, given Britain's historical reluctance to make a 'continental commitment', the guarantee was dramatic enough. Global responsibilities, added to occupation duties (in Germany, Austria and Italy's African colonies) and the Soviet threat, meant that conscription was maintained until 1962, far longer than after the Great War, though by 1948 the total size of the armed forces had dropped to one million. To the Treasury's annoyance the cost of the three services still amounted to a tenth of GNP in the mid-1950s, and during the Korean War defence expenditure leapt to almost a third of government spending. Such figures highlighted the material costs of the Cold War and the continuation of the world role, costs which Britain could less and less afford. Indeed, ironically, in 1952 the Conservatives had to cut back on the massive rearmament programme initiated by Labour during the Korean War.

The 'First' Cold War

In July 1945 Orme Sargent, soon to become FO Permanent Under-Secretary, wrote a memorandum, 'Stocktaking after VE-day', in which he argued that Britain must make itself the leader of Western European countries as well as the Commonwealth in order to be treated by the US and USSR as an equal. The FO was already interested in a 'Western bloc' in Europe as a way to establish British leadership, provide for defence in depth on the continent and contain German power. Insolvent as Britain was, however, Churchill was sceptical about her ability to act as paymaster to such a bloc and there were fears that Moscow and Washington might be antagonised by British attempts to form an exclusive alliance system in Europe. Despite Bevin's persistent interest in a Western bloc down to 1948, it became clear that Britain needed the US to stand up to the USSR and provide military and economic support to Europe. Britain had little reason to welcome a breakdown in East–West relations and the public hoped cooperation among the Big Three would be maintained, not least to prevent another German revival. The new peace-keeping body, the United Nations (UN), was established in 1945 and plans were laid for the permanent members of the UN Security Council – the US, USSR, Britain, France and China – to meet in a Council of Foreign Ministers (CFM) and draft peace treaties with ex-enemy states. The CFM held several meetings, and peace treaties with Italy and other German allies were concluded in February 1947. But even at the first CFM, in September 1945, it was clear that the Soviets and Anglo-Americans were divided. There were suspicions about the establishment of Communist-led governments in Eastern Europe and doubts about whether this policy was a defensive one or a springboard for further Soviet expansion. The process of 'Stalinising' Eastern Europe continued apace after 1945, with rigged elections, imprisonment of opponents and the eventual creation of puppet governments. In some countries the process took a long time, suggesting opportunism in Stalin's policy: Communists only seized control of Czechoslovakia in a coup in 1948. Two years earlier, however, Churchill, now Leader of the Opposition, had made his Fulton Speech, talking of an 'iron curtain' across Europe and calling for an Anglo-American alliance. Many newspapers in Europe and America were initially critical of Churchill but it was not long before his view was widely accepted. As in the inter-war years, the USSR was seen as both an ideological and a power-political menace, threatening to stir up trouble *within* Britain through Communists and their sympathisers, and menacing the Imperial position *abroad*, especially in the Near East. Even before Fulton, Bevin was concerned about Soviet ambitions in the Near East where the Royalist–Communist feud in Greece, Russian border claims against Turkey and the presence of the Red Army in northern Iran suggested sinister Soviet designs in a resuscitation of the 'Great Game'. Fears soon grew about Stalin's ambitions elsewhere: in France and Italy large Communist parties, which had established themselves as leaders of the wartime resistance movements and promised social reform, shared power in coalition governments in 1944–47; in Germany the Soviets established Communist domination of their occupation zone, had ambitions of sharing control of the industrially vital Ruhr valley (part of the British zone) and demanded huge reparations; and, on the other side of the world, Communists were increasingly successful in the civil war in China.

At first it was far from certain that the US would support Britain or resist Stalin. As in wartime, America and Britain shared common values but had distinct interests which did not always overlap. Isolationist feeling lingered in America, there was a strong desire to bring US forces home after the war and there was reluctance too about 'pulling British chestnuts out of the fire'. The US kept Britain out of the Japanese occupation and excluded it from obtaining atomic secrets under the 1946

McMahon Act, despite Britain's contribution to developing the atom bomb during the war. Washington provided a £3.75 billion loan in December 1945 to Britain but only on commercial terms and some Conservatives even opposed it as 'mortgaging the Empire'. But March 1946 saw the US and Britain work together in pressing Stalin to withdraw from Iran and the following months saw an increasing realisation in America that the USSR represented a threat and that Britain alone was too weak to resist. In mid-1946 the Americans and British agreed to fuse their occupation zones in Germany and, in effect, America took over British costs in running their zone, which amounted to £120 million that year. Then in September it was announced that US occupation forces would stay in Germany until stability was assured. The declining strength of Britain and the rise of the US to Western leadership were most obviously demonstrated in early 1947 when Bevin, under Treasury pressure, agreed that Britain could no longer maintain the Royalists in Greece. Within weeks the US agreed to provide aid to Greece (and Turkey), Truman announcing the fact in a speech to Congress which simplistically portrayed a world divided into totalitarian and free states, where America must support the free. The 'Truman Doctrine' was followed in June by the Marshall Plan, whereby America offered to assist a comprehensive economic recovery plan in Europe. The Marshall Plan promised to boost trade, rebuild the German economy and undermine support for Communism in France and Italy, and Bevin led the way in accepting it. When the Soviets refused to enter the Marshall Plan, Europe was split down the middle and after September 1947, with the formation of the 'Cominform' propaganda agency, an intense ideological battle between Communism and liberal democracy was underway. Following the breakdown of talks in the CFM over a German peace treaty in December, and goaded by the Czech Coup, Bevin and his American and French counterparts concentrated on building up Western strength. There were a number of developments in 1948: Marshall aid began to flow under the supervision of the Organisation of European Economic Cooperation (OEEC) formed in April 1948, which had a related body, the highly secretive 'Coordinating Committee' or COCOM, responsible for restricting trade with the Communists; in the security sphere, Bevin led the way in creating the Brussels Pact of March 1948 with France, Belgium, Holland and Luxembourg, after which difficult talks in Washington led to the North Atlantic Treaty in April 1949; and in Germany the British, Americans and French agreed in June 1948 to form a liberal democratic government. The threat of a revived Germany, allied to the West, led Stalin to blockade the enclave of West Berlin at the end of June, sparking the worst crisis in the Cold War so far. The RAF joined the Americans in keeping Berlin supplied by air and by the time the blockade ended in spring Stalin had only succeeded in solidifying the Western alliance under US leadership.

Whilst committing themselves to an American alliance and being anxious to involve America in European security, the British were determined to maintain their own independence and influence US policy in line with British interests, as 'Atlanticist' Britons had first dreamed in 1919. The end of any chance of British isolationism was not meant to remove the country's ability to take unilateral action. Yet very soon any great degree of independence was rendered all but impossible, given the need for US loans, the closeness of the 'intelligence alliance' and the creation, after July 1948, of US air bases in Britain, which acted as an 'unsinkable aircraft carrier'. With the successful test of a Soviet atomic bomb in August 1949 (an event JIC had not expected until 1954), the US air bases raised the danger of Britain becoming the prime target of a nuclear assault. The country might be utterly devastated in a matter of days, and it was unclear how much influence London would have on the use of US nuclear weapons. Yet the number of US bases and facilities kept growing, reaching over 100 by the late 1970s. Bevin resisted the US on a number of fronts nonetheless, refusing for example to be goaded into accepting supranational institutions in Europe. After 1947 the Americans saw a united Europe as the best guarantee of economic growth and resistance to Communism. Bevin, however, wished to lead a group of sovereign European states, as in the OEEC and Brussels Pact, rather than lose Britain's independence to some common European institution. When the idea was raised for a European parliament he channelled it into the virtually powerless Council of Europe, formed in 1949. On the economic side he showed some interest in European customs union, but the Treasury and Board of Trade were committed to a 'multilateral', global system of freer trade and sceptical of a European group's ability to match American economic power. Half Britain's trade was with the Sterling Area and only about a quarter with the OEEC. In January 1949 the Cabinet approved a joint paper by the FO and Treasury which stated that Britain must not cooperate with Europeans beyond the point at which it lost its own independent economic viability. If Europe were to be invaded by the Red Army Britain must be able to survive alone, as in 1940. In September 1949 the Americans effectively recognised Britain's importance as a *world* trading power when they supported Sterling during its devaluation from \$4.03 to \$2.80, and thereafter the French were seen in Washington as the likely leaders of European integration. Against this background it is not surprising that Britain took no part in the Schuman Plan, launched in Paris in May 1950, which led in 1952 to a supranational authority governing the coal and steel industries of France, Italy, Belgium, Holland, Luxembourg and the new government of West Germany, known together as 'the Six'.

Another example of Britain's desire for independent status was Bevin's wish to possess an atomic bomb with 'the Union Jack flying over it'.[8] For a time, after taking the decision to build such a weapon in 1947, there were hopes of becoming the world's second nuclear power, but a bomb was not actually tested until 1952, by which time both Superpowers were on the way to building much more powerful Hydrogen bombs. The British developed a viable atomic delivery system in the V-bombers, which began to fly in 1955, but once again it was not long before the Superpowers went further and tested intercontinental ballistic missiles, leaving Britain behind. The COS were quick to urge the logic of nuclear deterrence after the war and, as early as 1952, hoped to cut the costs of Britain's nuclear arsenal by relying more on atomic bombs. But it was clear that genuine deterrence of the Soviets relied on the huge US nuclear arsenal and, if it came to war, London needed US help to target the Soviet air and submarine bases which could threaten the British Isles. How far the British obtained US help is unclear: there were hopes of obtaining American atomic weapons in the event of war, Churchill received a briefing on the US war plan in 1952 and there was some freeing of American nuclear information to Britain two years later. But as Soviet nuclear capabilities grew, the Eisenhower administration threatened 'massive retaliation' in the event of conflict, and the effectiveness of the British deterrent in isolation was called further into doubt. The most reassuring point was that Western experts did *not* actually expect the Russians to start a Third World War until the late 1950s, if at all. Then again, as the outbreak of the Korean War in June 1950 showed, such an event was not impossible. The aggression by Communist North Korea against the pro-American South, and the rapid commitment of US troops at the head of an international force, which included some British and Commonwealth troops, marked a new stage in the Cold War. The focus of world attention moved to East Asia, where China had already fallen to Mao Zedong's Communists in September 1949 (destroying British commercial and financial interests which had barely begun to recover from the world war). Large-scale US involvement in Korea helped generate a demand for imports in America which further boosted the Western European economies, but on the negative side 'hot war' in Korea led to a costly drive in NATO for rearmament. There were fears too that Stalin might use the war to draw the US into a large-scale conflict, leaving Europe open to Soviet pressures. The British had a clear interest in standing up to aggression in Korea: policy-makers were preoccupied with the supposed 'lessons' of the 1930s when Hitler had not been resisted early enough and both Hong Kong and Malaya were vulnerable if the war spread. But Britain was never more than a secondary player in the Korean War, which only further emphasised US leadership of the

West. There was a clear desire in London to restrain America from action which might spark off general conflict and Bevin was doubtful too at first about the controversial US proposal in September 1950 to rearm Germany as a way to strengthen the West's conventional defences in Europe. Chinese entry into the war in November increased British nervousness still further but actually Truman was ready to localise the war in Korea and work, slowly, for an armistice which was finally achieved in July 1953.

Anglo-American differences continued in East Asia after Korea. In 1954 Washington was none-too-pleased with Eden's readiness to accept the creation of a Communist North Vietnam as the cost of ending war in Indochina; and in 1955 the British were critical of Eisenhower's apparent preparedness to risk nuclear war with China over the strategically useless Quemoy and Matsu islands, which were held by the anti-Communist Chiang Kai-Shek but within artillery range of the Chinese mainland. There were also disagreements over general Cold War tactics of covert action, propaganda and economic warfare activities. The British were fearful that bellicose attitudes in Washington might push the Soviets so far that Stalin would launch a preventive war, or that revolts would be encouraged in Eastern Europe which the West could not assist. Perhaps because of their propensity to conciliate strong enemies, their traditionally non-ideological approach to world affairs, their geographical vulnerability to Soviet attack or their declining military strength, the British were always less ready to run risks in the Cold War than the Americans. The end of British involvement in covert operations in Albania, growing doubts about the wisdom of flying spy-planes over the USSR, the readiness of PUSC (51)16 to contemplate a *modus vivendi* with Soviet Communism and the willingness of Churchill to work for a summit with the Soviets all reflected this. So did British eagerness after Korea to ease trade restrictions with the Eastern bloc, with Churchill, like Lloyd George in 1921, hoping to use expanded commerce to develop a more reasonable relationship with the Soviets. And the British were critical of the US determination to humiliate the Soviets over the crushing of the East German uprising of June 1953. Churchill himself may be seen as the father of European *détente*, for his belief in talking to the Soviets was not simply based on personal vanity: trade, talk and other contacts might break down Communist suspicions; the advent of the Hydrogen bomb might make Moscow see the uselessness of threats; and if, in the short term, the West proved ready to tolerate Soviet rule in Eastern Europe, then Cold War tensions might ease and in the long term the Communist bloc might break up. The US government, however, was determined to concentrate on building up Western arms, negotiating with the Soviets on specific issues and avoiding any settlement which condoned Russian control of the 'slave peoples' of Eastern Europe. The Anglo-American relationship then was as complex as ever, marked by strong elements of common interest and competition, but with the US now far more powerful than Britain and not always ready to listen to London's advice.

The end of Empire in India and the Middle East

It has been seen that, even had the British possessed extraordinary insight into future trends and been prepared to embrace such a policy, a rapid abandonment of Empire was impossible because of the dangers of anarchy, damage to commercial interests (including the stability of Sterling) or Soviet expansion. Yet it is true that the habits of Imperial rule died hard. The Colonial Office was ready to extend the franchise in African and West Indian colonies and, following riots in 1948, to prepare the Gold Coast for early self-government: Kwame Nkrumah became Prime Minister there in 1952 and his country obtained independence as 'Ghana' in 1957. But in practice in most colonies British governors retained wide powers and it was believed that proper preparation for independence would take up to half a century. It was also felt necessary to create larger, more economically viable federations of colonies in the West Indies, East Africa and, most controversially, Central Africa. All these three eventually failed, but there was greater success in Malaysia, which won its independence in 1957. In the short term British rule was seen by the Colonial Office as beneficial, the ideal of 'trusteeship' prevailed and the mother country's role was seen as being to foster good education, efficient administration and economic development. The last became much more important at this time, reflecting the wider faith in government intervention bred by the war. It was not, however, an altruistic policy: Bevin had hopes of developing Africa as an outlet for European investment and a source of raw materials which would boost British power. There were persistent hopes, as Britain became more dependent on America, of using Imperial resources to provide Britain once more with the resources for unilateral action. But after 1950, despite the success of Malayan rubber as a dollar earner, it was evident that proper economic development in most colonies would be a long task that Britain – which set aside only £12 million for development in 1945 – could not afford. Some projects, notably the East African groundnut scheme, proved costly failures. Economic interest in Africa and the West Indies declined sharply under the Conservatives and many colonies were seen as liabilities, making their independence uncontroversial even for the most determined Imperialist. Britain still hoped development aid might placate liberal opinion at home and help secure markets in the colonies after independence, thus maintaining an 'informal' Empire, but India and others tended to develop their own economic policies once they were free of British rule. Then again not all colonies were eager for independence and London had certain legal obligations to fulfil: Gibraltar, the Falkland Islands and Bermuda were still loyal to Britain at the end of the century, the lease on most of Hong Kong did not expire until 1997, and until 1971 there were security commitments to the Persian Gulf autocracies in Oman, Kuwait and Bahrain. There seemed to be some moral duty, however badly fulfilled, to resolve ethnic problems in such colonies as Palestine and Cyprus before independence; and there was a related problem in trying to build multiracial, democratic states in Rhodesia, Kenya and elsewhere where there were substantial white settler communities. Also there *were* areas where, for a long time, the British wished to remain for security reasons. Cyprus, Malta, Aden and Singapore were strategically placed bases which helped give reality to Britain's world role. Fear of Communist takeover directly influenced the speed of transition to independence in British Guiana and Aden. Most importantly between 1947 and 1956 the British wished to maintain a presence in the oil-rich Middle East, whose strategic importance had been demonstrated in the Second World War, which could act as a barrier to Russian expansion and which, most importantly, was the most substantial base for British power after the loss of India.

Indian independence did not lead to the loss of the Empire which had largely been built around its defence. Although, unlike Malaya and Burma, India escaped Japanese conquest during the war, the conflict had a dramatic effect on British rule. Subject to strict British controls on their agriculture, industry and labour, Indian leaders were no longer ready to accept the gradual evolution to Dominion status promised in 1935. In 1940 Gandhi called for his country's immediate independence but Churchill, always a reactionary where India was concerned, opposed concessions. Once war came to the Far East 50 000 Indians, led by Subhas Chandra Bose, fought on the Japanese side but, however disenchanted, most Indians refused to go so far. British prestige, the most important element in their ability to rule India at low cost, was crippled at Singapore and in March 1942 the Cripps Mission was sent to India in the vain hope of reaching agreement on the country's political future. Gandhi and others believed they could use Britain's predicament to obtain far-reaching concessions but there were divisions within both the Congress Party and the British government and, in the short term, both sides moved to extremes, though without a wholesale descent into violence. The Congress Party was banned, after launching a civil disobedience campaign, with strikes and demonstrations under the slogan 'Quit India', in August 1942. The British arrested 90 000 opponents including all the

Congress leaders, an event which gave added importance to another political force, Ali Jinnah's Moslem League, which increasingly came to favour the creation of a separate 'Pakistani' state for India's Moslem minority. Especially after 1941 the war brought inflation, food shortages, even (in Bengal) famine, and its end brought unemployment, creating the threat of mass disorder which the British – who had always had a small number of white officers and officials ruling a huge native population – could not possibly control. The 1942 arrests proved the last time coercion could be used. By now, after inter-war reforms, Indians outnumbered Britons in the civil service, local police forces were under the control of provincial Indian parliaments and the loyalty of the Indian Army (which had mushroomed from 150 000 to 2 250 000 during the war) to British officers was no longer guaranteed. The most hopeful factor was that the Congress leaders, despite their imprisonment, had no interest in encouraging army mutinies or communal unrest: it was obvious that the days of the Raj were numbered, even if no one expected them to end as rapidly as they did, and India's politicians had a vested interest in securing independence without violence and upheaval. In contrast to Churchill, Attlee was well disposed to independence and, in any case, the 'Labour government was deprived of both of the traditional methods of imperial rule: coercion, which became impractical, and collaboration, which was unforthcoming'.[9] The principal threat of violence came not from another clash of wills between London and Congress, but from Jinnah's 'Pakistan demand' which led to inter-communal bloodshed in 1946. A Cabinet mission after the war could find little agreement between Congress and the Moslem League, and the Viceroy, Lord Wavell, was ready to contemplate a precipitate withdrawal if violence continued to mount. Wavell was soon replaced, however, by Lord Louis Mountbatten, devious and indiscreet, but with royal connections which provided British rule with a sufficient residue of respect to escape from India with a sense of honour and even success. In February 1947 the Cabinet decided to regain the initiative and neutralise any new 'Quit India' campaign through a promise of independence by July 1948. In fact independence was granted on 15 August 1947, with more inter-communal massacres as Congress reluctantly accepted that partition was inescapable. Ceylon (now Sri Lanka) soon followed, as did Burma. India became the world's largest democracy, still with considerable British investments and trade, but pursuing a 'non-aligned' policy between East and West. Pakistan proved a more reliable ally, joining the Baghdad Pact and SEATO, but it oscillated between military and democratic rule. Furthermore, the two countries fought wars over the control of Kashmir in 1948–49 and 1965, calling into doubt the unity of the multiracial 'New Commonwealth'.

Indian independence did much to reshape the Commonwealth after 1945, because it created the first non-white Dominion which, in contrast to earlier practice, wished to go beyond self-government to full independence and even become a Republic. After considerable study it led in 1949 to a radical new relationship between former Imperial possessions. There was to be no written constitution, no common citizenship, not even a common monarchy. Instead, George VI was titled 'Head of the Commonwealth' and the loose organisation did little more than hold regular meetings. How successfully it could survive, let alone grow in importance, was unclear even at the outset. The beginnings of apartheid in South Africa after 1948 and the rise in the Conservative Party of opposition to coloured immigration from the Commonwealth, showed the difficulties of maintaining a multiracial group of states and Bevin himself was sceptical about any structure which allowed Commonwealth states to pursue their own policies without reference to the ideal of 'diplomatic unity'. For critics the Commonwealth was too loose an organisation to have any importance. Made up of fully independent states with different races, religions, international interests and political systems it was far too disparate to act together. And, with Imperialism out of fashion, and fears that ex-colonial powers would try to maintain 'neo-colonialist' relationships, not all ex-colonies joined the Commonwealth. Burma, given independence in 1948 under politicians who had collaborated with the Japanese, was the first example, and Ireland took the opportunity in 1949 to become a Republic outside the Commonwealth. Yet for all its disunity and vagueness the 'New Commonwealth' was surrounded by a degree of idealism at first and most former Imperial territories *did* join. Its unwritten constitution and hopes of pragmatic growth were well suited to British constitutional experience, and its very lack of uniformity made it adaptable. Most importantly it gave the British the important psychological reassurance, as the supposed triumph of Indian independence had done, that they were not set upon a course of retreat but were evolving a new role, not 'surrendering' the Empire but seeing it metamorphose into a more modern, acceptable form of relationship. In the short term too it did have its practical aspects, most notably the formation of a 'Commonwealth Division' in Korea and the Colombo Plan for the development of southern Asia. Neither did the 'New Commonwealth' put an end to the Sterling Area under which most Commonwealth states continued to hold currency balances in London where they earned low interest and underpinned Britain's financial importance.

Whatever the ability of the British to emerge with self-respect from India, nothing could disguise the later evidence of unwelcome retreat from the Middle East. Attlee, in 1946, would have been prepared to withdraw from the region, trusting locals to resist Soviet expansion. With British forces overburdened, defence costs high and the nature of warfare changing due to the advent of missiles and nuclear weapons, the value of the Suez base was called into doubt. But the Middle East did have one obvious economic resource, oil, which Britain required in growing quantities, Bevin saw the region as vital to the defence of Communist-threatened Greece and the COS argued that air bases in Iraq could be used to launch nuclear attacks against the southern USSR. Perhaps just as important was the wartime habit of treating the Middle East as essential to British power. It was strategically placed between Europe, Asia and Africa and was one area where British predominance was maintained. Neither was there an early, widespread crisis of British domination here, as there had been after 1918. The British were even able to extend their influence for a time by occupying former Italian colonies in Libya and East Africa. However, Palestine did present Bevin with serious problems because the war, and its accompanying Holocaust, generated irresistible demands for increased Jewish immigration. Jewish settlers, no longer enamoured of British policy after the 1939 White Paper and its effective promise of an independent Arab-dominated Palestine, began a policy of terrorist attacks, starting with the murder in November 1944 of the local British representative, Lord Moyne. The US, with its strong Zionist lobby and ambitions of breaking British economic predominance in the region, favoured the creation of an 'Israeli' state. By late 1946 the need to deal with outrages like the bombing of the King David Hotel pushed the British garrison up to 100 000 men. Outside the FO and Arab world there was little sympathy for Palestinian Arabs and Bevin was unable to resist the implications of the Balfour Declaration and the US alliance, which pointed towards greater Jewish political rights. In February 1947, at the same time as its decisions to leave India and Greece, Attlee's Cabinet decided to put the future of the mandate in the hands of the UN. It was that body which decided in November, following the lines of the 1937 Peel Commission, to partition Palestine between Arab and Jew. But in contrast to India, where an announcement of British withdrawal had beneficial results and partition proved a workable, if imperfect solution, the Palestine example justified Churchill's accusation that Labour was set on a policy of 'scuttle'. Rather than a graceful exit, British forces left in May 1948 with violence breaking out all around them and bitter criticism from both Jews and Arabs. In the subsequent Arab–Israeli War (1948–49) almost all Palestine became part of the new Israeli state which looked to America as protector. The British-officered Arab legion kept East Jerusalem and the West Bank in Jordanian hands, and the British preserved military links to Jordan and Iraq, but the war led most Arab opinion to become anti-Western.

The nationalisation of the Anglo-Iranian Oil Company, in which the British government had a majority share, by the radical Mohammed Mossadeq in 1951 provided another humiliation for Labour. Although MI6 helped overthrow him two years later, the British monopoly of Iranian oil production was lost forever, with American companies taking a large share. The most important point in Britain's Middle Eastern position, however, was still Egypt and specifically the Suez base. In 1936 of course the British had secured control of Suez through a treaty with the Cairo government, which was at that time fearful of Italy. During the war, as in India, the British assumed close control of Egyptian agriculture, raw materials and labour, and 1942 proved a year of political crisis: in May British tanks surrounded the palace and forced King Fuad to appoint a Wafd Prime Minister, who might mobilise Egyptian resources effectively. But cooperation with the British, alongside the corruption of its leaders, damaged the nationalist credentials of the Wafd among the growing, educated middle classes in the towns, and led to the rise of the more extreme 'Movement for National Liberation', which included Communists, the Moslem Brotherhood and army officers. The British also upset the Egyptians by insisting on moving the Sudan towards independence in 1956: constitutionally the Sudan was an Anglo-Egyptian condominium and, despite unrest there in the late 1940s, the Egyptians could not believe the Sudanese wanted independence from Cairo as well as London. During the traumatic birth of Israel the Egyptians also became more determined to assert themselves as the leading Arab state. Thus the impact of war, the rise of the US and internal political developments combined in Egypt as elsewhere to put pressure on the British position. But in the Egyptian case they were particularly vulnerable because their presence never had a secure legal base, the 1936 treaty only held good until 1956 and, with the Italian threat removed, the Egyptians had no obvious reason to make concessions. The all-important Suez base relied on labour and water supplies from Egyptian territory. In 1951 the British hoped to 'internationalise' their presence in Egypt by creating a Middle East Command, supposedly to protect the region from Soviet expansion. It was hoped to persuade Australia, New Zealand and South Africa to help with the area's defence, as they had in the world wars, and even to win US approval for the scheme. But the Egyptians did not feel threatened by the USSR and were not to be persuaded by such a thinly disguised attempt to continue British influence. In 1952 the decrepit Egyptian monarchy was overthrown by the radical, nationalist 'Free Officers', first under General Neguib, then in 1954 under Colonel Nasser. They were even less likely to make concessions to London. Despite being accused by the 'Suez Group' of backbenchers and even Churchill of 'appeasement', Eden proved ready that year to agree to withdraw from the Suez base. From a weak negotiating position, the only concession he won was that it could be 'reactivated' by Britain if certain Middle Eastern states were attacked over the next seven years. It seemed possible to preserve Britain's Middle Eastern predominance by concentrating on other bases, in Libya, Cyprus or, more importantly, the 'northern tier' states of Turkey, Iran, Iraq and Pakistan who joined Britain in the Baghdad Pact in 1955. Of these only Iraq was an Arab state but its Royalist Prime Minister, Nuri el-Said, was a bitter rival of the radical Nasser for Arab leadership. Like the Middle East Command, the Baghdad Pact could be seen as an attempt to 'internationalise' Britain's Middle East presence, but it appeared anti-Egyptian as well as anti-Soviet. Not only did the moderate King Hussein of Jordan refuse to enter it but in January 1956 he sacked the British Commander of the Arab Legion, General Glubb. Even before the Suez crisis, therefore, the British position in the Middle East was being called into question.

The Suez crisis was sparked by an American decision to cut off financial aid to Nasser after he accepted arms purchases from the Eastern bloc. Nasser was bullying, erratic, eager to pose as the leader of the Arab world, but no Communist: rather, like India's premier, Jawarhal Nehru, he was a leader of the non-aligned movement who wished to define his own foreign policy without reference to the Cold War. He had wanted US help to finance a major development project, the Aswan dam, but the Americans were already losing patience with him and the CIA was involved in joint planning with the British to destabilise both his government and that in Syria. Having lost American money, Nasser rapidly found an alternative source of money by nationalising the Suez Canal, in which the British were the largest shareholders. Suez of course was long-recognised as a vital linchpin of global trade and communications. Having succeeded Churchill, and leading a party which had savaged Labour over its weakness before Mossadeq five years before, Eden could not accept this latest affront to British power. He believed deeply in Britain's Great Power status, drew ludicrous comparisons between Nasser's regional ambitions and those of Hitler, and felt it possible to act without American approval – even though Britain was badly placed to act militarily, since it now lacked any naval base between Malta and Aden. The post-war years had been marked by frequent Anglo-US differences in the Middle East not only because of business rivalries and the Israeli question but, more widely, because of American fears that British Imperialist behaviour could drive the Arabs into Soviet hands. (There was a contrast here with East Asia, where it was the British who feared that American extremism and bellicosity would lead the West to ruin. Periodic suggestions that America should agree to back Britain in the Middle East, if Britain automatically supported Washington in the Far East, came to nothing.)

Yet America had helped resolve the Iranian problem and, given both the origins of the Suez crisis in the Aswan decision and the involvement of the CIA in schemes to undermine Nasser, Eden may have expected that America would tolerate tough action. (A British-backed group of anti-Nasser conspirators was uncovered by the Egyptians in August.) After vain attempts to resolve the crisis by diplomatic means, Eden, who at least recognised that Britain could not act alone, found military allies in Israel and France: the Israelis, though not close to Britain, had tense relations with Egypt; the French were substantial shareholders in the Suez Canal and, faced by Arab nationalism in Algeria, hoped to give the movement a bloody nose in Egypt. Secret collusion between the three countries (publicly denied by Eden) led to an Israeli invasion of Egypt in October, which the British and French used as an excuse to launch an invasion of Egypt, supposedly to protect the Suez Canal. Few were fooled by such a ruse and the real intention was to topple Nasser – though who would replace him was not clear (another Egyptian nationalist would presumably have followed similar policies; and a Franco-British stooge could hardly have survived for long). The military operation was successful in occupying much of the canal, but slow in execution and in early November the British, to French consternation, insisted on a halt. At home there were demonstrations against the invasion, Labour was united in condemnation and even FO, military and intelligence officials tried to distance themselves from it. There was world-wide criticism and, within the Commonwealth, even Canada joined India and others in condemning the invasion. For the first time Britain was forced to use its veto power in the UN Security Council to protect itself. But the most important opposition came from the Eisenhower administration, which was also facing a presidential election and a crisis with the USSR, after an anti-Communist uprising in Hungary. The US saw the Suez operation as both an act of treachery – Washington was not forewarned of it – and a mistake, likely to offend the whole developing world and help Communist propaganda. The Secretary of State, John Foster Dulles, was openly critical of Britain and America brought pressure to bear on the Pound, the scale of which was exaggerated by Macmillan, now Chancellor of the Exchequer, who had been in favour of the invasion but also had ambitions of becoming premier. Despite Eden's unparalleled foreign policy experience, Suez became the worst post-war diplomatic blunder by any British government, seen in retrospect as a seminal moment in the decline from Great Power status. It would be wrong to draw too many conclusions from one, unique episode, however, and the implications of Suez are easily overstated. Nationalist pressures from within the Empire, Britain's lack of economic strength and reliance on the US were *already* apparent as forces driving the retreat from Empire – although 'at no stage up to ... Suez did *all* these relevant factors come together in a way that might cause Britain serious difficulty in its Imperial role'.[10] What Suez did show was Britain's inability to wield large-scale military power, even in cooperation with its ally of 1914 and 1939, France. The crisis also revealed that the Commonwealth would no longer automatically follow London's lead. Yet many Conservatives were unapologetic, never forgiving the junior FO minister Anthony Nutting, who resigned in protest over the invasion. Eden was made a scapegoat for the failure and, suffering renewed ill-health, resigned in January, to be succeeded by Macmillan who won the next election. Even in foreign policy 'the affair itself did not in the short term appear to have a major effect on the British government's strategy'.[11] Relations were patched up with the Commonwealth and America, and whilst the French, still smarting from the behaviour of 'perfidious Albion' during Suez, signed the Treaty of Rome in March 1957, Britain held aloof from the new European Economic Community. In the Middle East the British continued to support the Baghdad Pact, were as close as ever to Nuri el-Said and maintained their predominance in the oil-rich Persian Gulf. Only over the following decade did it become apparent that the 'three circles' approach had failed as a means to uphold British power and indeed overstretched it.

Notes

1 Barnett C., *The Audit of War* (London, 1986), 304.
2 Gamble A., *Britain in Decline* (London, 1994 edn), 38.
3 Pollard S., *Britain's Prime and Britain's Decline* (London, 1989), 271.
4 Kavanagh D. and Morris P., *Consensus Politics from Attlee to Major* (Oxford, 1994), 91.
5 Kennedy P., *The Realities Behind Diplomacy: Background Influences on British External Policy, 1865–1980* (London, 1985), 362.
6 Young J., *Britain and European Unity, 1945–92* (London, 1993), 15.
7 Earl of Kilmuir, *Political Adventure* (London, 1964), 193.
8 Bullock A., *Ernest Bevin: Foreign Secretary, 1945–56* (London, 1983), 352.
9 Owen N., 'War and Britain's Political Crisis in India'. In Brivati B. and Jones H. (eds), *What Difference did the War Make?* (London, 1993), 125.
10 Goldsworthy D., 'Aspects of Colonial Policy during the Churchill and Eden Governments', *Journal of Imperial and Commonwealth History*, **18**(1), 1990, 103.
11 Sanders D., *Losing an Empire, Finding a Role: British Foreign Policy Since 1945* (London, 1990), 101.

7
Without a role? 1957–1972

Policy-makers in an era of retreat

The years between the Suez crisis and entry to the European Economic Community (EEC) saw a continuing poor performance by the British economy, the rapid decline of the Sterling Area, the independence of almost all that remained of the formal Empire and deep uncertainty among political leaders about the country's place in the world. It was an American commentator, the former Secretary of State, Dean Acheson, who remarked in 1962 that 'Britain has lost an Empire and ... not yet found a role'. This was pithy but inaccurate – the Empire had not exactly been 'lost' and in the 'three circles' the British still had more than one role – and the leaders of both main parties were reluctant to agree with him. Yet if British politicians had an excuse for failing to appreciate the pace of their relative decline in the first post-war decade, there was less and less excuse thereafter. True, they did liquidate the formal Empire at a speed which is difficult to criticise; but, despite this, they failed to adjust the attitudes which accompanied greatness. In particular they still hoped to retain military and naval facilities world-wide and play a major role in the Cold War. Indeed, when Labour returned to office under Harold Wilson in October 1964, after 13 years in Opposition, there was hope of rekindling faith in the Commonwealth, renewed belief in development programmes for the third world, a determination to preserve a presence 'East of Suez' and strong reliance on the American alliance to prop up British power. In view of the Communist menace in Asia and the secure military balance in Europe, it even seemed logical in Labour's first defence review to limit Britain's commitment to NATO in order to remain in South-east Asia and the Persian Gulf. It took three years before it was accepted that this costly position could not be maintained. In 1965 Commonwealth disunity was exposed once more because of a second Indo-Pakistan conflict and the unilateral declaration of independence by a white supremacist state in Rhodesia. Such developments as the creation of a Commonwealth Secretariat (to plan meetings and policy statements) could not reverse the trend. The same year witnessed the escalation of the Vietnam War which led to Labour backbench criticism of America. Even if it had the trappings of a Great Power, such as its permanent seat on the Security Council, Britain simply lacked the resources to remain an effective world power with a global trading currency and a 'special relationship' with Washington. In 1957 the country still had about 17 per cent of world manufacturing exports (well ahead of Japan and France), the age of 'consumerism' had dawned and the economy was continuing to grow. It was possible to return Sterling to 'convertible' status (that is freely changeable into other currencies) for the first time since 1939 but this proved a mixed blessing. Convertibility helped boost the fortunes of the City as an investment centre, and by 1960 Britain had more overseas investment (about £10 million worth) than ever. Yet such success could not disguise the fact that British growth, which averaged about 2.5 per cent in two decades of global economic expansion after 1952, though comparable to the US, was well behind that of France (4.5 per cent), Germany (nearly 5 per cent), Italy (just over 5 per cent) and Japan (a remarkable 8 per cent). Already, in 1957, Germany was beginning to overhaul Britain once more in manufacturing output and trade; Japan followed in the 1960s and France about 1970 when Britain's share of world manufacturing exports fell to 10 per cent; and by the end of the 1970s British GDP was half Germany's and less than a half of Japan's though still (a fairly consistent figure since 1950) an eighth that of the US.

Even in the mid-1950s, when they decided against entering talks on the original EEC, ministers and officials were aware of the declining value of the Commonwealth trade preference system, as former colonies developed new trading partners. The Treasury and Board of Trade hoped that the US-led 'multilateral' (global, non-discriminatory) trade system – whose features had much in common with the Victorian dream of a world based on free trade – would be best for British profitability in future. But Britain continued to slip in comparison to its commercial competitors. The Macmillan government (1957-63) changed the tone of policy about 1960, when it decided to apply for EEC membership and adopted new policies for state planning of the economy. However the EEC bid failed and the economy remained troubled by balance of payments problems and the so-called 'stop–go' phenomenon in which periods of expansion resulted in higher imports, inflation and the selling of Sterling, forcing Chancellors of the Exchequer to deflate. Around 1960 these difficulties called into question the value of the Sterling Area, which was supposed to provide Britain with both prestige (as a global economic power) and a more stable environment for trade and finance. It was now much harder for London to act as banker to a currency zone with huge potential liabilities. 'Runs on the Pound' could emerge quite suddenly as periodic dips in the economy and certain global crises (such as the 1967 Middle East War), combined with currency speculation and increasing trade union militancy, led speculators to buy other currencies. The first line of defence was Britain's gold and currency reserves, but since these were seldom in a healthy state after the war it was usually necessary to put up interest rates or taxes. The Sterling Area was therefore both at the mercy of Britain's own economic weakness and a contributor to that weakness. It increased Britain's financial liabilities and prevented governments from pursuing monetary policies suited to Britain's own needs. Yet still those governments sought to preserve it. In 1964 Labour might have blamed the Conservatives for Britain's poor balance of payments and devalued the Pound immediately, but Prime Minister Harold Wilson had been involved in the 1949 devaluation and did not wish Labour to take the blame for such a step again. Determined to demonstrate both British resilience and his own party's ability to govern, he instead opted for an import surcharge, but such a step offended Britain's trading partners and only proved a palliative. The need to defend the Pound ruined Labour's attempts to introduce a proper Economic Plan, forced another bout of deflation in July 1966 (following a damaging seamen's strike), and ended in failure. In November 1967, despite US support, the Pound had to be devalued from $2.80 to $2.40. Thereafter, there was widespread currency upheaval in the West as the high growth rates of the 1950s and 1960s fell off, inflationary pressures mounted and the US, lodged in the Vietnam quagmire and far less dominant in the world economy than it had been in the 1940s, proved unable to prop up a stable currency system. Newly independent territories in Africa and the West Indies saw little need to trim their own economic policies to benefit Sterling and the early 1970s saw a move to the uncertain world of 'floating' exchange rates, with the Pound being floated in June 1972. Britain was not the only country in difficulties, but its growth and inflation rates in the late 1960s and early 1970s *were* still worse than those of Japan, Germany and France, and steps were now taken to dismantle the Sterling Area. The years 1967 to 1972 were ones of marked British retreat. They also saw the end of the presence East of Suez and a decision to concentrate British political energies in Europe. The value of holding on to the Sterling Area was clearly very doubtful by 1967 and the decision to enter the competitive European market was seen by the Heath government (1970–74) as the way to reinvigorate the British economy as a launching pad for recovery as a Great Power.

The vain defence of Sterling confirmed that attempts to play a world role without the necessary resources could damage the economy and, in turn, the world role itself. Similar problems plagued defence policy. In 1957 the White Paper issued by the Defence Secretary, Duncan Sandys, goaded by Macmillan, followed COS advice by putting greater reliance on nuclear deterrence over conventional arms. Despite criticism from NATO allies, this allowed a reduction in the British Army of the Rhine from 77 000 to 51 000 by 1963. More important for the public, it allowed an end to conscription in 1962. 'National Service' had been popular neither with those conscripted nor the military, who preferred to train professionals for long periods of service. The end of conscription theoretically gave Britain an advantage over its European neighbours, whose young men continued to be absorbed into military service rather than productive employment. But even if nuclear weapons were cheaper than conventional ones, the Sandys White Paper did not bring defence spending under control, and the armed forces continued to take a higher proportion of GDP (about 8 per cent in the late 1950s) than in other NATO countries, apart from America and Portugal. Whatever cuts were possible in the Rhine Army, the world role continued to demand a large navy and air force, as well as military garrisons, able to use a number of scattered bases, from Gibraltar to Simonstown (South Africa), and from Aden to Singapore. In 1965 there were still over 60 000 servicemen and 80 naval vessels East of Suez, supposedly maintaining order from which the whole of Western trade benefited. In Research and Development the British had considerable expertise and resources, but tried to do too much and continued to fall behind the Superpowers. The explosion of a British Hydrogen bomb in 1957 suggested that Britain was still a major player but the Conservatives were forced to abandon the Blue Streak missile, for delivering nuclear warheads, in 1960, when Britain's V-bomber force was already becoming obsolete. Both America and Russia had entered the 'space age' and now possessed intercontinental ballistic missiles. Britain had little choice, therefore, than to try to purchase such missiles from America, hence an initial decision to buy the Skybolt system and, in December 1962, when Skybolt was cancelled, the submarine-launched Polaris (which fell under Royal Navy control rather than that of the RAF). There was, perhaps, an alternative strategy of cooperation with France, which became the fourth atomic power in 1960, but cooperation with France was impossible if Britain wished to keep receiving American nuclear information. As military chiefs knew, Britain had become so reliant on the Americans that the concept of an 'independent nuclear deterrent' was nonsense, yet the government continued to use the term. Nuclear weapons gave an *appearance* of power and allowed the COS to influence American nuclear targeting policy, but they did not give Britain real freedom in the world and could only realistically be used in cooperation with America. The British asserted that they and America were 'interdependent', but actually London was in a *dependent* position. Similarly in the 1960s Britain became reliant on US spy satellites in the intelligence field and also on advanced conventional weaponry. In the 1965 White Paper, the Wilson government, under Treasury pressure, aimed to reduce defence spending below £2 billion a year by 1970 and hold it at that level – the first time since the 1930s that a specific limit had been put on such expenditure. Despite Wilson's own emphasis on the need for technological investment in the economy, the Paper included the scrapping of several British aircraft projects, notably the long range jet aircraft, TSR-2, to be replaced by the American F-111. It was the devaluation crisis of 1967 which finally forced the abandonment (announced in January 1968) of the presence East of Suez. The decision upset America, Malaysia, Singapore, Australia, New Zealand and the Gulf States but, despite the second thoughts of Edward Heath's Conservative government, was fulfilled by the end of 1971. In parallel with the continuing Imperial retreat Denis Healey was responsible, as Defence Secretary in 1964–70, for involving Britain in closer cooperation with other European countries on defence, notably in the 1969 'Eurogroup', a European pillar of NATO. NATO was important, not only for British defence, but also, after the 1967 Harmel Report, for pursuing a policy of *détente* with the USSR. By 1972, with their much reduced role, if not reduced ambition, the British had cut defence spending below 6 per cent of GDP, or 11 per cent of government spending. Not that this eased the tax burden: expenditure on both social security and education had outstripped defence and standard income tax rose to over 30 per cent of personal income.

If Britain's position as a trading power and global military power was in decline, this was not necessarily true of its diplomatic importance. It has already been seen that diplomatic reputation and skill can, at least for a time, counter the impact of declining economic power and limited military might. British standing in the world *did* suffer because of the Suez failure, but its position as the world's third nuclear power and third trading nation at the end of the 1950s still counted for much, it retained a permanent seat in the UN Security Council, was the leader of the Commonwealth and had a role in numerous other international organisations, which had grown in importance since 1945 in the management of international affairs, creating a world of institutions. These organisations included various bodies created by the UN – such as the UN Educational, Scientific and Cultural Organisation (UNESCO) and the UN International Children's Emergency Fund (UNICEF) – NATO, the Council of Europe and, in the economic field, the General Agreement on Tariffs and Trade (GATT), the International Monetary Fund (IMF) and the Organisation for European Economic Cooperation (OEEC) (which in 1960, when it was joined by America and Canada became the Organisation of Economic Cooperation and Development, or OECD). Neither did a relative decline against its leading competitors mean a reduced workload for the Foreign Office. With modern communications and an increasing number of independent states, the volume of telegrams handled by the Office more than tripled between 1957 and 1972. Policy management had to continue adapting in an age marked by swifter news reporting and rise of television. There were a number of important developments in the FO in 1964 including: the creation of a small, new Planning Staff; the beginning of daily, morning meetings between senior officials in the office of the Permanent Under-Secretary; and the Plowden Report, which recognised the need for a substantial diplomatic service, with high morale, to reinforce British influence in the world, and proposed the merger of the FO and Commonwealth Relations Office (CRO). Such a merger was achieved, creating the Foreign and Commonwealth Office (FCO), in October 1968 and reducing the costs of overseas representation. Two years earlier the Colonial Office had been absorbed into the CRO, an important bureaucratic reflection of the end of Empire. The same phenomenon seems to have influenced the next report on FO activities, that by Sir Val Duncan made in 1969, after the decision to withdraw from East of Suez. The report had its positive aspects, recommending for example that the News Department be strengthened in order to influence foreign media opinion and it put greater emphasis on trade promotion as a function of diplomacy – in contrast to FO attitudes earlier in the century. But overall, under Treasury pressures, Duncan urged further savings, with a concentration of diplomatic efforts on such 'core' areas as Western Europe and North America. Logical as this seemed, it harmed British interests over the following decades in other important regions like the Middle East and East Asia.

Elsewhere in Whitehall, April 1964 had finally seen the creation of a fully integrated Ministry of Defence (with a single Defence Intelligence Staff), ending the system of separate service ministries, though not the rivalries between the armed forces. An independent Chairman of the COS had first been appointed in 1955, being known after July 1958 as the Chief of Defence Staff, but individual chiefs still had right of access to the Minister of Defence and even the Prime Minister. One potential threat to the FCO's control of foreign policy was the creation by the Wilson government of a separate Overseas Development Administration, but this was never well-resourced and Heath placed it under FCO control in 1970. The Treasury faced a more serious threat to *its* power after 1964, in the form of the Department of Economic Affairs which was designed to break the policies of limited spending, piecemeal economic planning and concentration on the defence of Sterling which, it was felt, had inhibited British growth. The new Department, initially under the dynamic deputy Labour leader, George Brown, was also keenly in favour of EEC membership. But in 1969, its efforts at economic planning in turmoil, it ceased to exist and the Treasury, more pragmatic in its European views, reasserted itself. The early 1960s were particularly difficult years for the intelligence services with George Blake of MI6 being revealed as a spy, the exposure of the British agent Oleg Penkowsky in Moscow and the confusion caused by the 1963 Profumo Scandal. Relations between Labour and MI5 were evidently difficult, with some MI5 officers even holding absurd suspicions that Harold Wilson was a Soviet 'mole'. Wilson in fact strengthened the coordination of intelligence in 1968 with the creation of a Joint Intelligence Organisation in the Cabinet Office, to look at *all* information (not just secret intelligence) reaching the government and prepare reports for the JIC. And British counter-intelligence work received a boost to morale in September 1971 with Foreign Secretary Douglas-Home's brave decision to expel over one hundred Soviet officials, who were known to have intelligence links. One of the most important, overdue and lasting reforms of this period, however, was at the top, where Churchill's increasingly inadequate creation, the Defence Committee, was replaced by a Defence and Overseas Policy Committee, still under the chairmanship of the Prime Minister but meeting about once per week and reviewing most major issues in the area of external policy.

Prime ministers, the American alliance and East-West *détente*

The position of the Prime Minister, supported by the Downing Street staff, remained a most important factor in foreign policy making. Macmillan and Wilson were determined to play a leading role on the world stage, ideally in close alliance with Washington, in a period which saw an ever-increasing number of bilateral and multilateral 'summit' meetings. Summits were more convenient thanks to jet transport; they allowed prime ministers to emphasise their importance, bask in media attention and resolve problems at the highest level; but such familiarity between leaders caused concern among diplomats who found themselves sidelined and were concerned that their leaders might be insufficiently expert on certain matters or liable to conclude unwise agreements for the sake of appearing successful. Despite the Suez blow, Macmillan sought to resolve 'the problem of being poor and powerful at the same time'[1] by avoiding further bellicosity and staying close to America, whilst continuing to play the rcle of a Great Power. He quickly rebuilt relations with Eisenhower at Bermuda in March 1957 (despite the doubts of the

'Suez Group'), preserved the nuclear arsenal (not only as a deterrent but also as a source of prestige and a link to America) and continued the Churchillian policy of fostering *détente*, with a visit to Moscow in February 1959. He also had high hopes of making the Commonwealth more effective and was, indeed, determined to maintain the 'three circles' policy in full: concentration on any one circle, it was feared, would harm British links with the others. The Conservatives rallied to him, respecting both his patriotism and his reputation for 'unflappability' and, helped by the continuation of economic growth, he won a healthy majority in the 1959 election, after which he became more innovative in his policies. Not only did he adopt greater government intervention at home, but he redoubled his efforts to secure a summit of the major powers, quickened the pace of decolonisation in Africa and pushed the government towards the first negotiations for EEC membership in 1961. He also did much to achieve the 1963 Test Ban Treaty with America and Russia, which helped neutralise the Campaign for Nuclear Disarmament, a middle-class pressure group formed by Socialists and humanists in 1958. Yet Macmillan was an improviser and pragmatist, much less self-confident than he appeared and slow to tackle the twin challenges of modernisation at home or reduced commitments abroad which he only partially recognised to exist. His welfare spending and toleration of inflation worried some Conservatives. The East–West Summit meeting, which he had done so much to organise, collapsed in failure in Paris in May 1960, after the Soviets shot down a US spy-plane, and there were signs that Britain might not have many more chances to sit at the top table. Already, in 1959, Eisenhower and Khrushchev had met, face-to-face, at Camp David in America without the need for a British mediator, and 1961 saw another US–Soviet summit in Vienna. Macmillan's own efforts at *détente* were criticised in NATO especially because he chose to visit Khrushchev only three months after the latter had threatened to drive the Western powers from Berlin. The German leader, Konrad Adenauer, whose own country's economic and military might were recovering apace, was especially concerned at London's tendency to 'appease' the USSR and considered Britain to be 'like a rich man who had lost all his property but does not realise it'.[2] The Test Ban Treaty, with its prohibition of nuclear tests underwater and in the atmosphere, was valuable as an environmental measure – an area of growing international concern – as well as for *détente*. But Macmillan only pursued it vigorously after Britain had carried out its own H-bomb tests *and* after the 1962 Cuban Missile Crisis, which showed his limited influence during a frightening Superpower crisis. It was in America's interests to foster 'special relations' with Britain in areas where the British could prop up Western positions (in Western Europe or Malaya for example), but Cuba was too vital to

Washington, too peripheral to London, for the US to listen to British views. As to the government's decolonisation policies, they ought more properly to be identified with the Colonial Secretary, Iain Macleod. And the EEC application (discussed more fully below) was hedged round with conditions, proceeded only slowly and ended in failure at the hands of French President Charles de Gaulle in January 1963, after which the days of Macmillan's premiership were numbered.

Macmillan deserves praise for recognising, before many in his party, the 'wind of change' sweeping Africa towards independence under black majority rule and for seeing EEC membership, not as a retreat, but as a way to boost the British economy in a more competitive (yet also 'interdependent') environment, win greater influence in Europe and counter the growing tendency of US officials to deal with the EEC rather than Britain as their main transatlantic partner. Yet Macmillan continued to act as though Britain were a major global player and relied on personal dealings with fellow leaders to secure his aims. The FO was rather better in understanding the implications of Suez: the Office 'had adapted to [the] new climate by adopting a more measured and realistic attitude ... However, for the politician, driven by ambition and reputation, it was important to keep the myth of British power and influence alive.'[3] During the EEC negotiations Macmillan, from his lofty position, took little interest in day-to-day dealings and concentrated on personal meetings with de Gaulle and Adenauer to win the elusive breakthrough; his *détente* policy proposed little concrete other than a summit meeting; and in his dealings with America he relied heavily on personal links with his old wartime colleague, Eisenhower, and the succeeding President, John Kennedy, with whom warm relations proved possible despite a 27-year age difference. Macmillan was not the only Prime Minister to rely on personal friendships and such a policy brought successes, including Eisenhower's willingness to increase nuclear cooperation in 1958 and Kennedy's readiness, against the wishes of some of his advisers, to supply Polaris at the Nassau Summit of December 1962. Being seen in close friendship with US presidents also helped disguise the fact that the Empire was ebbing away and Britain was excluded from the EEC. But such personal links could offend other European leaders, most notably de Gaulle who was determined to distance France from American domination; they carried a certain price (Macmillan supported the deployment of US nuclear missiles in Britain in 1957 and the presence of US Polaris submarines at Holy Loch in Scotland); and they could not be institutionalised in the long term. Indeed, once Kennedy was assassinated and Macmillan had resigned, Anglo-American relations rapidly worsened, especially after the new premier, Douglas-Home, upset the abrasive Lyndon Johnson by publicly insisting on Britain's right to trade with Fidel

Castro's Cuba. Macmillan, then, was quite capable of coming to terms with the inevitable, but not necessarily with anticipating it quickly enough. And ultimately he was unable to escape the implications of his own carefully nurtured image of detached grandeur.

Harold Wilson was a rather less grand, but no less pragmatic, manipulative and determined individual who also recognised, albeit imperfectly, the need to modernise at home and reduce commitments abroad, and who hoped to remain, somehow, a special ally of Washington and a leader of world importance. He even declared in 1965 that Britain's borders lay on the Himalayas, a claim made hollow when the Soviets, rather than Britain, succeeded in resolving Indo-Pakistan differences after their recent war. Just as Macmillan had kept the competent but uncharismatic Selwyn Lloyd as Foreign Secretary in the late 1950s, so Wilson preferred to appoint foreign ministers, like Patrick Gordon-Walker (1964–65) and Michael Stewart (1965–66 and 1968–70), who could run the FO efficiently but would not steal the limelight from Downing Street. He had more trouble, in 1966–68, with the colourful, outspoken and frequently drunken George Brown, who eventually resigned over the failure of the Prime Minister to consult him sufficiently. When Labour came into office it was supposedly committed not only to decolonisation, but also the abandonment of the nuclear deterrent, and such other idealistic steps as a ban on arms to South Africa. But power-politics and commercial self-interest soon took hold: within months decisions were taken to maintain Polaris and fulfil a South African order for Buccaneer war planes. As seen above, although Labour's faith in the potential of the Commonwealth soon receded, it was not until 1967 that the Wilson Cabinet accepted devaluation, withdrawal from bases East of Suez and the belief that Britain must enter the EEC if it were to remain a major power. Indeed, when de Gaulle vetoed another, hasty bid to 'enter Europe', the British decided to leave the application 'on the table' in the expectation it would be taken up in future. Wilson's first visit to Washington as Prime Minister, in December 1964, was quite successful for even in decline Britain's Imperial heritage had its uses for Washington. In British Guiana, for example, a joint Anglo-American intelligence effort kept the leftist Cheddi Jagan out of office after independence, and in the Indian Ocean the British provided America with a military base on the island of Diego Garcia. Nonetheless, as time went on Wilson's value to the President became less. Faced by public doubts and overstretched elsewhere, Labour would not send even a token force to fight alongside the Americans in Vietnam. This upset Johnson, who had to make do with the fact that Wilson, despite the anti-Americanism of the Labour Left, avoided criticism of US policy. Wilson also pointed out that Britain was helping the cause of stability in South-east Asia by maintaining tens of thousands of troops in Malaysia, which was threatened with attack by the radical government of Ahmed Sukarno of Indonesia. But the overthrow of Sukarno by the CIA in 1965 and withdrawal from East of Suez meant that Britain was no longer the peace-keeper for the West in the Indian Ocean and Persian Gulf. 'The whittling down of overseas commitments saved money. But it also had the effect of weakening Wilson's hand in Washington.'[4] The Americans, who had tried to dissuade London from taking the East of Suez decision, feared they would now have to take over British positions in these regions, as they already had in the Eastern Mediterranean (with the Truman Doctrine) and in the Middle East (with the Eisenhower Doctrine of 1957). Thus, Richard Nixon, who succeeded Johnson as President, played a forthright role during the next Indo-Pakistani War in 1971, and to fill the power vacuum in the Persian Gulf the Americans began the fateful policy of strengthening Iran as a regional policeman. Meanwhile in NATO, Germany had arguably become a more valuable ally than Britain for the US by 1969, with larger armed forces, a leading role in the EEC and a position on the front line against the Soviets. Wilson did try, like Macmillan, to act as a mediator between East and West, most notably with his efforts in early 1967, during meetings with Soviet premier Alexei Kosygin, to broker a ceasefire deal in Vietnam. But by then de Gaulle, better able to distance himself from Washington, had become the chief European exponent of *détente*. In contrast Britain, however poor the relations between Wilson and Johnson became, still cooperated closely with America in the intelligence, atomic, monetary and commercial fields. For such reasons Wilson was never trusted by the North Vietnamese as a peace-maker, or for that matter by de Gaulle. Despite a host of disappointments, Wilson survived in office until 1970. He still tried to keep up the appearance of a 'special relationship', inviting Nixon to a showpiece Cabinet meeting in 1969, and Britain continued to show signs of its Imperial mission, controversially supporting the Nigerian government against the Biafra secession (1967–72) and, in a somewhat farcical manner, 'invading' the tiny West Indies island of Anguilla in March 1969 after it declared independence from the former colony of St Kitts and Nevis. But in the June 1970 election Labour, Conservatives and Liberals all agreed that EEC membership was the best option for Britain's economic and international future.

Wilson unexpectedly lost the 1970 campaign to his uninspiring opponent, Heath, who in many ways stands out from post-war premiers in his foreign policy outlook. Where others were only in favour of EEC membership for pragmatic reasons, Heath embraced it with enthusiasm. Although he accepted increased Western contacts with the Soviets in 1971–72, including conventional arms reduction talks and recognition of

East Germany, he appeared more interested in improved relations with Communist China, which had now fallen out with the Soviets. And rather than flying to Washington at the first opportunity, Heath refused to use the term 'special relationship'. 'The intimate access to the President which prime ministers had enjoyed was reduced to formal diplomatic exchanges.'[5] It was not that he was anti-American in any way. Far from it. He recognised the need for the US alliance and his loyalty to NATO was unquestioned, as was that of his Foreign Secretary, the ex-premier Douglas-Home. Nor did Heath abandon all ambitions of being a major world player. He reluctantly confirmed the withdrawal from East of Suez but signed a five-power defence pact with Malaysia, Singapore, Australia and New Zealand to emphasise Britain's interest in South-east Asia after the Singapore base was closed in October 1971. But he believed that the way to strengthen Britain's role in the world and restore her economic competitiveness was to join the successful EEC group, he saw that the relationship with America had become normal rather than 'special', and he was less eager than Macmillan or Wilson to compensate for failings at home by cutting a dynamic figure abroad. It should also be noted that problems in the Anglo-American relationship were not one sided: Heath was as shocked as other Western leaders when, in August 1971, America abruptly ended the Bretton Woods monetary system and put a hefty surcharge on imports. Apart from EEC entry, he was ready to leave day-to-day foreign policy to Douglas-Home and had plenty of problems to tackle at home, with increased inflation, widespread strikes and mounting violence between the Protestant and Roman Catholic communities in Northern Ireland. There was even talk of Britain becoming 'ungovernable' and, with the rise of nationalist parties in Scotland and Wales, some fear that the end of overseas Empire might be followed by the break-up of Britain itself. Certainly the Northern Ireland situation could be interpreted as Britain's last great Imperial problem; and the loss of the colonies and continued economic underperformance also suggested to Scottish Nationalists that their country would fare better as an independent unit. Yet such problems are easily exaggerated. The early 1970s were years of stagnant growth and high inflation throughout the West, other European countries had local secessionist movements (Spain in the Basque country, France in Corsica), many too were blighted by terrorism. The extent of intermarriage, economic ties and social cohesion between England and Scotland was greater than it had been with Ireland. Certainly the Heath government did not face as difficult a situation as, say, Italy, with double-digit inflation, a rapid turnover of government and incessant strikes combined with the terrorism of the Red Brigades and criminal activities of the Mafia. Then again, Britain's experience of 'stagflation' and strikes *was* worse than France or Germany. For Heath salvation was supposed to come from across the Channel and on 22 January 1972, in his most significant achievement as Prime Minister, he signed the treaty which would carry Britain into Europe the following year. At the same time, beyond the control of any individual, the signs of British retreat from the wider world went on. As part of the agreement with France's Georges Pompidou on EEC entry, Heath promised to continue running down Sterling's role as a reserve currency. There was now no question of Britain attending the trio of summits held between Nixon and Soviet leader Leonid Brezhnev in 1972–74. And along the old Imperial lifeline through the Mediterranean and Red Sea, the last vestiges of power were disappearing: Prime Minister Dom Mintoff asked British forces to leave Malta in December 1971; in Libya in 1972 Colonel Muhamur Gadaffi (who had overthrown the monarchy) tore up his country's defence treaty with Britain; and Somalia, formed from British and Italian Somaliland, had become a Soviet ally in 1969.

The end of Empire in Africa

It has been seen that the process of decolonisation was a fitful rather than gradual affair. Despite the withdrawal from India and Burma in 1947–48, plans were only made for the independence of a handful of colonies during the next decade, one of which was another reasonably wealthy and advanced Asian possession, Malaya. Liberal sentiment, US criticism and periodic disturbances had failed to bring the Empire crashing down and Britain was still a major power in the Persian Gulf and South-east Asia in 1957. The independence of the Sudan the previous year had more to do with the loss of Britain's hold on Egypt than with the experience of the African Empire: in Black Africa the preparation of Nkrumah's Ghana for independence in 1957 was seen as a unique experiment and in most of the African colonies (as well as in the West Indies) the Colonial Office still expected that British rule could last decades. Many of the public still associated the Empire inextricably with British greatness; trade with the Empire-Commonwealth, though declining as a proportion of the whole, was still substantial, falling from 40 per cent in 1957 to 25 per cent in 1972; and most of the African colonies, though poor, were not troublesome. The main exception was Kenya with its 'Mau-Mau' movement. Surprisingly the Suez crisis, with all its supposed lessons, does not seem to have quickened the pace of withdrawal or ended the belief that Britain must keep order in the world for the sake of its commercial and financial wealth. Macmillan was evidently concerned about the burden of the colonies, many of which presented few opportunities for trade or investment and lacked any strategic use. But initially he had to concentrate on winning the 1959 election, a task which would not be helped by further evidence of national retreat. Even in the Middle East Macmillan, a hawk over Suez, had hopes of rebuilding British influence in cooperation with moderate, pro-Western states like Iraq and Jordan, and against Nasser. In July 1958, however, the Iraqi monarchy was brutally overthrown, after which Iraq joined Egypt and Syria in the radical Arab camp. The loss of its major local ally was a blow to Britain's position, as significant in Middle Eastern terms as the Suez crisis, and it effectively ended any chance of London pursuing a major role in the region, yet Macmillan quickly accepted the new reality. A joint Anglo-American operation helped prevent such radicalism spreading and did something to assuage British bitterness over US attitudes towards Suez: British paratroops flew to Jordan to protect the young King Hussein and a larger force of US marines landed in Lebanon. But after this, British activity was largely concentrated in the Persian Gulf where, in 1960, London sent reinforcements to Kuwait to deter an Iraqi invasion before granting the protectorate full independence. Together, the operations in Jordan and Kuwait showed that Britain, whilst taking care to act in unison with America, was willing to use armed force in limited circumstances. But coercion was no longer to be used to retain Imperial positions in the face of strong local sentiment and after the 1959 election Colonial Secretary Macleod initiated a swift and determined policy of decolonisation, especially in Africa, the exact motivation for which is still debated. Macleod himself, with his lower-class background, liberal opinions and lack of obsession with international power, undoubtedly had some importance but his policy had already been advocated by others in the Colonial Office and Commonwealth Relations Office. Liberal opinion was concerned about the dangers of becoming oppressive in order to retain the Empire. The murder of several Mau-Mau inmates at the Hola prison camp in Kenya and the discovery, after riots in the capital Blantyre in 1959, that Nyasaland (now Malawi) was run as a virtual police state by its white rulers, may have prompted Macmillan's government both to abandon earlier efforts to prop up white supremacy in these colonies and to move them rapidly to self-rule within their existing borders, rather than in federations. But the decolonisation movement under Macleod was much more widespread than Kenya and Nyasaland, and may have been influenced by changes in other European Empires. In Paris, the Fourth Republic was brought down in 1958 by the Algerian colonial war and the new President, de Gaulle, was quick to promise independence to France's sub-Saharan possessions. In the Congo, abandoned with unseemly haste by Belgium in 1960, the dangers of tribal divisions, anarchy and external (including Soviet) intervention were plain for all to see. The British, pragmatic as ever, and keen (as in India in 1947) to retain the initiative, decided to bend willingly before the 'wind of change' – whilst not emulating the Belgians' haste. Certainly nationalist pressure from the colonial peoples does not seem to have been the prime reason for decolonisation at this time. Educated, middle-class nationalist leaders there certainly were, but their power in many colonies was limited and sometimes even they saw the speed of British departure as too swift.

What may have been more important was the need to stand close to America and resist Soviet Communism: 'The Africa official committee [with representatives from several departments] argued ... that withdrawal from dependent territories would be the way to ensure a pro-Western or politically neutral Africa',[6] and the Commonwealth Relations Office was keen to see a coherent British external policy across the board, based on the Western alliance and prosecution of the Cold War. It has also been argued that, for Macmillan, 'the process of shedding the Empire was an attempt to swap dwindling tangible assets for increased intangibles':[7] the African colonies had little commercial or economic value, but by departing gracefully, before strong nationalist movements emerged, Macmillan would win prestige, keep them well-disposed to Britain and improve the chances of Commonwealth unity in future. To have held on would have involved expenditure on development programmes and an increasing danger of colonial wars. In retrospect the Conservatives can be said to have retreated from Africa with as good grace as Labour quit India. Yet whilst there were few disasters in the process, it was not an untroubled one, and whilst the British public proved surprisingly quiescent about withdrawal from Empire, not all Conservative backbenchers were as understanding. Some dubbed the day of Macmillan's wind of change speech 'Black Monday' and formed the Monday Club to promote right-wing causes in future. Such MPs disliked both the retreat itself and the fact that white settlers were now expected to live under black majority rule. There was naturally a strong affinity between British people and their relatives who had settled, some very recently, in Kenya, Rhodesia and South Africa, and Conservatives were less than universal either in welcoming a multiracial Commonwealth or in condemning the apartheid regime in South Africa, which left the Commonwealth in 1961 after the widely condemned massacre of black demonstrators at Sharpeville. There were particular difficulties with the Central African Federation of Southern Rhodesia (now Zimbabwe), Northern Rhodesia (Zambia) and Nyasaland. The federation, first suggested in 1939, had come into being in 1953 but, whatever the economic logic of its creation, the black majority disliked its domination by white settlers who were concentrated in Southern Rhodesia. Serious public questioning of the federation began in Britain with the Blantyre riots, which were followed by the Devlin Mission to investigate local conditions in Nyasaland. The local nationalist leader, Hastings Banda, was first imprisoned but then, soon after Macmillan's wind of change speech in 1960, released. Backbench criticism of Macleod over this helped bring his replacement at the Colonial Office in 1961 but the federation was nonetheless dissolved in 1963. Nyasaland and Northern Rhodesia then became independent, but in Southern Rhodesia (soon simply referred to as Rhodesia) the white settlers, a minority even in their own country, began to consider a unilateral declaration of independence from Britain without granting democratic rights. (The 50 000 white settlers in Kenya, in contrast, made do with certain guarantees of their land holdings.) By the end of 1964 almost all Britain's African colonies and some of the West Indies had become independent. So too had Malta and Cyprus, though both retained British bases, for a short time in the first case, into the twenty-first century in the second. Cypriot independence proved particularly difficult to achieve partly because until the mid-1950s British leaders insisted they would 'never' leave such a vital base, but also because of local differences between Greek and Turkish inhabitants. The Greek majority led by their Archbishop, Makarios III, were keen not only to win independence but also to achieve '*enosis*', or union with Greece, and their more extreme members joined the terrorist organisation, EOKA. But Britain had obtained Cyprus in 1878 from Turkey, which was now a member of NATO and the Baghdad Pact, and Turkish Cypriots, amounting to a fifth of the local population, had been favoured with positions in the British colonial administration and police force. Tortuous negotiations were needed before fortuitous circumstances in 1959–60 allowed the Greeks and Turks to agree on independence as a single state, without *enosis*. But by 1963 this settlement had begun to break down into intercommunal violence and in 1974 the island was divided between the two communities. Britain, though a guarantor of the 1960 agreement, chose not to intervene. There was violence too in Kenya, Uganda and Tanganyika in January 1964, when British troops intervened, at the request of local leaders, to put down army rebellions. Thereafter, however, the British avoided conventional intervention in their former African colonies, preferring to concentrate on covert means of assistance via MI6.

Between 1964 and the end of 1968 the Labour government granted independence to all the rest of Africa except Rhodesia, as well as to Aden, the Indian Ocean colony of Mauritius, and most of the West Indies (though a few remaining possessions there did not receive independence until the 1970s). There was some disappointment with the instability of the newly independent African states, many of which fell to military rulers and few of which retained genuine democratic institutions. Economic problems, tribal differences and political inexperience brought down even Nkrumah's model government and suggested that there *had* been inadequate preparation for independence. Given the anti-Imperialist, anti-Western atmosphere of post-independence Africa, the British government was wise not to criticise its former charges too much, however, especially if Wilson wished to rekindle faith in the Commonwealth. But one problem which the Prime Minister could not escape was Rhodesia, where a hard-liner, Ian Smith, had been elected Prime Minister in April 1964 by the colony's white electorate. Despite the Labour government's readiness to compromise on some of the details, its overall insistence on the formula 'No independence before black majority rule' was unacceptable to the ruling 'Rhodesia Front'. Smith, as long expected, unilaterally declared independence in November 1965 and there was considerable pressure on Wilson from black African leaders for Britain to intervene with force. But Labour had no desire to fight a costly war, far away in Africa, many British people were sympathetic to Smith, and Rhodesia was protected by its position adjacent to South Africa and the Portuguese colony of Mozambique. Wilson preferred to use economic sanctions and, backed by the US and a UN Resolution, promised to bring Smith down in 'weeks not months'.[8] Sanctions were criticised by some Conservatives, barely satisfied black Commonwealth leaders, and failed to work. In long talks, aboard HMS *Tiger* in 1966 and on HMS *Fearless* in 1968, Smith refused to give way. South Africa and Portugal helped breach the sanctions policy and Smith's regime faced no great difficulties until a left-wing coup in Portugal in 1974 led to Mozambique becoming independent under a pro-Soviet government. To Labour's dismay, Rhodesia, along with South African apartheid, the Indo-Pakistani wars and increased restrictions on Commonwealth immigration into Britain, kept the Commonwealth divided throughout the 1960s and into the 1970s. Edward Heath, however, in another contrast to his predecessor, never showed much faith in the increasingly divided organisation, whose leaders now included military dictators and mass murderers. At the 1971 leaders' conference in Singapore – the first held outside London – the Commonwealth was described vaguely as a 'voluntary association' of equal states and most time was spent by African members in criticising Heath and Home for their decision to resume new arms sales to South Africa.

Wilson and Heath also experienced Imperial problems beyond Africa, especially with the East of Suez policy, first in maintaining it, then in its abandonment. In 1964 of course, despite African decolonisation, a presence in the Persian Gulf and Indian Ocean still made sense to British leaders, a fact which confirms yet again the fitful, reticent manner of Imperial retreat. These regions were important for Western trade and investments, as well as (in the Gulf's case) for oil, and with the Americans committed elsewhere it seemed essential for Britain to continue 'policing' them. Yet even in 1964 there were signs of serious difficulties. The worst problems were in Aden, strategically placed on the southern coast of Arabia, at the juncture of the Red Sea and Indian Ocean, which the

COS saw as the natural location for a military base after Suez. Aden itself was a well-populated urban centre, where strong Arab nationalist feeling, sympathetic to Nasser, was already apparent among the young skilled workers of the port. Yet after 1959 the British not only tried to repress such feeling but also sought to unite Aden Colony with the much less developed, anarchic hinterland, where numerous petty sheikhdoms vied for power. The British hoped that the traditional, feudal elements in the proposed South Arabian Federation, which came into being in 1963, would control the radicals. Instead the sheikhs persisted in bickering among themselves and Aden itself became a centre of pro-Nasser terrorist activity. By 1966 the British had effectively lost control of the situation, as they had earlier in Palestine, and were forced to promise Aden its independence in two years' time. Ultimately they lost the base, alienated Arab opinion once more and, uniquely in the history of decolonisation, had to hand power directly to a Marxist regime. Fortunately things were not quite so difficult elsewhere. In 1965 another British-created federation, Malaysia, faced crisis when its wealthiest component, the mainly Chinese city of Singapore, declared its independence under the formidable Lee Kwan Yew, but both states went on to become stable and wealthy. The desperate efforts which the British made to prevent Lee's secession may have convinced him that they would indeed remain East of Suez for decades. Instead of course they announced their departure within a few years. Heath's five-power pact with Malaysia, Singapore, Australia and New Zealand was only partial compensation and, with war still raging in Vietnam, no one could be quite certain that, with the British gone, the rest of South-east Asia would remain untroubled. Also offended by the East of Suez announcement were the sheikhs of the Persian Gulf. 'Withdrawal from the Gulf was determined ... by Treasury calculations and a fading of the imperial will in Westminster'[9] and there was little attempt to assuage the feelings of local rulers who wanted Britain to stay and had been assured it would. For Labour the Gulf sheikhdoms were something of a political embarrassment in any case: Britain had only ever had rights over their defence and foreign policies, not their autocratic methods of internal rule. The sheikhs were further upset when Heath confirmed the East of Suez decision, after earlier promising to reverse it. He of course had decided that Britain's route back to greatness lay, not in the Middle East, where so many hopes had been buried since Bevin's day, but in Europe.

The road to Europe

Between about 1960 and 1972 EEC membership rapidly emerged as *the* major external concern of the British public. Even in 1961, when

Macmillan made the first application for membership, one opinion poll showed that most Britons either did not know what the EEC was or thought Britain was a member! Until then European integration had only excited the interest of Whitehall departments, a few politicians and the business community. But by 1972 the issue inspired strong popular opinions and, unusually for an international issue, divided the Labour and Conservative front benches, with Heath making it a centrepiece of his programme but Wilson critical of the terms of entry the Conservatives negotiated. Many businessmen, represented in the Confederation of British Industry, were in favour of joining the 'common market', which now seemed to hold greater promise for trade and investment than the Commonwealth, but the National Farmers' Union feared the impact on farmers of the EEC's agricultural policies and most trades unions saw the EEC as an exploitative, capitalist club. Among the Press, the *Guardian* and *The Economist* supported entry from as early as 1960 but Lord Beaverbrook's *Express* newspapers, long time propagandists for the Empire, were determinedly opposed. Whatever the strength of opposition to the EEC, the accepted wisdom about British post-war policy towards Europe is that the country 'missed the bus': if only Bevin in 1950, or Eden in 1955, had joined in the early attempts at integration, it is argued, Britain could have made itself the leader of the EEC and shaped its policies from the outset; instead it was left trailing in the wake of France and Germany, and was forced to accept the costly, inefficient Common Agricultural Policy. In fact Bevin had tried to take the lead in Europe through such intergovernmental organisations as the OEEC and Brussels Pact. But the group of states known as 'the Six' (France, Germany, Italy, Belgium, Holland and Luxembourg) was *not* ready to accept British leadership on these terms. The French especially, after three German invasions in living memory, were anxious to form supranational institutions, involving a pooling of sovereignty, in order to control Germany within a European framework. This basic idea had already inspired the 1929 Briand Plan and led in 1950 to the Schuman Plan, bringing the iron and steel industries of the Six under a single 'High Authority'. The new liberal West German government under the anti-authoritarian Adenauer was ready to enter the Schuman Plan because it offered an opportunity for reconciliation with France, anchoring the new Germany in a democratic group of states and giving Germans a European idealism to replace the old nationalism and militarism. Post-Fascist Italy also saw European integration as a way to rehabilitate itself in the world, whilst Belgium and Holland could hope to gain from freer access to the German and French markets. Britain, in contrast, still did half its trade with the Empire-Commonwealth, never had much desire to limit its independence within international organisations, did not share France's obsessive fear of Germany, had no Fascist past to expunge, and possessed large, competitive coal and steel industries, freshly nationalised, which felt no need for integration with Europe. Bevin doubted that either the High Authority or the subsequent scheme for a European Defence Community (to rearm Germany as part of a 'European Army') would succeed. He was right about the latter: it collapsed under the weight of its contradictions and French doubts in August 1954. But he was wrong about the Schuman Plan, which in 1955 became the foundation stone of the EEC.

The 1950 decision to avoid talks on a supranational institution meant that Britain was excluded from important talks between its continental neighbours. But it did not necessarily rule out membership of the negotiations for a 'common market', initiated by the Six at Messina in June 1955. In 1954 Britain had become an associate member of the Schuman Plan and Eden had helped turn the Brussels Pact into the Western European Union (WEU), mainly a defence pact between Britain and the Six but also with regular ministerial meetings. The Messina conference issued an invitation to Britain to join the economic community negotiations, held in Brussels, and the Eden government *did* send representatives. They were led, however, not by a major political figure, but by a Board of Trade official, Russell Bretherton, who soon correctly concluded that, despite the recent failure of the Defence Community, the Six were determined to create a new supranational institution in the economic field. In Whitehall, despite a Foreign Office desire to remain in the talks, an official committee soon concluded that it was not in British interests to join such a body: Commonwealth preferences were still too important to abandon in favour of a European future; the Board of Trade wished to concentrate on freeing trade at a *global* level, from which the City's investment houses and insurance services would gain most; and the Treasury feared losing its control of the British economy. (Given the economic and commercial significance of the common market proposal, it was the Treasury and Board of Trade which dominated discussion of it in the late 1950s.) Ministers took little interest in the issue but agreed to distance themselves from the Brussels talks. However, it was also clear to officials that, if successful, the 'common market' *could* prove a powerful economic, and perhaps political competitor. Hitherto Britain had been careful to avoid any hint of 'sabotaging' integration on the continent. Such sabotage would upset not only the Six but also the Americans, and it might put at risk Franco-German reconciliation, which was seen as desirable by everyone in the Western alliance. But now, at the very least, it seemed Britain should suggest some counter-proposal to the common market. Therefore in November 1956 Macmillan (by then, Chancellor of the Exchequer) put forward a plan for a European free trade area. The aim was not to prevent the EEC coming into being, but to embrace the Six in a wider, non-supranational arrangement, which would preserve British access to continental markets. But from the start the Six were suspicious of Britain's intentions and it was not obvious why they should allow it access to their own markets whilst it preserved special arrangements with the Commonwealth. The British plan was only to apply to industrial goods not agriculture and was therefore of limited value to France, Italy and Holland. Furthermore, November 1956 was precisely the time when Britain and France fell out over the Suez operation. In the aftermath of the crisis, in January 1957, the Foreign Secretary, Selwyn Lloyd, in a memorandum reminiscent of Bevin's dream of a 'third force', suggested to the Cabinet that, having been ill-treated by Washington, Britain *should* commit itself to a European future and even create a European atomic power. But other ministers opposed this and in March Macmillan travelled to Bermuda to restore relations with Eisenhower. That same month the Six gathered in Rome and signed the treaty giving birth to the EEC. Not only did they create a common market in goods, they made promises of further integration including the Common Agricultural Policy (CAP). Talks on the British free trade area scheme began in October 1957, but soon became bogged down in technical detail and 13 months later were brought to an abrupt end by de Gaulle.

In 1959 the British, rejected by Europe but still confident of their own importance, led the way in creating a 'European Free Trade Association' (EFTA) with Austria, Switzerland, Portugal and three Scandinavian states, Norway, Sweden and Denmark. 'The Seven' hardly amounted to a powerful group, however. Their total population was less than that of 'the Six' and Britain was easily the largest member. Over the following few years, British trade grew more rapidly with the Six than the Seven. Macmillan probably intended EFTA as a lever to force the EEC into some kind of trade deal, but such hopes came to nothing and the Americans were critical of EFTA as dividing Western Europe into two commercial blocs. By 1960 the British were in an unenviable position. Commonwealth trade continued to decline, decolonisation was proceeding apace, Macmillan's hopes of playing an East–West mediator had come to nothing and EFTA was of limited use but the EEC had proven successful. Selwyn Lloyd now warned Macmillan that 'the Americans will think more and more of the Six as the group which they have to consult'.[10] Some officials, including the new Permanent Secretary at the Treasury, Sir Frank Lee, were convinced that EEC membership could stimulate economic growth, force industry to become more competitive and bolster Britain's political position in the world. As seen above, debate began to develop in Whitehall, among business, agriculture and the Press, about the value of membership. Britain was, in a sense, faced by an age-old danger: the continent, or its Western half, was coming to be dominated by one power. The power on this occasion, however, was not an expansionist, militarist state like Napoleonic France or Nazi Germany, but a voluntary, democratic organisation of nations. With the USSR already a menace, the US in favour of European integration and Britain's own economic fortunes in decline, London lacked the strength, allies or will to break up the EEC and hence the only viable policy was to try to enter and influence its policies from within. Bevin had earlier feared that membership of supranational bodies would destroy British independence, but after de Gaulle came to power it was clear that the EEC had *not* impeded French independence. De Gaulle was as patriotic and independent a French leader as any before him. The supranational elements in the Treaty of Rome were less than those in the Schuman Plan and the driving force was not the central executive body, the Commission, but representatives of the individual states, who met in the Council of Ministers. Once inside the Council, the British might be able to ally with France to oppose further supranationalism; they might even be able to return to their role of playing the arbiter between France and Germany. Thus it appeared that EEC membership need not destroy British independence and in fact might prove the best means to achieve traditional aims, providing a more valuable outlet than the Commonwealth for trade and investment, offering the British people higher rates of economic growth and bolstering political standing on the world stage. Significantly, in 1961 Britain for the first time exported more to Europe than to the Commonwealth. Becoming a European backwater, in contrast, could prove increasingly detrimental to the nation's wealth, social cohesion and international importance.

The Cabinet decided to apply for EEC membership in July 1961, but the bid was surrounded by difficulties. Macmillan had only won round his Cabinet and party with difficulty. Many were concerned about the interests of British agriculture, the Commonwealth and also Britain's new allies in EFTA. Macmillan made it clear that Britain would have to be satisfied that these three areas would all be protected before he would enter the EEC. Indeed the Prime Minister's public announcement of the application was so low key as to suggest that even he himself was lukewarm about the application. He certainly overestimated British strength *vis-à-vis* the EEC. The entry talks did not start until October, with Edward Heath, then Home's deputy at the FO, leading the British team and they proceeded only slowly. The conditions which Britain demanded to protect Commonwealth trading interests proved particularly difficult, but Macmillan could hardly abandon the Commonwealth at this point, however divided it had become. A Commonwealth leaders' conference, in London in September 1961, showed that the Canadians,

Australians and New Zealand were all concerned about their commercial interests, even if they could understand Britain's motives for seeking EEC membership. Canada's premier, John Diefenbaker, was even interested in revamping the Ottowa Agreements. The government was also faced, in the summer of 1961, by a determined attack on the application from the Labour leader, Hugh Gaitskell, who declared that it would 'end a thousand years of history'. From the start Macmillan hoped that his own personal diplomacy might secure British membership and especially tried to win over de Gaulle. However, de Gaulle had a love–hate view of the British, disliked their close links to Washington and was quite happy being the dominant leader in the EEC himself. Macmillan had some hope of winning the Frenchman over by offering him a nuclear alliance but, as seen above, because of the terms of Anglo-American cooperation in the same field, this idea came to nothing. To put real pressure on de Gaulle to let them into the EEC, the British would have had to move much more quickly in the talks and to have abandoned most of their preconditions. As it was, the evidence of domestic division and Commonwealth doubts about entry in the summer of 1962 came just as de Gaulle was cementing his hold on French politics. He ended the colonial war in Algeria and in October his supporters won a general election handsomely. Three months later he vetoed the British application, using the Nassau Agreement as an excuse: by deciding to take Polaris missiles from Kennedy it could be argued that Macmillan had once again effectively put the US alliance before Europe. Actually Macmillan faced a difficult dilemma. He knew an American deal might upset de Gaulle, but could hardly compromise British Great Power status by giving up possession of the nuclear deterrent – especially when the EEC application was still in doubt.

De Gaulle's veto shut the door to EEC membership even as the value of the Commonwealth and American alliance continued to decline. Macmillan had concluded that there was no alternative to EEC membership if Britain wished to remain a major power and, although for the next few years a second application was out of the question, it is not surprising that in 1966–67 Wilson's government, too, decided that the door to Europe must be opened. Wilson himself had no emotional liking for a European commitment, but the continued underperformance of the British economy, the impact of Rhodesia on the Commonwealth and the pressures to retreat from East of Suez all pointed to a European future and both the FO and the Department of Economic Affairs urged a second application. In October 1966 the Cabinet agreed that Wilson and his pro-European Foreign Secretary, Brown, should make an exploratory tour of EEC capitals in the New Year to ascertain the chances of entry and in April 1967 it was decided to make a formal application. Brown, in another echo of Bevin's 'third force' ideas, hoped to create 'a politically integrated Europe capable of standing up to the Russians and Americans'.[11] But there were still serious doubts from the Labour Party, including some Cabinet ministers, and many predicted that de Gaulle would veto the second application, as happened in November. The fact that the application was pressed in the face of such a predictable rebuff showed how desperate Britain's position had become. The urgent necessity of EEC entry – now seen by most experts as the *only* course for British foreign policy to take – was confirmed by the decision to leave the application 'on the table', even after de Gaulle's action. That it was finally taken up by the EEC in 1969 had more to do with de Gaulle's resignation than any developments in British policy. Pompidou, his successor, wanted Britain as an ally against both the rising power of Germany and pressures from the smaller members for greater supranationalism; he also probably recognised that Britain would have to pay much of the cost for the CAP, which was about to come into existence. Formal talks on entry began within weeks of Heath's election victory, with Conservative ministers using the negotiating papers which had been prepared under Labour. This did not prevent Wilson from attacking the terms which Heath obtained, but it is significant that it was the *terms* and not the *principle* of membership which Wilson criticised: he never opposed EEC membership outright at this time, even if some of his front bench did. There were several reasons why Heath succeeded in entering the EEC where Macmillan and Wilson had failed. His own undoubted commitment to Europe and his attitude towards the US were probably no more vital than the decision to keep Britain's preconditions for entry to a minimum. New Zealand dairy produce and West Indian sugar were given some protection in the entry terms but gone was Macmillan's hope that Commonwealth producers might retain a market equal to that which Britain had earlier guaranteed them. It proved easier to win over Pompidou, at a summit meeting in Paris in May 1971, than it had been to convince de Gaulle of Britain's European commitment. The terms announced in July fell short of the 'sell-out' which Labour claimed but were potentially costly. In return for access to the common market, Britain had to accept the CAP as it stood, was unlikely to receive much in the way of agricultural subsidies but would have to pay about one fifth of the EEC budget. The government won a parliamentary vote in favour of the principle of entry in October, despite negative opinion polls (in 1961 and 1967 the public, though volatile on the issue, had favoured entry). The vote exposed differences in both parties, revealing that Europe was an issue which cut across party loyalties. Nearly 40 patriotic Conservatives, fearful of a loss of sovereignty and critical of EEC 'protectionism', opposed the government; but almost 70 Labour 'pro-marketeers', led by Roy Jenkins, supported Heath. Pushing through detailed legislation during 1972 proved a time-consuming and controversial process, not completed until July. But Heath attended an EEC leaders' meeting in October in high spirits. He denied that EEC membership would impede British sovereignty in any fundamental sense and was confident that – even if he could not explain exactly how – European competition would invigorate British industry. And he hoped to see new institutions created in Europe, including a regional development fund, which would be of specific benefit to Britain. Formal entry on 1 January 1973 was followed by 11 days of celebration, called the 'Fanfare for Europe', intended to symbolise the new future. But the general public greeted it with depressing indifference.

Notes

1 Turner J., *Macmillan* (London, 1994), 154.
2 Prittie T., *Konrad Adenauer* (London, 1971), 263–4.
3 Rawnsley G., 'The Anglo-American Alliance during the Cuban Missile Crisis', *Contemporary Record*, **9**(3), 1993, 599.
4 Pimlott B., *Harold Wilson* (London, 1992), 388.
5 Campbell J., *Edward Heath* (London, 1993), 342.
6 Ovendale R., 'Macmillan and the Wind of Change in Africa', *Historical Journal*, **38**(2), 1993, 457.
7 Hemming P., 'Macmillan and the End of Empire in Africa'. In Aldous R. and Lee S. (eds), *Harold Macmillan and Britain's World Role* (London, 1996), 118.
8 Wilson H., *The Labour Government 1964–70* (London, 1971), 196.
9 Balfour-Paul G., *The End of Empire in the Middle East* (Cambridge, 1991), 6.
10 Public Record Office, Kew, PREM 11/2998 (Selwyn Lloyd to Macmillan, 15 February 1960).
11 Brown G., *In My Way* (London, 1971), 207.

8
Reluctantly European, 1973–1997

The 'Europeanisation' of government

British entry to the European Community (EC) on 1 January 1973 might have been expected to lead Britons to feel greater affinity with their continental neighbours and end ambitions for a world role. A generation had grown up which had only dim memories of the war. Britain was only one of America's allies, the Commonwealth meant little, and both Conservative and Labour governments had decided that EC membership was the wisest course to safeguard national power and wealth. Yet there were many reasons why British people found it impossible to embrace a European future with verve. Although entry to the Community represented a dramatic step, which affected foreign, financial, commercial and industrial policies, and had profound constitutional and legal implications, governments were determined to maintain well-established policies including the maintenance of British influence in global affairs, maximising freedom of trade and resisting the spread of Communism, and they hoped to minimise their loss of control over decision-making. Even a leading pro-European like Douglas Hurd was determined as Foreign Secretary in 1989–95 that Britain should 'punch above its weight' in world affairs. Indeed, the EC simply became a new forum in which to press old policies and there were few, beyond such pressure groups as the Federal Trust, who viewed European union with enthusiasm. 'For the British people European integration was at best a necessity, not ... an ideal.'[1] This pragmatic approach is easy to understand given the country's past, especially its position as an island power, able to avoid the intensity of day-to-day contacts which continental states experience. Its island position has allowed it to escape wars and revolutions elsewhere in Europe and to evolve an unwritten constitution, which makes it reluctant to embrace ambitious blueprints for greater EC integration. It also developed a strong national identity, and had often defined itself in contradiction to Europe. A long-term commitment to European security in NATO only emerged after 1949 of course, when decades of bitter experience showed that a military role on the continent could not be escaped: in general, Britain, whilst ready to play a role in the continental balance, has preferred throughout its history to intervene only in exceptional circumstances. In 1945 the reinforced sense of separateness bred by the war did not prevent Bevin from considering far-reaching cooperation with other Western European states, but the idea of 'pooling sovereignty' with them, as in the Schuman Plan, was anathema. In contrast to France (with its desire to control Germany) and Germany (with Adenauer's dream of lodging his country in a liberal democratic group), national interest simply did not point Britain in the direction of supranationalism. Britain also had a long tradition of free trade, whereas France and Italy, for example, were wedded to protectionist policies.

The situation changed by 1970 because of the retreat from Empire, comparatively poor economic growth and fear of the EC's growing power. Yet the fact that membership was accepted, in part, as a defensive measure rather than a positive act, was significant. Also, by 1970, the EC had developed a highly protectionist agricultural policy which Britain was forced to accept but from which, as an industrial power with a small, efficient agricultural sector, it would benefit little (although the CAP, whose costs were borne by consumers, did reduce the price to the Treasury of subsidising British agriculture). Once inside, Britain hoped to point the EC in certain directions – open to external trade, with a minimal supranational element and a reformed CAP. But in a multilateral structure where two or three countries were as powerful as Britain, and where states had many different views, reform proved difficult to achieve and soon the pragmatic British believed they had gained little from membership. The country not only suffered rising food costs (because of the CAP) but had to pay a proportion of Value Added Tax and *all* earnings from tariffs, the net contribution to the EC being estimated by 1980 at a billion pounds. Britain's own economic performance continued, in the first decade of membership, to lag behind the original EC members. In the second decade Margaret Thatcher's government succeeded in achieving a single European market, again emphasising London's belief in free trade, but at the same time the political drive towards supranationalism revived and rather than strengthening British power Europe seemingly threatened to take decision-making away from Whitehall to the Commission in Brussels. Britain was used to multilateral diplomacy, but it had led the Empire-Commonwealth, considered itself second only to America in NATO and thus found it hard to adjust to an organisation where it was less important than France and Germany; the Franco–German alliance prevented Britain from pursuing its traditional 'balance of power' role between them; and its own political practices, such as the first-past-the-post electoral system, one-party government and unitary state, did not make cooperation easy with politicians used to proportional representation, coalitions and (in some cases) strong provincial governments. In short, Britain's constitutional and economic background fitted badly with the EC from the outset and, as one of the wartime 'Big Three', it found it harder than other, smaller or recently defeated powers to adjust to sharing decision-making with others. For all that, EC membership did bring access to a large market, allowed Britain an important say in European policies and buttressed liberalism and capitalism until the Soviet menace was overcome. Trade with the EEC grew from one-third of the British total in 1973 to about half in the 1990s, though the balance was in favour of the EEC (especially West Germany). The Labour Party became more firmly committed to membership in the 1990s, after promising 'negotiated withdrawal' in the 1983 election, and serious Conservative politicians avoided talk of withdrawal for two decades. Even if Britain retained a considerable volume of trade and investments beyond the EC, it was not obvious how it could thrive by leaving. Yet the Community was a very unusual form of organisation, its supranationalism, protectionism and elitism persistently grated against British traditions and premier John Major's hope, expressed in 1991, of being 'at the heart of Europe' was difficult to fulfil.

EC membership had a profound effect on policy-making in London, in both the external and domestic spheres. On joining the Community, Britain accepted not only the CAP and a common tariff, but a vast number of regulations drawn up since 1958. More regulations continued to emerge from the Commission, over which parliamentary oversight was quite inadequate. Community law covered only certain areas, and could not replace British practice entirely, but the European Court did mark a new court of appeal which could prove embarrassing to governments (by, for example, insisting on an equal age of retirement for men and women). With the Single European Act in 1987 the need to harmonise European economies extended the Commission's activities further with, it should be said, the British government's agreement, and discussion of a common currency raised the spectre of a full economic union in which monetary policy, social spending and taxation might all be geared to European norms. At that time, EC policies began to attract greater criticism from the right-wing Press and began to divide Conservative opinion, just as Labour had been divided over Europe in the 1970s. Entry to the EC was never a simple 'foreign policy' decision therefore: this particular international body affected all areas of national life and showed how impossible it had become to divorce domestic and international affairs. However, entry did certainly affect external policy-making too. The basic structure was still recognisable. The Overseas Policy and Defence Committee (OPD), JIC and COS remained in being and, apart from the formation of the powerful Department of Trade and Industry by Heath, the structure of key ministries (FCO, MOD, Treasury) was familiar. No dedicated ministry for European affairs, such as existed in many member states, was created (although such a step was considered in the late 1980s). But ministries *were* forced to alter their departmental structures to cope with entry. Some predicted that the FCO would become less vital in foreign policy after EC entry, as domestic and international issues became meshed together, but actually the Office found a new role as the lead department on EC policy matters. It trained its diplomats in the techniques of 'permanent negotiation' in EC institutions, improved its grasp of financial and economic issues, and emulated practice elsewhere in the Community by appointing a Political Director – a more independent senior figure, travelling abroad frequently and having a key role in meetings of international organisations. The Cabinet Office was restructured, with a European Secretariat to cope with coordinating (though not defining) policy towards Europe in Whitehall and to service the OPD's European subcommittee, chaired by the Foreign Secretary. Britain established a permanent delegation in Brussels, to which a number of Whitehall officials were seconded; and a group of ministers – especially the Foreign Secretary, but also the Chancellor of the Exchequer, Trade Secretary, Agriculture Minister and others – now faced regular meetings with their European counterparts. EC membership marked another upturn in the practice of 'multilateral diplomacy' which had expanded greatly over the century across the world. With regular meetings of the EC Council of Ministers now added to the UN, NATO, Council of Europe, Western European Union and Commonwealth (as well as bilateral meetings) foreign secretaries might easily travel over 100 000 miles each year and rarely remained in Britain for ten days at a time. James Callaghan, Foreign Secretary in 1974–76, set up a VC-10 airliner as a 'flying FO', able to visit several countries at short notice without having to fit in with airline or RAF schedules. Being seen at so many international meetings benefited British prestige and prime ministers too found more opportunities for summitry. In 1975 the EC agreed to bi-annual leaders' meetings as the best way to make high-level policy decisions and annual summits also began between the 'Group of Seven' leading industrial states, America, Japan, Germany, France, Britain, Italy and Canada. The end of the Cold War brought yet more international organisations into being, including the World Trading Organisation and Organisation for Security and Cooperation in Europe, as well as regular EC–US Summits. High profile prime ministerial involvement in foreign policy was nothing new but under Margaret Thatcher (1979–90) it led some right-wingers to favour a 'mini-FO' in Downing Street, where her foreign policy adviser, Charles Powell, wielded formidable influence. Thatcher played a particularly forceful role in European policy where she was increasingly at odds with the FCO and Treasury over monetary integration. The FCO indeed, even under the 'Thatcherite' Geoffrey Howe (1983–89), was seen by some Conservatives as a kind of 'enemy within', oversympathetic to foreign opinion and likely to 'sell-out' to Europe.

The most obvious evidence of the EC's impact on foreign policy was the adoption in the 1991 Maastricht Treaty of a Common Foreign and Security Policy (CFSP). When Britain entered the EC there was some enthusiasm for the idea of a single European outlook on international issues. This had its antecedents in the 'third force' concepts of Bevin, Selwyn Lloyd and George Brown, and its supporters included Heath and Thatcher's first Foreign Secretary, Lord Carrington. After all, together the EC states had a larger population than either the US or USSR, represented the largest market in the world and had to have a common view on many matters for the common market to function. Something of a common policy did prove possible in the Middle East in the 1970s and there was a structure for European Political Cooperation, initiated in 1970 and involving bi-annual meetings of foreign ministers (increased to four times per annum in 1973). Heath saw entry to the EC, of course, as a way to resolve domestic economic underperformance *and* strengthen Britain in the world by acting in unison with others. 'But international organisations, even of the stature of the EC, are not panaceas and they tend to resist all efforts to move fast.'[2] Whatever the attractions of a 'third force', it proved difficult for EC members to concert a view on most issues, and Britain's own interests (in nuclear and in intelligence cooperation with Washington, for example) were not necessarily shared by its European partners. The main impact on British policy was the need to share information with European countries which it would, in the past, only have shared with Washington. The end of the Cold War, German reunification in 1990 and the break up of Yugoslavia all added to the pressures for greater coordination and led to the Maastricht agreement on CFSP, which was followed by the creation of a CFSP Unit in the FCO, designed to coordinate policies with other EC foreign ministries. The British approach was typically pragmatic and evolutionary, aiming at 'efficiency' rather than ornate organisational structures, but the extent of consultation grew remarkably quickly and helped, for example, to secure EC support in resisting the Iranian *fatwa* against the writer Salman Rushdie. The FCO's Policy Planning Staff, greatly strengthened in 1987, engaged in joint planning with other EC states (as it did with NATO). But CFSP only worked on an intergovernmental (not supranational) basis and on major issues coordination was as difficult as ever, being humiliatingly exposed by the hesitations of EC policy-makers during the Bosnian civil war of 1992–95.

'Thatcherism' and policy-making

Not all developments in foreign policy-making could be laid at the door of the EC. The intensification of interdependence in the 'information age' was met not only by European cooperation but by global activity, seen in the Group of Seven meetings and such developments as the 'Earth Summits' on the environment (1992 and 1996) as well as by the growth of new pressure groups like Greenpeace. There were regional groups in Africa (the Organisation of African Unity, OAU), Latin America (Organisation of American States, OAS) and South-east Asia (Association of South-East Asian Nations, ASEAN) designed to give countries in those areas greater weight in world affairs, and in the 1970s Britain and other industrialised states had to cope with the new-found strength of the petroleum-exporting countries, represented in OPEC (Organisation of Petroleum Exporting Countries). The whole Western world faced OPEC oil-price rises in 1973 and 1979 which added a new twist to inflation and condemned it to years of low growth, culminating in the Depression of 1979–82. Britain's vulnerability to outside economic pressures was especially highlighted by the 1976 Sterling Crisis when the IMF only agreed to assist the Labour government if it introduced stringent austerity measures. Britain was also becoming a multicultural society, thanks to immigration from the West Indies, East Africa and South Asia, and many of its people now had a close interest in, for example, Islamic solidarity, Indo-Pakistani relations or opposition to apartheid. The information age brought rapid currency flows and changing patterns of investment which, linked to the power of multinational companies and the need to keep the City competitive as an investment centre, left Britain at the mercy of changes in the world economy. In one sense this was nothing new: a large volume of overseas trade had long made the country vulnerable to such shifts and, before 1914, the City already stood at the centre of an interdependent world. But in 1900 the British were powerful enough, relatively speaking, to feel they benefited most from, and had some control over, a system based on Sterling and oiled by their banking, insurance and shipping services. In the 1970s there was far less sense of control, and the economic situation bred radical solutions, one of which was the Socialist dream of a centrally planned, egalitarian state, another the free enterprise, individualist approach which triumphed in the 1979 election victory of Thatcher's Conservatives, promising lower taxes, privatisation and tight control on government spending. After this election Labour split, with Roy Jenkins leading a Social Democratic Party, and the front benches of the major parties began to diverge widely on foreign policy: the new Labour leader, Michael Foot, believed in unilateral nuclear disarmament. A divided opposition and an improving economy helped

Thatcher win re-election easily in 1983 and 1987, but the growth delivered by the Conservatives was fuelled by an expanding market in America, liberalisation of credit controls and, most vital, the sale of North Sea oil, which disguised a continuing trade deficit in manufactures and low domestic investment. Unemployment was consistently high, the value of Sterling was volatile (even after the removal of the old problem of Sterling Area balances) and by 1990, when Thatcher lost office, another depression was approaching, alongside 10 per cent inflation and a massive trade deficit. On some interpretations of the statistics, Britain was even overtaken as an industrial power by Italy. Yet the victory of Thatcher's successor, John Major, in the 1992 election and the distinctly non-Socialist policies adopted by Labour after 1994 under Tony Blair, showed that the 'Thatcherite' solution had come to stay. Government intervention in the economy was to be reduced where possible, even if its cost to the tax burden was as large as ever; and the 'dependency culture' bred by the universal nature of the welfare state would be replaced by a more entrepreneurial, self-sufficient outlook. In order to remain competitive and attract 'inward investment' it was argued that Britain must keep its salary costs and social spending low. The City, having modernised itself in the 'Big Bang' of 1986, remained one of the world's main stock exchanges but was now a centre for activity by German, Japanese or Middle Eastern investors as much as by Britons.

Conservative free enterprise doctrines led to an ever-increasing emphasis in foreign policy work on trade promotion, already seen in the Duncan Report. This was part of a general move since the war towards creating *functional* specialisations in the FCO (on, for example, trade, energy or arms control) alongside the traditional expertise in a region or country. There had long been informal links between businesses and government: ministers and senior civil servants moved in the same world as financiers and industrialists and, from the Victorian era, companies had frequently urged government to assist them in winning contracts. But formally the FO had tried to preserve an impartial position, by keeping its distance from private business interests, and even after the Eden reforms of the 1940s few FO mandarins had much economic experience. By 1997, however, trade promotion, in cooperation with the Department of Trade and Industry, had become the prime focus of many embassies' activity. It was also the purpose of most ministerial and royal visits abroad and in 1996 the 'New' Labour Party suggested that some ambassadorial positions should be filled from the private sector. Such a policy was not without its critics. One of Britain's most experienced ambassadors, Anthony Parsons, learnt from bitter experience in Iran in 1979 (when the pro-Western government was overthrown) that concentration on commercial promotion harmed political reporting: 'the Embassy was primarily organised ... for the promotion of British exports and ... even the political officers had a brief to be on the look out for fresh export opportunities'.[3] Another area in which Conservative policies affected foreign policy was in spending restraint. Again, as seen earlier in this book, expenditure restrictions are hardly a recent phenomenon, but radical cuts in FCO activity were first suggested, under Treasury pressure, in 1976 by the Central Policy Review Staff (a 'think-tank' based in Downing Street) and by 1997 there was real concern, in such areas as FCO representation abroad, overseas aid and the BBC World Service, that spending cuts and managerial reforms were causing real harm to British interests abroad. Despite a refurbishment of the FCO in 1984 and the reputation of its occupants as privileged and spendthrift, morale in the middle sections of the diplomatic service was poor in the 1980s and many left. Between the creation of the FCO in 1968 and the break-up of the USSR in 1991 the number of countries with British representatives increased from 136 to 168 but the number of staff serving abroad fell by 1500 to 6600. Development aid (almost half of which was now channelled via the EC) was targeted in the 1980s on governments that were to Britain's taste, both in their respect for human rights and their belief in free enterprise; and by emulating America and leaving UNESCO in December 1985, the Thatcher government demonstrated that it would not underwrite international bodies which pursued 'anti-Western' policies. (There was a growing feeling, too, that the UN had taken multilateralism to absurd lengths, spawning agencies that were wasteful, corrupt and unnecessary.) Most money from the Overseas Development Agency went to former colonies, but the amounts were becoming more restricted, and whereas Africa received less attention, in 1989 assistance was suddenly expanded to Eastern Europe through such means as the 'Know-how Fund', designed not for development aid as such, but to help Communist systems transform themselves into free enterprise economies. Threats to the BBC World Service, with spending cuts and, in 1996, managerial changes, seemed particularly destructive to those who recognised the power of the media in the information age. Given the importance of the English language and the trust in which the BBC was held (notwithstanding links between the FCO and World Service), it seemed foolish to put such an asset at risk. The BBC arguably played an important role in breaking up the Communist system in Europe, especially after the Soviets ended their policy of 'jamming' transmissions in 1987–88, and the ability to shape perceptions – of friends, enemies, or neutrals – had become an important weapon in international relations. The BBC, and the news agency Reuters, were areas where Britain could compete with America, whose 'cultural imperialism' via film studios and television companies was otherwise overwhelming – the British government having also failed to see the international significance of fostering a large-scale film industry.

Where defence was concerned, Conservative policy was contradictory, wishing on one hand to restrict spending, on the other to pose as the party of strong armed forces. By 1979 expenditure on the services had fallen to 5 per cent of GDP, but it was still higher than France or Germany. Even a focus of activity in NATO still involved Britain in paying for home defence, the British Army of the Rhine, a substantial naval presence in the Atlantic and the maintenance of Polaris. In addition, there was unrest in Northern Ireland and periodic emergencies elsewhere, notably wars in the Falkland Islands (1982) and Persian Gulf (1990–91), as well as UN actions such as the 'peace-keeping' operation in Bosnia. And, as throughout the century, weapons costs were escalating all the time. When Britain tried to modernise its own forces it could prove costly and unsuccessful, as with the Nimrod early-warning aircraft in the 1980s, but cooperation with other countries, in projects like the Eurofighter, carried its own uncertainties as to whether all the consortium would see the development through. The old dilemma of multiple roles and limited finance had not therefore disappeared with the withdrawal from East of Suez, even if resources were now better matched to commitments. In 1981 Defence Secretary John Nott insisted on cuts in the Royal Navy (reduced to about 100 vessels, from 300 as recently as 1957), only to be faced with the Falklands War the following year. In the elections of 1983 and 1987 the Conservatives were determined to use defence as a weapon against Labour, especially attacking its views on nuclear weapons and Thatcher secured a replacement for Polaris in the form of the American 'Trident', another submarine-launched ballistic missile of great destructive power. The real opportunity to cut costs while maintaining an adequate defence therefore only came with the end of the Cold War. In 1990 the 'Options for Change' paper decided to proceed with Trident but otherwise advocated reductions in all three services, whose total personnel would fall by 60 000 to 250 000. Building on this, the 1996 White Paper announced that the last RAF base in Germany would close in 2002. By 1997 defence expenditure was down to 2.7 per cent of GDP, ironically about where it had been a hundred years earlier, though still above the European average of 2.3 per cent. At the same time, whilst being keen to work closely with America and preserve NATO, Britain was cooperating more with France on defence matters and ready to see the Western European Union (almost a forgotten structure for a generation after its creation in 1954) adopt a more important role. Spending cuts and the end of the Soviet threat caused low morale in the armed services and uncertainty about their role, but in 1995–96 the Joint Operational Doctrine study pointed to a new direction in planning, based on the Gulf War experience and designed to achieve united action by the three armed services, whilst keeping costs low. Emulating American practice, the emphasis was on 'rapid reaction', high mobility, airpower, intelligence and psychological operations over the armoured columns which had dominated training fields during the Cold War.

Just as Conservative ideology created tension in defence policy between cost-cutting and military might, so attitudes towards political freedom and national security pointed the government in different directions. On one hand a belief in individualism and open government helped produce a number of innovations. In 1979 the government introduced a comprehensive system of parliamentary oversight over Whitehall, including a Foreign Affairs Committee able to question the Foreign Secretary, FCO Permanent Under-Secretary and others. The Committee, whose proceedings were televised after 1984, asked embarrassing questions about the sinking of the Argentinian battleship *General Belgrano* during the Falklands War, investigated a range of specific issues (from FCO expenditure to the Single European Act) and was critical of the FCO's performance on such matters as trade promotion in the 'Pacific Rim' in the late 1980s. But it was far less inquisitive and knowledgeable than equivalent committees in the American Congress and its precise impact on policy-making is difficult to judge. More traditional means of pressure from MPs had more notable effect at key junctures. Thus criticism in the Conservative '1922 Committee' of backbenchers helped force Lord Carrington from office over the Falklands War, and in 1990 a right-wing revolt ended any prospect of large-scale immigration from Hong Kong. In the mid-1990s, when Major had only a slim majority in the Commons, it was possible for a group of a dozen 'Euro-sceptic' MPs to threaten the government consistently. The ability of parliament to embarrass government over foreign policy was also demonstrated by questioning of the Pergau Dam development project in Malaysia, which could potentially have damaged the environment, and by the 'Arms to Iraq' affair which showed that businessmen had secretly been encouraged to sell arms to Saddam Hussein's regime when many believed this to be against British policy. Further evidence of Conservative openness came with the 'Waldegrave initiative', which led to greater releases of documents, including intelligence materials, under the '30-year rule'. Other changes, notably the rising status of women in the foreign service, had more to do with social evolution than Conservative beliefs. Until 1972 women had to resign from the FCO on marrying; a generation later they still found it virtually impossible to reach the top of the service, but a few had become ambassadors and in 1996, for the first time, most new entrants to the FCO's elite 'fast stream' were female. Ethnic minorities were still under-represented, but after 1991 homosexuality was no longer a bar to a diplomatic career. Yet alongside such improvements there was a strong tendency, especially under Thatcher, towards secrecy in government. On grounds of national security, but also in line with labour relations policy, trades unions were banned at GCHQ in 1984 – provoking an unprecedented public debate about that highly secret institution. Thatcher drew widespread criticism for preventing publication in Britain of the memoirs of a former MI5 officer, Peter Wright, when his book *Spycatcher* was freely available abroad. In the early 1980s there were also suspected campaigns of 'dirty tricks' against the revived CND by MI5. And the government's reform of the Official Secrets Act in 1989 was disappointing. For years the original 1911 Act had been criticised, especially for its 'catch-all' nature, but in clarifying it Thatcher refused to accept a 'public interest' line of defence, still less any commitment to a US style Freedom of Information Act. Despite parliamentary pressure for democratic control of the intelligence services, only a weak oversight committee of privy councillors was set up in 1994. Then again, the end of the Cold War allowed some relaxation in the secrecy surrounding MI5, including the naming and public appearance of its head. In 1995–96 there was also public debate about allowing MI5 to widen its attention, from tracking down subversives and tackling the IRA, to dealing with drug traffickers and organised crime: both these groups had an important 'international' dimension and there was already close cooperation against criminal organisations by European intelligence and police forces (another example of the 'Europeanisation' of policy). Even in the 1980s there were some insights into intelligence work. For example, the 1983 Franks Report on the Falklands War was critical of the JIC's failure to predict the conflict. It was felt that the FCO, which chaired the JIC, had interpreted intelligence according to its own diplomatically based expectations. Thatcher put the Chairmanship in the Cabinet Office but the change did not prevent later failures, in 1989, when the collapse of Communism was predicted by none of the West's intelligence (or academic) experts, and in 1990 when Saddam Hussein's invasion of Kuwait was almost as surprising. One other important development under Thatcher was the creation of a successor to the Information Research Department (IRD). By the early 1970s IRD 'employed 400 staff, which made it the biggest department in the Foreign Office and absorbed a yearly budget of £1 million'[4] on covert propaganda. Its size, expenditure and the nature of its work made it unpopular even in the FCO. But in 1973 it too began to face spending restrictions and staff cuts. Its work – which included counter-subversion within Britain as well as anti-Soviet activity – was unpopular with the incoming Labour government and in May 1977 it was closed down. Thatcher, however, was determined to have efficient covert agencies fighting the Cold War and the result was the creation of a new IRD, known as the Overseas Information Department, as secret in its activities as its predecessor.

The fag-end of Empire

Although Churchill's vision of 'three circles' was first expounded in 1949, when the Empire was still vast and NATO a fresh creation, the idea that Britain must defend possessions outside Europe and remain a close ally of America persisted long after entry to the EC. Certainly, even by 1973, the Commonwealth had become the least of the 'three circles'. The unity provided by a common colonial past, the English language and such institutions as the Commonwealth Games could not offset the political and economic, religious and racial differences between its members, who were free to leave the organisation at will. By 1980 the Commonwealth accounted for only 15 per cent of British trade. Yet it *did* stay together, partly because it was such a flexible and tolerant structure, and there was even talk of it winning new members. The bi-annual Commonwealth summits from 1973 to 1979 all proved quite friendly and respect for the monarchy – still rather more than a decorative institution – was confirmed by Elizabeth II's Silver Jubilee celebrations in 1977. Most members were impressed by Heath's readiness in 1972–73 to give refuge to Asians expelled from Uganda by its eccentric and violent military dictator, Idi Amin. In 1975 Wilson pleased the Commonwealth by supporting a world commodity agreement to help the developing countries (an idea which was never realised). And in 1979 Thatcher fared well at the Lusaka conference because of her government's efforts to settle the Rhodesian secession. But the desire of most members to increase pressures on South Africa to abandon apartheid created grave difficulties at the Nassau conference in 1985. With Portuguese colonies in southern Africa independent and Rhodesia (as discussed below) having become 'Zimbabwe' under black majority rule, the idea of increased sanctions against the beleaguered system of apartheid was popular with black Africans and with Britain's own strong anti-apartheid movement. But Thatcher refused to support such a policy. She argued that sanctions would harm poor blacks most; but her party was suspected of sympathy for the South African government. There were more arguments at Vancouver in 1987 and again at Kuala Lumpur in 1989, where Foreign Secretary John Major negotiated a common statement by the 49 member states only to have Thatcher cast it aside in favour of isolation. South Africa finally eased as a problem in 1990, when the South African leader, F.W. de Klerk, released the black African leader, Nelson Mandela, from a long imprisonment. In 1994 Mandela became President himself, taking his country back into the Commonwealth and showing remarkably little resentment of British Conservatives for their past policies.

If the Commonwealth proved a weak base for the projection of British power, the remnants of Empire still made demands on British resources and diplomatic skill. Responsibilities still had to be wound down peacefully or protected, if necessary by force. The settlement of the long-running Rhodesian dispute was the first great foreign success of the Thatcher government, rather ironically since many Conservatives were unsympathetic to black majority rule and, for a time, Thatcher seemed likely to accept a Rhodesian government under Bishop Abel Muzorewa, who was tainted by collaboration with Ian Smith. The collapse of Rhodesia was probably only a matter of time anyway, since Smith's regime was hard-pressed in the late 1970s by economic sanctions and black guerrilla movements, but a peaceful settlement owed much to the diplomatic skill of Lord Carrington and the FCO. Elections brought independence in April 1980 under Robert Mugabe, with certain guarantees for the country's white farmers. The Falklands War in 1982 was a more sudden and violent problem, destructive of Carrington's career and harmful to the FCO's reputation, but a dramatic success for the strong-willed Thatcher. The Falklands had been under British rule since 1833, but were on the edge of the Antarctic, thousands of miles from Britain and with only 2000 inhabitants. The islands were heavily dependent, economically, on Argentina but negotiations in the 1970s between the FCO and Buenos Aires on their long-term future (perhaps with joint ownership) had come to nothing and Thatcher ended all such discussion. John Nott's decision, during the spending cuts of 1981, to withdraw the islands' main if paltry defence, the ice patrol vessel HMS *Endurance*, encouraged the increasingly unpopular Argentinian dictatorship of General Leopoldo Galtieri to seize the islands, thereby fulfilling a long-running national aim. But in contrast to the expectations in Buenos Aires, Thatcher was determined to meet this affront to British dignity. US attempts at mediation failed and President Ronald Reagan decided to provide help to Britain, notably in satellite intelligence, despite the problems caused for Washington by Latin American sympathy for Argentina. By 14 June, with 1000 casualties and the loss of several ships, the Falklands had been regained in a remarkable long-range operation which showed the continuing value of the Royal Navy. Hitherto, Thatcher's government had been quite unpopular, presiding over high inflation and rising unemployment, but the 'Falklands factor' did much to restore Conservative fortunes as well as reviving national self-confidence, which had been at a low ebb for a decade or more (arguably, where world affairs were concerned, it reversed the depressing effect of Suez). Although foreign policy did not specifically figure much in the

1983 election, memories of the war helped guarantee a handsome Conservative win. Thatcher was also able to secure, for the first time, a close ally in Howe as Foreign Secretary. Thereafter she rejected all pleas to negotiate a settlement with Argentina and adopted the expensive policy of 'Fortress Falkland'. Few asked whether, first by ending talks with the Argentinians in 1980, then by withdrawing *Endurance*, the government had been partly responsible for encouraging war in the first place.

The withdrawal from Britain's last major Crown Colony showed a very different approach to international relations. Hong Kong had been shown in 1941 to be virtually indefensible and, though it had returned to British rule after the war, it had long been vulnerable to Chinese pressure. Anglo-Chinese relations were marred by the 1949 Communist revolution and the subsequent liquidation of Western business interests; they were especially poor during Mao Zedong's 'Cultural Revolution' in the late 1960s but improved under Heath, when Mao opened the country up to Western contacts once more. Britain was under increasing pressure to negotiate over the future status of Hong Kong, for the simple reason that most of the colony was held on a lease from China, which was due to expire in June 1997. Hong Kong island, which had been fully ceded to Britain, was too small to be viable on its own and the idea of resisting a Chinese takeover was unthinkable. China was a massive military power, with a quarter of the world's population and a valuable area, from the 1970s once more, for trade and investment. Talks began tentatively in 1979 with the British hoping to retain some rights in Hong Kong in the long term but China demanding full sovereignty. For China the restoration of areas lost during the colonial era was an important issue of national pride. The talks reached their most important stage in 1983 under Howe, who established a surprisingly good relationship with his Chinese opposite number, Wu Xueqian. In an agreement of September 1985 Howe conceded that the colony would return to Chinese sovereignty in 1997 but it would preserve a special, autonomous status (and a residue, perhaps, of British influence) for 50 years after that, with its own government institutions. A few critics saw this as a surrender of an economically prosperous, Westernised city to Communism, but it is difficult to see what else even a patriot like Thatcher could have done faced by the legal and power-political realities of the situation. The agreement paved the way for a successful state visit by the Queen to China in 1986 and survived, despite a number of problems over the next decade. Fears of a repressive Chinese policy reached their height in 1989, when the Communists crushed pro-reform demonstrations in Tiananmen Square in Peking; the Chinese were insistent that, before 1997, the British should return home over 40 000 refugees who had fled to Hong Kong from Vietnam; and the period after 1992 saw almost permanent tension between the Chinese government and the British governor, Chris Patten, who introduced democratic reforms into Hong Kong's government. A violent Chinese response was unlikely, if only because Peking had an interest in a peaceful transition of power, but Patten's policy offered little long-term protection to the Hong Kong population and in the short term may have harmed British commercial interests in China which, with the termination of Empire, were becoming Britain's prime interest in the Far East.

As one academic noted in 1988 'British foreign policy ... understands that it ignores Asia at its peril'.[5] Apart from Hong Kong, East Asia was vital to the Pacific balance of power – now the concern primarily of America, Russia and China – and to the world economy, with China and the 'tiger' economies of Singapore, Malaysia, Taiwan and South Korea, added to Japan, forming the strongest region of economic growth in the world. The retreat from East of Suez had too easily been thought to imply an ever-declining British interest in the Far East. Certainly the end of formal colonial rule had been accompanied by a decline too in those informal means of financial and commercial exploitation which had been a feature of the Imperial era. However, such exploitation had given way to a new competitive and egalitarian relationship in which money was still to be made by British companies in East Asia but where East Asian manufacturers could also sell goods and invest in the UK. In 1994–95 South-east Asia became Britain's eighth largest market, valued at £5 billion. Indeed, Euro-sceptics pointed out the irony that the fastest growing markets in the world were not in Europe but in former British colonies in Asia. Britain, still an island trading power, which must export to live, could not ignore these markets. Any idea of reviving the Commonwealth trading system was pure fancy, however, whilst the ability of German and French companies to make profits in China, India, Malaysia and elsewhere showed it was possible to combine a European commitment with an ability to trade competitively world-wide. Certainly, after Hong Kong returned to China, there were no more economically valuable areas under British control anywhere in the world. British dependencies like Gibraltar, Bermuda and the Falklands only had a population between them of about 200 000 people. Malcolm Rifkind, who succeeded Hurd as Foreign Secretary in 1995, summed up British foreign policy in September of that year, emphasising that, though the country's principal aims were still national defence and peace in Europe, the wider world remained of vital importance beyond the end of Empire: 'We export one quarter of all we produce; a greater share than Japan or the US ... Germany or France. We are the world's third largest outward investor ... Britain is the world's leading centre for international bank lending, foreign exchange, aviation and marine insurance.' The global market, the power of multinational companies, the communications revolution and environmental problems all pointed to the need for cooperation in the European Union and other groups. But Rifkind insisted, 'the nation state remains the basic building block of the international system' and in such areas as the former USSR and Yugoslavia nationalism was resurgent. British interests, dictated by its need to export and invest, would be reflected in a pragmatic approach to European integration and the encouragement of open markets in Eastern Europe and the wider world. The speech suggested Britain was still committed to doing a great deal in the world but – an old problem – was vague about where effort and resources should be concentrated.[6]

The American alliance and the end of the Cold War

Although Heath could never be described as anti-American, his desire to reduce the 'special relationship' from its exalted plane and his neutral line during the October 1973 Middle East war, linked to such developments in America as the campaign to reduce troop levels in Europe, created the impression of poor Anglo-US relations. With 'stagflation', oil price rises and the situation of 'Mutual Assured Destruction' between the Superpowers, the 1970s proved a depressing period on the world stage, eased somewhat by fragile progress with *détente*. When Harold Wilson re-entered Downing Street in February 1974 relations with the EC were marred by a renegotiation of Heath's terms, but European *détente* reached its high point in the August 1975 Helsinki Agreements. At Helsinki the West effectively recognised Soviet domination of Eastern Europe as the price for opening the Communist world up to the potentially subversive influence of Western trade and a belief in human rights. The Labour Left, convinced that the Soviet threat had previously been exaggerated to justify high arms expenditure, hoped that nuclear disarmament could now be pressed more vigorously and, committed not to renew Britain's nuclear deterrent, the government made a costly, failed attempt to update Polaris with the so-called Chevaline Project. Wilson and his successor (in 1976) Callaghan were rather more successful in improving relations with Washington, despite the continued suspicion of the Left. Callaghan indeed became the most trusted European colleague of the luckless President Jimmy Carter (1976–80). But in general, abroad as at home, pessimism was inescapable. As Foreign Secretary, Callaghan had warned the Cabinet in April 1974 that 'our place in the world is shrinking: long-term political influence depends on economic strength – and that is running out'.[7] Income per head was now half that of Germany. And a decision by NATO in 1977 to boost defence spending by 3 per cent showed that *détente* had not ended competition with the Soviets. True, by 1978, despite losing its majority in the Commons, Callaghan's government had begun to cut government spending, brought inflation back below 10 per cent and achieved a current account surplus. But the strikes of the 'winter of discontent' which followed ensured Thatcher's victory in the May 1979 election. At home her policies marked a decisive (but not unheralded) shift from the 'post-war consensus' to a low tax, free enterprise doctrine which was likened to Victorian liberalism. Her foreign policy, in contrast, was curiously traditional in aim, if more resolute in execution than in the recent past. The first female Prime Minister in the Western world had already earned the epithet 'Iron Lady' for her pronounced anti-Communism, to which she was able to give free rein when in December 1979 the Soviets invaded Afghanistan. The invasion fatally undermined the Left's claim that Moscow was primarily a defensive power and put an end to the era of *détente*. A strong supporter of NATO, when Thatcher looked abroad for allies she found the closest not in Europe but in America, especially when Ronald Reagan, a fellow right-winger and free-marketeer, became President in January 1981. Perhaps it was her wartime upbringing which bred suspicion of Germany, contempt for France and an over-estimation of British power. Yet, as seen over Rhodesia, she was no prisoner of right-wing beliefs, nor did her 'conviction politics' and notorious lack of diplomatic finesse rule out compromise. The 11 years of her premiership saw some surprising developments. Sceptical about European integration, she contributed much to one of its greatest advances, the Single European Act. Whilst doggedly resisting political concessions to IRA hunger strikers in 1980–81, she effectively acknowledged the international dimension of the Ulster problem in November 1985 by creating the Anglo-Irish Council. Despite her anti-Sovietism she also proved ready to emulate Churchill and (of all people) Macmillan, by encouraging a revival of East–West contacts in the mid-1980s.

Thatcher's toughness, patriotism and anti-Communism were much to the taste of the new US President, and they formed the closest partnership between British and American leaders since Macmillan and Kennedy. Whatever the differences between London and Washington, they continued to share a democratic and capitalist outlook, and a common interest in, for example, resisting Soviet expansion, maintaining the West's nuclear deterrent and trying to stabilise the Middle East. Thatcher was determined to resist pressure from Labour and the revived Campaign for Nuclear Disarmament (CND), and to deploy intermediate range Cruise and Pershing missiles in Europe to offset Soviet SS-20s. The decision to do so was taken in December 1979, just before the Afghanistan invasion, and carried through in 1983 amid considerable controversy and fear as the 'Second Cold War' reached its height. Thatcher was able to use her link to Reagan to secure a replacement for the long-range Polaris nuclear missile in the form of Trident, and she overcame private doubts to praise the President's 1983 'Strategic Defense Initiative', designed to build defences against a Soviet nuclear attack. In the wider world, Britain's rediscovered readiness to involve itself in the role of policeman proved useful both in the Persian Gulf (an old haunt), where the Royal Navy's Armilla patrol helped keep oil tankers safe during the Iran–Iraq War, and in the Lebanon, where a small British force joined the Americans, French and Italians during a 1984–85 'peace-keeping' operation. In April 1986 Britain was also, controversially, the only European state to provide active help to the American bombing raid against Libya, whose leader, Colonel Gadaffi, was accused of aiding international terrorism – another growing menace to Western security since the late 1960s. Lebanon and the Gulf, alongside the Falklands, confirmed Britain's ability to play a forceful role beyond Europe, so long as operations were limited in aim and had US support. The point was further demonstrated during the 1990–91 Gulf War when Thatcher urged Reagan's successor, George Bush, to resist Saddam Hussein's invasion of Kuwait and Britain's air force and army took a leading role among America's allies in the successful campaign to liberate the oil-rich sheikhdom. Anglo-American friendship was not however untroubled. In October 1983, when the Americans invaded the West Indies island of Grenada (which had fallen to a radical left-wing movement), Thatcher showed her displeasure: Grenada was a Commonwealth state and Britain had not been consulted about the American action. Britain was also ahead of the Americans in 1983–84 in supporting a more imaginative policy towards Moscow, which Reagan condemned as an 'Evil Empire'. MI6 were warned by one of their most successful spies, Oleg Gordievsky, about how nervous the Kremlin was because of Reagan's uncompromising policy, and the FCO, as concerned as ever about the dangers of conflict, began to develop 'Howe's Ostopolitik' of increased contacts with Eastern Europe. As with Churchill in the 1950s, the aim was not to condone totalitarianism but to undermine it, in this case by encouraging individual Eastern European states to look for cooperation with the West and by building contacts with reformist Communist leaders. Thatcher saw the logic of this, visiting Hungary in February 1984 and attending the funeral of the Soviet leader, Yuri Andropov, the following month. She identified Mikhail Gorbachev as the next Soviet leader and encouraged American contact with him, without however becoming part of the Reagan–Gorbachev summits which later took place.

With the collapse of Communism in Eastern Europe in 1989 Thatcher, the victor of three elections, seemed in an enviable position. Victory in the Cold War had followed the Rhodesia and Falklands successes abroad. At a summit in London in July 1990 NATO indicated that nuclear war had become extremely unlikely and that its main role was now to develop links to the East. But just as the Conservatives' domestic fortunes became more troubled in 1988–90, so the dramatic changes abroad exposed the weaknesses of a foreign policy based, Macmillan-style, on personal contacts rather than economic strength. 'Whereas in the 1940s Britain was one of the chief architects of the post-war order ... by 1989 [it] was largely reduced to the status of observer of the transformation of its security environment.'[8] The end of the Cold War removed the main reference point of Thatcher's policy, Bush proved less close a partner than Reagan and the Prime Minister was unsympathetic to German reunification which came about in October 1990. The FCO and most of the rest of Whitehall saw a single German state as inevitable at this time and Thatcher seemed out of touch with reality on this matter. She was quite correct on the other hand – as others were not – to expect that German reunification would lead to a deepening of European integration, and her eagerness to stabilise Eastern Europe while preserving, and expanding, the Western alliance fitted well into the American approach. Even the beginning of the Gulf War in August 1990 and a revival of influence in Washington, however, could not save the situation. In November 1990 disagreements in the government over Europe, added to fears about the electoral implications of a new 'poll tax' at home, helped bring Thatcher's fall from office. She was, however, able to secure the election of her own favoured successor, the little-known John Major. Though he inherited Thatcher's mantle, Major was the product of a post-war upbringing, more pragmatic, far less charismatic but also less jingoistic and readier to deal more positively with the EC. Much of the content of British policy remained the same – significantly Major was quick to make a visit to Washington – but the style had changed. Despite the Prime Minister's early hopes of creating a country 'at peace with itself', and becoming a leading player in Europe, the new government faced a daunting situation. At home, the drive to cut social spending and make Britain competitive bred considerable insecurity, depression had returned and an election was due within 18 months. Abroad, despite the reduced fears of nuclear war, there was equal uncertainty, bred by the end of the Cold War, upheaval in the USSR, novel challenges such as 'global warming', new talks on European integration, the danger of a division of the world into powerful trading blocs and, of course, the Gulf War. The last was, in one sense, quickly resolved: isolated even in the Arab world and condemned by the UN (where the US and USSR were now in agreement), Saddam Hussein was driven from Kuwait in January–February 1991 after the astonishingly successful, American-led operation 'Desert

Storm'. But in another sense the Gulf remained a problem, for Saddam remained in power and, though subject to sanctions, continued to threaten the peace of the region, as well as oppressing national minorities in Iraq. It was largely thanks to Major's efforts that in April the allies established 'safe havens' for the Marsh Arabs in the south and the Kurds in northern Iraq. But in January 1993 air strikes were launched against Iraq because of its refusal to abide by the 1991 ceasefire agreement, and in 1996 only the British were ready to give strong support to American bombing raids, launched in retribution for Saddam's continued meddling in Kurdish areas.

'Britain in the 1990s [was] part of a world that [was] immensely different from that of the 1970s.'[9] In 1973, with the first oil price increase, peace in Vietnam and British entry to the EC seemed far away indeed. Europe, which had been the centre of Cold War tensions in the 1940s and 1950s, was now just one region of a complex world. Yet foreign policy was still based on the old aims of peace, free trade and the American alliance. Britain supported the formal end of 'containment' at NATO's Brussels Summit of November 1991 and the 'partnership for peace' with Eastern European states, initiated at another summit in January 1994. In seeking stability in Europe, London was anxious to retain a full role for America, avoiding any return (however unlikely) by that country to isolationism. But a desire to retain the US alliance did not mean that Britain would always support Washington's line. Throughout the bloody Bosnian civil war the British participated in peace-keeping operations by both the UN and NATO, but they refused to take a pronounced anti-Serb line such as the Americans might have preferred. To avoid casualties among their own forces, and aware from past experiences of the dangers of becoming bogged down in inter-ethnic conflict, the British preferred to play a minimalist role. It was significant that US rather than European efforts led to an uneasy settlement of the conflict in the November 1995 Dayton Accord, but Britain did contribute to the 'Implementation Force' which oversaw the enforcement of the agreement. By then the UN's reputation as a force for peace, which had revived so strongly around 1990, was severely tarnished. For some British policy smacked once more of 'appeasement', though in contrast to the 1930s it was not obvious that Serb aggression, localised in the former Yugoslavia, need pose a threat to the wider peace or the balance of power in Europe. The Bosnian war was only one problem to bring about a worsening in Anglo-American relations under Major and Bush's successor (from January 1993), Bill Clinton. The end of the Cold War also ended one powerful element driving Britain and America together, and American society, more multicultural than ever, now had little interest in notions of 'Anglo-Saxon' solidarity. Even on the issue of free trade, where London and Washington often shared a common approach, there were disagreements in 1996 after America threatened legal action against companies investing in Cuba. Pressure on Cuba's Marxist regime was part of a general campaign under Clinton against so-called 'pariah states' (including Iraq, Libya and North Korea) but Britain and other European states argued that the US action was an illegal, unilateral infringement on their commercial rights. Even worse arguments were generated by the Irish problem. The December 1993 Downing Street declaration, in which Britain denied any 'selfish strategic or economic interest in Northern Ireland', was welcomed in America and followed nine months later by an IRA ceasefire. But the British were enraged at the speed with which Clinton was willing to welcome representatives of the IRA's political wing to Washington. The resumption of IRA terrorism in February 1996, and the adverse reaction this caused in America, helped restore relations somewhat but the close Thatcher–Reagan partnership had long gone. The end of the Cold War may have left Britain more secure, in one sense, than it had been since the 1920s: a military threat was highly unlikely. But with the Commonwealth a virtually meaningless entity, the US alliance soured, the nuclear deterrent of questionable value and the forces of interdependence ever-growing, Britain's ability to shape the international environment was ever-more limited. Nor did Europe provide the solution to domestic and overseas challenges which Heath had hoped in 1973.

Britain in Europe

Heath himself spent barely a year as the leader of an EC government and the experience proved frustrating. None of the lofty plans made at the Paris Summit of October 1972 came to much. Most importantly, the goal of Economic and Monetary Union (EMU), designed to provide a stable basis for expanded trade, was undermined by depression, inflation and the differing economic policies of the member states. There was an attempt to tie European currencies together, within a certain value of each other, in the so-called 'snake' but Britain only remained a member for six weeks. Heath's attempt to boost demand in the domestic economy ahead of entry simply generated more inflation and membership itself led to the predicted higher food prices. Neither did the Germans, already contributing much to the costs of the CAP, wish to pay for Heath's idea of a European regional development fund which might have channelled EC money to Britain. Such a fund was only formed, on a modest basis, under the subsequent Labour government, whose main European aim was to renegotiate the terms of entry won by Heath. Renegotiation proved a limited affair. A slightly better deal was secured for

Commonwealth exports and a 'correcting mechanism' was agreed to limit the size of British budgetary contributions to the Community, but there were no changes to the Treaty of Rome, the CAP or the basic fact that Britain paid more into the EC than it got out. The terms still left a divided Cabinet with critics like the left-wingers Tony Benn and Michael Foot ranged against social democrats such as Roy Jenkins. But the ever-resourceful and manipulative Wilson was still able to hold Labour together by putting the final decision on whether to remain in Europe to the electorate in a referendum. This provided a remarkable, unique opportunity for the British people to have their say on a major international issue. In fact, by the time the referendum was announced in January 1975 opinion polls were already moving in favour of the EC and when it was held, on 5 June, there were numerous factors which influenced two-thirds of the electorate to approve membership. Wilson and a majority of the Cabinet (though not of the wider Labour Party) were in favour; the European Movement spent millions on the campaign; and whereas most moderate politicians (Conservative, Liberal and Labour) advocated a 'Yes' vote, their opponents were a diverse gathering which included both extremes of British politics. Neither do the British people seem to have been convinced that there was any viable alternative to continued membership if national wealth and power were to be shored up. Yet, of course, this still did not mean that there was much idealistic commitment to the EC. The three-year premiership of James Callaghan showed continuing doubts about the country's Community spirit. Callaghan was as unexcited about the EC as Wilson, and needed to strike a balance between 'pros' and 'anti-marketeers' in his own party as well as coping with the Euro-enthusiasm of the Liberals, on whom he relied in parliamentary votes. Britain supported the 'southern enlargement' of the EC to Greece, Spain and Portugal, but partly in the hope that this would make it more difficult to centralise the Community. Five-yearly direct elections to the largely ineffective European parliament were agreed but differences in Britain delayed them being held until June 1979, by which time Callaghan was out of office. And although it was Roy Jenkins who, as President of the Commission after 1977, first advocated a renewed attempt at monetary coordination, Labour refused to join most other EC members in founding the Exchange Rate Mechanism (ERM) in March 1979, which tied currency values closely together.

So troubled was Labour's European policy that many welcomed Thatcher's arrival in power as likely to produce a more positive attitude. But, despite having criticised Callaghan's refusal to join the ERM, she pursued the same policy and soon proved an even more determined critic of the inefficient, expensive CAP, the powers of the unelected European Commission and, above all, the billion pounds net contribution which

Britain now paid into the EC. A cost-cutter at home and a resolute leader abroad, her crusade to reduce the net contribution was perhaps a natural aim, but the abrasive style in which it was pursued shocked Carrington, the FCO and her fellow EC leaders. The last group expected to be treated as partners and equals, not foreign foes. She rejected early offers of compromise as inadequate, refused to recognise British payments as the EC's 'own resources' and was unmoved by arguments that Britain should simply abide by the terms of entry. In May 1980 her tactics had some success, with a rebate of nearly £800 million per year, but it was only a provisional settlement, reluctantly accepted in Downing Street. A long-term settlement was only achieved at the 1984 Fontainebleau Summit, which established a new system of rebates. By then the other EC leaders were desperate for a deal because they also needed to increase VAT payments as a way to cover the costs of the CAP, and this decision required unanimity. Some praised Thatcher's achievement as a triumph for British interests won by determination and toughness, an example, like the Falklands War, that appeasement no longer dictated policy. But others pointed out that the total amount of money won back was a fraction of national wealth, that the extra VAT payments marked an important concession and that the budgetary episode had damaged the country's standing in the EC. Indeed the whole first decade of British membership had been one of disappointment, both for the country itself (which failed to see any dynamic positive results from entry) and the Community (which was put in the doldrums by economic uncertainty, arguments with Britain and slow progress with institutional reform). However, by 1984 both France's President, François Mitterand, and West Germany's Chancellor, Helmut Kohl, were ready to exploit the revival of economic growth in Europe to deepen integration further. Kohl, like Adenauer before him, urged Europeanism on Germany as a route away from nationalism and militarism of the past to liberalism, wealth and peace; whilst Mitterand's socialist economic policy at home had run into the sand and he urgently needed an alternative. Both leaders believed that European cooperation could deliver security and growth, allowing the continent to match the economic and technological might of America and Japan. For the first time since the 1950s, Paris and Bonn strongly agreed on a policy which might increase the supranational element in EC institutions. Predictably this was not to British taste and there was some fear of a 'two-tier' Europe developing, in which an inner group of states, led by France and Germany, would integrate faster than Britain and the rest. As yet, however, Thatcher felt no need to be left behind. Though an opponent of institutional reform, she *was* greatly interested in attempts to improve Europe's competitiveness, both within the Community and without. In particular, Conservatives championed a 'single market' in which members would trade freely, not only in goods, but in services and where such barriers to trade as customs regulations and safety laws would be simplified or removed. In March 1985 an EC Summit in Brussels agreed to pursue such a policy, and three months later, in Milan, it was agreed to achieve the single market by 1 January 1993. The price for securing this, however, was that the Prime Minister had to accept a study of institutional reforms too: had she refused the others might have gone ahead without Britain, a step which would have disturbed industry, the City and many Conservative pro-Europeans. The result was the December 1985 Single European Act which extended the scope of EC activities, strengthened the parliament and greatly widened the use of qualified majority voting in the Council of Ministers. The last step was enormously important because it reduced individual members' power of veto on an issue, but Thatcher agreed to it, largely, it seems, in order to secure the single market. The Act was easily ratified in Britain in 1986 and few Conservatives recognised that the single market itself involved a large increase in the responsibilities of the European Commission, which was charged with bringing it into effect.

Within a few years it was clear that the rest of the EC did not simply wish to create a Thatcherite free market. French Socialists, including the new President of the Commission, Jacques Delors, as well as German Christian Democrats, were determined to protect individuals from social distress once the single market was achieved. Opportunities for business and industry were to be matched by a Social Charter, which guaranteed certain rights and conditions for the rest of society. At the same time the disciplines of the ERM had succeeded in bringing down inflation in most member states, and interest revived in a fully fledged EMU. The Delors Report of April 1989, which resulted from a study of EMU by a committee of bankers, proposed to work towards a single currency in three stages, beginning with ERM membership. EMU could be seen as a natural step to follow the single market, making international trade easier and boosting growth. The Treasury, under Nigel Lawson, was increasingly in favour of ERM membership as a way to stabilise the value of the Pound and control inflation in Britain, and Howe's FCO believed that joining the ERM would strengthen Britain's diplomatic strength in Britain ahead of any talks on the EMU. But, as forthrightly stated in her Bruges Speech of September 1988, Thatcher believed in a single market only alongside strong nation-states, which could best provide stability and protect democracy. She wanted Europe to be open to trade with the wider world, not a closed, protectionist system, and she had no desire to see the EC interfere in social and budgetary policies: 'We have not ... rolled back the frontiers of the state in Britain ... to see them reimposed [by] ... a European super-state'.[10] A single currency and central bank would mark a vast increase in the EC's power, undermine the independence of member states and lead to further economic and budgetary coordination among its members, very different to the Community of competing states which Thatcher wished to see. At first she tried to slow down progress on the Delors Plan, refused to enter the ERM and encouraged both Lawson and his successor, Major, to develop alternatives to the single currency. But the EC Summit in Strasbourg in December 1989 agreed to begin talks within 12 months of an EMU treaty. Thatcher recognised that the prospect of German reunification made the French more anxious to limit German independence: Paris believed this was best achieved by replacing the Deutchsmark with a European currency. As the intergovernment talks approached, other Cabinet ministers were keen to get Britain into the ERM so as to play a strong role in the talks. A clamour built up throughout Westminster and in most of the Press for ERM membership and Thatcher finally succumbed in October 1990, a month before losing office. Doubts about the wisdom of her European policy contributed much to that event. The single market had been an important achievement and she had never advocated withdrawal from the EC, but her abrasive style and her particular vision of Europe seemed ill-suited to the delicate negotiations which were about to begin. Most Conservatives hoped that, whilst protecting British interests, her successor would take a more positive role in Europe.

Such hope did not prove misplaced. Indeed, especially when viewed in the light of his later problems, Major's European policy in his first 18 months was a great success. He adopted a more *communitaire* negotiating manner, supported by the pro-European Douglas Hurd, and sensibly chose to improve personal relations with Chancellor Kohl, whose support helped avoid disaster when a new treaty on integration was signed at the Maastricht Summit in December 1991. In some ways Maastricht looked dramatic: a 'European Union' (EU) was declared; there was a further strengthening of European institutions; and two new areas of cooperation, CFSP and 'Justice and Home Affairs', were begun (on the basis of intergovernmental rather than supranational cooperation). But whilst all the other members agreed to a Social Charter and EMU, Major won the right to 'opt out' of both and thus appeared to preserve a free hand for Britain. He also had some success in pressing the principle of 'subsidiarity': that European institutions should only intervene where action was not better pursued at national or local level. This was sufficient to please Thatcherites in his own party, allowed him to avoid domestic controversy on Europe and even led to the EU becoming a side issue in the 1992 election. Neither of the main parties stood to gain by opening up their internal differences on it. Once the election was over, however, Major's European nightmare began. His reduced majority made it easier for 'Euro-sceptics' to embarrass him in the Commons, many Thatcherites grew critical of his leadership style and Maastricht became an important symbol of Britain's restricted independence in the world. It was clear that, while the opt-outs had solved the short-term problem, the treaty had nonetheless pushed European integration still further and in the long term Britain faced a dilemma: how could it avoid membership of a single currency if other EU members went ahead? Would non-membership damage its competitiveness in Europe and lead Frankfurt to replace London as an investment centre? Since the mid-1950s the main question for Britain in Europe had not been whether it wished to take part in integration, but whether it could afford *not* to take part if other countries went ahead. The treaty was ratified in 1993, but only after some close votes, especially when its Conservative opponents threatened to unite with the Labour Party and vote in favour of the Social Charter – in the hope that defeat on this issue would lead ministers to revoke the whole document. The Maastricht debates would not have been so bitter, however, had it not been for evidence of the damage that involvement in currency integration could do to the economy. Britain's ERM membership had been troubled from the start, bringing down inflation but strangling economic growth and triggering a resurgence of unemployment. Britain had arguably joined at too high an exchange rate and at the wrong time, just as German reunification pushed up interest rates in the anchor-economy of the mechanism, forcing other members to do the same. When currency pressures pushed Britain out of the ERM on 'Black Wednesday', 16 September 1992, it damaged Major as badly as devaluation had harmed Wilson a quarter of a century before. Even the lower interest rates which followed failed to restore the Conservatives' reputation as reliable economic managers. Furthermore, it allowed Euro-sceptics to argue that, far from harming British competitiveness, non-involvement in EMU would be beneficial, allowing Britain to maintain economic and monetary policies which suited it best.

As by-election losses continued to reduce his majority, and the right-wing Press adopted a determinedly anti-European line, Major was repeatedly forced to demonstrate his patriotic credentials at the cost, like Thatcher, of alienating European opinion. More than ever European issues had an impact on domestic politics and vice versa, and a Prime Minister had to try, somehow, to dovetail both. Opposition to the nomination of Belgium's Jean-Luc Dehaene as President of the Commission in July 1994 and bitter arguments that same year about voting procedures when the EU expanded to Scandinavia and Austria, were followed in 1996 by the 'Beef War', when Major vetoed EU decisions in retaliation for a ban on cattle exports following a health scare. Austen Chamberlain's term for Britain's European policy – 'semi-detachment' – was again widely used and some Conservatives even began to consider what had hitherto been unthinkable, that Britain should consider leaving the EU, an idea which Major roundly condemned. He himself preferred to advocate an '*à la carte*' (or 'variable geometry') Europe in which each member could choose to cooperate, or not cooperate, on a range of issues; he was also at the forefront in urging an enlargement of the EU to Eastern Europe. Britain was heavily reliant on trade with the EU, its business community strongly favoured a full commitment to membership and on many issues it could work well with its partners: they reached a common position on the 'Uruguay Round' of world trade talks, they settled most details of the January 1995 enlargement quite amicably and London was respected for its record in implementing EU regulations. Neither was Britain the only country to disagree with its partners on European policies. Greece and Denmark were often at odds with the rest and it was rare for a decision to be taken without some controversy. Even in France and Germany grave doubts grew about the potential economic price of creating a single currency and, after the crisis of 1992–93, the ERM had become a shadow of its former self. But the potential of European issues to provoke division in Britain was particularly intense as the 1997 election approached. 'For Britain to be at the heart of Europe would require Europe to be in the hearts of the British',[11] and the symbolism of integration was no more living in the country than it had been 25 years before. Even on a cool-headed assessment of national interest, Europe presented Britain with a difficult policy choice. To the preparations for a common currency – on which vital decisions about membership had soon to be taken – was added in 1996–97 an intergovernmental review of the Maastricht Treaty which could lead to further institutional reforms and, in the view of Thatcherites, might nudge the hybrid European structure even more in the direction of the much-feared 'Superstate'. However, if Britain did not take a positive line on these issues, there was an increasing chance that an 'inner core' of EU members, led by Germany and France, might push on with a single currency and institutional reforms anyway, leaving Britain and others in a peripheral position, with the diplomatic and economic costs that might carry.

Notes

1 George S., *An Awkward Partner: Britain in the European Community* (London, 1990), 66.

2 Hill C. and Lord C., 'The Foreign Policy of the Heath Government'. In Ball S. and Seldon A. (eds), *The Heath Government, 1970–74* (London, 1996), 314.

3 Parsons A., *The Pride and the Fall: Iran 1974–79* (London, 1984), 40.

4 Crozier B., *Free Agent: The Unseen War, 1941–91* (London, 1993), 104.
5 Segal G., 'Asia of the Pacific'. In Byrd P. (ed.), *British Foreign Policy under Thatcher* (London, 1988), 118.
6 Rifkind M., 'Principles and Practice of British Foreign Policy', speech to the Royal Institute of International Affairs, 21 September 1995.
7 Callaghan J., *Time and Chance* (London, 1987), 326.
8 Richardson L., 'British State Strategies after the Cold War'. In Keohane R. *et al.* (eds), *After the Cold War* (Cambridge, Mass., 1993), 148.
9 Clarke M., *British External Policy-making in the 1990s* (London, 1992), 1.
10 Thatcher M., speech on Europe to the College of Europe, Bruges, 20 September 1988.
11 Wallace H., 'Britain out on a Limb?', *Political Quarterly*, **66**(1), 1995, 47.

Conclusion

Before drawing some conclusions about Britain's experience in world affairs from the Diamond Jubilee to the withdrawal from Hong Kong, it is appropriate to underline the scale of the changes which took place over that period. In 1897 Britain was the world's greatest financial, commercial and naval power, its currency underpinned the global trading system and its formal rule extended to a quarter of the Earth's surface. Despite some concern over how the Empire could be maintained over the coming century, late Victorians believed their greatness to be secure, based on both 'heaven's command' and the irresistible triumph of *laissez-faire* economics and constitutional liberalism. A hundred years later there was no Empire, the Royal Navy was a fraction of America's, the stability provided by the Gold Standard had long gone and the City lived on Eurodollars rather than Sterling balances. As an industrial power Britain, just being overtaken by America around 1890, had been surpassed by Germany, Japan and France, and was on a par with Italy. Britain appeared less and less able to control its international environment and was no longer the prime beneficiary of growing interdependence. Yet to concentrate on such points is to show an obsession with decline which is only one, albeit vital, factor in the story. The same century saw developments which many might consider positive. The Victorians' easy assumption of racial superiority and their right to rule over others, inculcating Anglo-Saxon values and Protestantism, had given way to a world of independent nations, where several East Asian states (apart from Japan) threatened to match British levels of wealth, and where Britain itself had become a secular, multiracial and multicultural society. In 1897 there was no proper democracy, no universal education and only a nascent popular Press; landed and financial wealth created a political elite which industrialists had begun to penetrate over the previous few generations. But by 1997 the aristocracy had lost its power (if not its wealth), and policy-makers had to consider (if only seldom to bow to) the views of an educated electorate and a sophisticated mass media. In the earlier period states were undoubtedly the prime actors in an anarchical international environment, only *within* the Empire (with the system of Imperial conferences) did regular 'multilateral diplomacy' exist, Britain had no close allies and war was an accepted way even for advanced European governments to resolve disputes. In the later period London operated through a number of alliances and international organisations, which helped manage the forces of interdependence, and war between Western European nations, perhaps between any liberal democracies, had become unthinkable. Despite environmental fears, AIDS and international terrorism, the end of the Cold War – with its Superpower rivalry, nuclear arms race and ideological divide – left Britain even more secure from conventional attack in 1997 than she had been in 1897. Domination of Europe by a hegemonic power seemed improbable, even if Germany and Russia remained powerful; violence in other regions, even as close as Bosnia, was unlikely to reach British shores; and the supposed menace of Islamic Fundamentalism had largely come to the fore only because that of Communism had receded. The main challenge that faced Britain was not how to deal with likely enemies, but how to manage relations best with its partners in the EU and Atlantic alliance.

Some changes over the century may be seen as neither positive nor negative, simply a reflection of human development and technological advance. In 1897 the dreadnought was nearly a decade away; in 1997 the Hydrogen bomb was four decades old. In the 1890s a Foreign Secretary might visit the FO a few days each week, avoid overseas travel for years and treat even his most senior officials as glorified clerks. Those officials were all male, mostly of aristocratic background, wrote with quill pens and had only a few typists to support them. In the 1990s work almost always intruded into a Foreign Secretary's weekends, he travelled tens of thousands of miles each year, worked with a varied (if still rather select) diplomatic service and was supplied with instant information from around the world via computers, televisions and 'fax' machines. Diplomats in the 1990s dealt with a range of problems which their Victorian forebears would have found remarkable: trying to dovetail national aims with those of their European neighbours; devoting time to energy shortages, drug trafficking, economic deprivation and illegal immigration; and working alongside an intelligence community, propaganda machine and agencies for cultural diplomacy or overseas development which had not existed a century before. Yet through all the changes there were some factors which always remained the same. Britain's geographical position, as both an island power and a European one, did not change. Neither did the basic insecurity of the international system. Britain was always reasonably safe from invasion yet vulnerable to any upsets in world trade – adequate imports being vital to its survival. Its island position helped foster peaceful internal development but bred a form of patriotism which made close cooperation with Europe difficult. Despite such episodes as the General Strike, the country's social cohesion and the foreign policy consensus among its leaders was remarkable from the 1890s to the 1990s and a major asset in world affairs. Concern with American, German and Russian power was evident, albeit in different forms and at varying intensity, across the century. And thanks to the peaceful nature of Britain's political evolution the foreign policy machine too had its consistent elements, headed by the Cabinet, with the Foreign Office the lead department and a concentration of day-to-day decisions in the hands of a narrow, paternalistic elite. British ministers and officials were largely able to dominate the external policy-making debate and were subject only to very general limits set by the public, such as the need to preserve naval predominance before 1914, to foster peace between the wars or to fight for national interests in the EC after 1973. This is not to say that international issues were divorced from domestic ones, however. There were always areas where foreign policy and domestic politics were closely linked: throughout the century security abroad was tied to wealth and tranquillity at home; opposition to the Soviet Union between the wars and during the Cold War was influenced by a desire to prevent the growth of Marxist doctrines at home; and in the EU in the 1990s (as in the Tariff Reform question earlier) external and internal considerations became inextricably intertwined.

In 1997, for all its declining economic power relative to leading competitors, Britain was as wealthy as ever and better off than most. It was no more threatened by 'globalisation' than were many other countries, and although the right-wing Press might rail against the powers of the European Commission, Britain was one of the strongest states in the EU. With one-hundredth of the world's population it nonetheless accounted for one-twentieth of the world's trade. In one sense the world of the 1990s, with its liberal trade system, widespread respect for liberal political values and world-wide use of the English language, could be seen as fulfilling the Victorian dream of a rational, progressive global system from which most countries gained. As late as 1982 Britain had demonstrated that it was still a considerable naval power, with an ability to campaign on the opposite side of the world, and looking at the century as a whole, the country could certainly count itself a success compared to such rivals as Germany, Japan, France and Italy. A victor in two world wars, vulnerable but never invaded, Britain had protected its liberal political system and, outside of Ireland, avoided persistent internal unrest. Defeat in either world war could have led to rapid and absolute decline: instead Britain was able to help shape the new international environment after both and in contrast to, say, Germany in 1918 'there was no wholesale destruction of the old framework, no patriotic revolt against ... national leaders, ... no frontal assault on the fundamental assumptions ... inherited from the Victorians'.[1] Victory in war, alongside the generally successful management of colonial retreat and the idea that Empire was being transposed into Commonwealth (rather than lost altogether), also helped avoid any popular outcry against the end of Empire or a political crisis such as France faced in 1958. It should always be remembered that even in the mid-nineteenth century Britain was never all-powerful. Its small population, scarcity of raw materials (other than coal) and insubstantial army were all deficiencies. Another mistake is to conflate the relative decline of the country and the absolute loss of Empire. Quite obviously the fall of the British Empire was more rapid than that of Rome but, unlike Rome, London remained a major power after the Imperial retreat. Its industry, investments and diplomatic experience still counted for something and it adjusted to new circumstances, where colonies and navies were less important indicators of power than the possession of a highly educated population and being at the forefront of the communications revolution. The end of Empire certainly *was* one vital aspect of Britain's declining power and prestige after 1945 – it would have been remarkable if the most successful state of the Imperial age had not suffered in the process of decolonisation – but the relative underperformance of the country in comparison to, say, France had more to do with industrial failings, whilst even the possession of the world's largest Empire in 1945 did not stop Britain being overtaken by the Superpowers. If Britain had forcibly resisted decolonisation it might have been even more ruinous. What may have had a detrimental effect after 1945 on Britain's economic and diplomatic performance was not the loss of Empire but the reluctance, especially after 1956, to give up more quickly the global presence and attitudes which went with it. Then again, the eagerness of ministers to retain Imperial positions after the Second World War, as after the First, shows that (in contrast to some historical opinion) they retained much of their determination and ambition – even if the experience of the Great War led to a deep craving for tranquillity in the population at large. Eventually British pragmatism and adaptability did win through: Conservative 'die-hard' opposition to colonial withdrawal melted away in the face of economic and electoral self-interest. Only in Rhodesia did a white settler community try to prevent decolonisation on the principle of majority rule; whilst, again in contrast to France, the armed forces proved loyal through the decolonisation process. The retreat from Empire was even viewed as a triumph, as the myth was fostered of an enlightened, constitutional Mother Country grooming its offspring in Africa and Asia for independence, in the way the white Dominions had been prepared before them.

In studying Britain and the world in the twentieth century historians have since the 1960s tried to look beyond traditional diplomatic history

– with its concern for individual policy-makers, specific crises and detailed areas of policy – to the *structural* factors which did much to dictate decisions, and to the totality of external relations, recognising in the process the interreliance of overseas and domestic policy. For, 'does not any foreign policy reflect the efforts of the nation state to shape an international environment congenial to ... the preservation of the ... economic ... and social order within its own borders?'.[2] International relations cannot be understood fully by looking at diplomatic documents. Strategic, ideological, economic, geographic, psychological and sociological factors must all be considered, as must the behaviour of allies (including, in Britain's case, the Dominions) and enemies. Political beliefs, business interests, the education system and popular xenophobia can be more vital than ambassadors, admirals, governors and prime ministers. It has often been argued by 'structuralists' that from the mid-Victorian era to the post-war world Britain, as one of the world's wealthiest powers and with such a vast Empire, was extremely constrained in its policy choices and prone to 'appease' its enemies by satisfying their demands rather than risking war. It needed to defend both its island home and far-flung Dominions and colonies. It relied on an orderly system of global commerce and finance, centred on the City of London, the success of which could be upset by riots, rebellions and wars almost anywhere. The Royal Navy had to protect the world's sea communications not only because of the formal Empire, but also because the island power's wealth was built on trade and investment and, with a densely packed population, it needed to import food and raw materials simply to live. After 1890 Britain was unable to hold onto all it possessed, to unite its Empire into a whole or to escape from the world into isolationism. Yet it can also be argued that, as a satisfied power, with liberal institutions and such a strong desire for order, it was less prepared than others to risk war; and its island position and parliamentary sovereignty made it less keen to enter firm alliances, so that limited concessions to rivals, securing the peace whilst protecting vital interests, became the policy norm. Over time the restrictions on British independence increased but the radical option of cutting naval spending and retreating from Empire was resisted by political leaders as too dangerous, liable to benefit rivals and lead to even greater insecurity. The costs facing the government at home were increased furthermore by the growth of an interventionist, social security state. Robert Holland has written that, from the Edwardian era to the 1970s, 'What economic policy was meant to do was to prop up the structure of Welfare at home and Greatness abroad which gave both the Right and Left a stake ... in the political consensus of the day'.[3] The attempt to pay for both policies, it may be argued, eventually meant that in the 1970s the country could properly afford neither. The present study has made no attempt to unravel the undoubtedly complex reasons for Britain's economic failings, but it is impossible to avoid considering the links between this subject and declining external power. These links permeate the established literature, and much of the mystery surrounding Britain's twentieth-century experience is because – in contrast to other examples of declining Empires from Assyria to Austria–Hungary – the single cause of overwhelming military defeat is not available to explain decline. Instead Britain's fall from predominance is widely accepted as being multi-causal, but it is difficult to weigh the importance of one cause against another, and some historians have elevated one cause – usually economic failings – above all others. There has also been a tendency to see the root causes of decline stretching back into the Victorian period and to interpret such events as the world wars merely as quickening a pre-existent process. But it is always dangerous to 'read history backwards' and the facts are, first, that British leaders had faced the constraints of an island position and the need to defend far-flung commercial interests from the seventeenth century onwards and, second, that awareness of relative economic decline took time to set in. Although concern about declining exports was apparent in the 1930s, and although the Second World War should have sounded alarm bells about Britain's industrial efficiency, deep pessimism about the country's economic performance did not set in until the 1960s, when many historians would agree that decline was well-advanced and the Empire was being given up: indeed in the 1960s and 1970s decline was seen as a *domestic* problem, not as having much to do with the loss of Empire.

Paul Kennedy, whilst not ignoring other elements, lays great stress on economic statistics and considers that 'the early British lead was a happy accident, conditioned by certain broad economic, and technological trends rather than by native virtues' and that once new competitors emerged to challenge Britain's industrial lead, 'long-term eclipse was inevitable'.[4] Ultimately British Imperial and naval power relied on its financial and commercial power, built in the eighteenth century, reinforced by its nineteenth-century industries, and in Kennedy's view, once economic strength failed to match Britain's commitments, as happened in the 1930s, decline could not be escaped. Such overstretch was apparent earlier, especially in 1916–18 when Britain tried to maintain both a large navy and a huge land army. Bernard Porter is even more openly fatalistic than Kennedy, and dismisses attempts to uncover 'where Britain went wrong', arguing that decline relative to some other states 'could not have been prevented: not by wise statesmanship, nor by more favourable world conditions, nor by any measures to restore ... Britain's economic health' because the reasons for its Victorian predominance lay in those same economic and social factors, its faith in free trade, individualism and an open society, which made it so vulnerable to disturbances in the rest of the world.[5] In contrast, Corelli Barnett believes that the right choices could have made a difference and that decline was linked to the moderate, unheroic, consensus-seeking attitudes of politicians and the popular desire for peace: Britain's predicament in 1940 'derived neither from bad luck nor from the failures of others. It had been brought upon the British by themselves.'[6] Yet looking across the century Porter does seem to have a case, for the British tried a range of solutions to their dilemma, all ultimately in vain. No variation of economic policy, whether *laissez-faire* or interventionist, based on Imperial trade preferences or the cold douche of EEC membership has carried Britain back up the league tables of comparative performance. And no variation of foreign policy protected Britain from war, growing insecurity and the loss of Empire whether it be the *ententes* or the US alliance, the restlessness of Lloyd George or the docility of Baldwin, Neville Chamberlain's brand of appeasement or Churchill's stern defiance, the semi-detachment of Austen Chamberlain (and Margaret Thatcher) or the Euro-enthusiasm of Heath. Yet a determinist outlook does little to explain the *exact* course of events, even over long periods of several decades. Whilst the rise of new competitors and the vulnerabilities created by a liberal, free market outlook may have created some problems for Britain, it is not obvious that they should have pushed the country, in terms of wealth per head, so far behind another liberal-capitalist state like America. True, America has a larger population and huge natural resources, but so did another 'continental' power, the Soviet Union, and these factors did not save it from disintegration in 1991. Neither is it obvious why post-war Britain should have been overtaken in national wealth by another island nation with limited resources, Japan; or why France, another Western European democracy and former colonial power with a similar population size, should have been so much more successful since 1958. Whilst it may be true that, *in the long term*, economic underperformance compared to other states fatally undermines political power, this is not very informative about what happens in the shorter term (even a period as long as a generation) and takes no account of other forms of power.

In contrast to Kennedy and Porter, other writers, notably David Reynolds and a group of Canadian international historians, emphasise that 'power is relative',[7] not only between different powers (which Kennedy and Porter accept) but between different time periods and local circumstances. Power can be an easy relationship to define: put crudely it is the ability of one country to make another country do something it would not otherwise do. But it is far more difficult to measure, because it includes both tangible and intangible factors. Britain without the Empire may have been weak compared to other Great Powers for much of the century in some of the more obvious indices of strength, such as population, land area and economic growth rates, but it fared well on others such as social cohesion, efficient government and a universal language. It fared worse than America over the period 1895–1997 as a whole but better than, say, Austria or Turkey, and until at least 1939 it was at the forefront of world powers. The precise conditions in which power is wielded can have an enormous effect and superior economic strength does not always guarantee military success, as seen most famously in the American defeat in Vietnam or the Soviets' in Afghanistan. Even in its Victorian heyday Britain, too, sometimes failed to make its military, economic and technological advantages tell against smaller, weaker powers, the prime examples being its own Afghanistan disaster in 1841–42 and the Boer victory at Majuba Hill (1881). Choice too is always an important element in policy-making, and however much states may seem at the mercy of impersonal factors it can be possible to select a course which breaks free of even the most inhibiting restraints. In the twentieth century France too saw its share of world trade fall and its Empire lost, as it was outstripped by the Superpowers, but in the late 1940s it adopted an economic modernisation policy which allowed it to surpass British growth levels, and in the 1950s its leaders chose the imaginative policy of European integration which gave Paris a leading role on the continent. For Paris European integration also proved far more successful at controlling German ambitions than had the earlier policy of *entente* with 'perfidious Albion'. Other states, too, have proved capable of imaginative leaps to transform their international position: the way President Nixon's first administration used the 'opening to China' to improve its position *vis-à-vis* the Soviets (while the Vietnam War was still underway) is another obvious example. The British were not without ideas to improve their strength but Tariff Reform, Appeasement and the 'three circles' policy all failed and, perhaps because of the country's pragmatism and evolutionary development, real leaps of imagination were non-existent. Pragmatism could be both beneficial (allowing the British to adjust without convulsion to new realities) and harmful (preventing such leaps of faith as the original signatories of the Treaty of Rome). Finally, *chance* should be noted, as a factor too often ignored by those historians preoccupied with 'structural' analysis. For, however much our understanding of international developments has been improved by looking at the 'realities behind diplomacy', history is also about contingencies, the coming together of particular forces, personalities and events at particular times. The complexity of international events breeds a vast array of interconnections and collisions between such forces and events, over which no country has control. Just to mention some key events before 1914 – discovery of gold in the Transvaal, the Japanese victory at

Tsushima, the assassination at Sarajevo: British foreign policy would have had a very different shape if none of these had occurred, even if, over the century as a whole, underlying factors like anti-colonialism, new industrial competitors and technological change did work to the country's detriment.

Whilst having more to say about policy-making in Whitehall, where 'bureaucratic politics' could have an important impact on the country's foreign policy choices, and whilst giving greater attention than past studies to the emergence of intelligence and propaganda services, the present study too has tried to show that Britain was, for most of the century, a leading power in the world and a successful one compared to most others. It is important not to place all the emphasis on economic decline, and read the political impact of such decline too far back in time. Although very many developments – colonial, economic, technological – were in train before 1939 and affected Britain's performance relative to leading competitors, national leaders were not obsessed by them and real obsession with 'decline' was a product of the post-war years. The country undoubtedly did have a craving for world peace and a readiness to make compromises to maintain this, but this did not mean it was ready to cave in to all challenges; its reliance on peace and trade was well-nigh inescapable given its island position and the need to import, but this did not prevent a decision in favour of war in 1914. Before 1914 Britain was losing its manufacturing predominance but not its financial lead, and it still controlled 48 per cent of the world's shipping, four times as much as its nearest rival, Germany. Although the Royal Navy had many challenges it beat the most serious rival, Germany, in the naval race. The Japanese alliance and the *ententes* might suggest that policy choices abroad were becoming constrained, but – again – Britain had never been all-powerful (in the 1860s, for example, it had little diplomatic influence over such an epochal development as German unification) and the *ententes*, like the building of the *Dreadnought*, showed the country's adaptability and readiness to take risks. In 1900–5 the Franco-Russian threat was serious enough to cause major policy changes, but such a combination, a threat both in Europe and to the Empire, would have caused problems at any time in the nineteenth century and Britain's policy cannot be said to have been driven by fear or weak-mindedness. This point is reinforced when one looks at its reaction to the German threat during the naval race and the Moroccan crisis. It was an extremely daunting situation – continuing tension with Germany and the need to preserve the *ententes* – that led to the naval commitments to France in 1912 which had such significant implications in July 1914, but Britain avoided formal alliance commitments and maintained greater diplomatic freedom than other Great Powers at the time. The First World War did not prove the absolute disaster it proved for the autocratic regimes of Central and Eastern Europe, and there were many signs of enduring British strength, including the creation of a substantial army, maintenance of natural unity, the mobilisation of the Empire and the evolution of more efficient government machinery. Yet whilst Britain was able to pay for its own war effort, the conflict gravely harmed the country's financial position, especially *vis-à-vis* the US, the most successful rival for predominance in the twentieth century.

The Great War also proved psychologically scarring, bred a popular desire for peace and, paradoxically, produced even more commitments to defend in future. This has led several historians to argue that it was between the wars that the realisation of British decline really dawned. Actually in the early 1930s Britain was one of a group of powers of roughly equal strength, but still in the lead in some respects, especially in Imperial and naval power. Even if America possessed the economic, financial and technological capacity to outbuild the Royal Navy, it lacked the desire and determination to do so, and this too must be read into any equation of power. In the next few years it again took a particularly strong, and unexpected, combination of aggressive militarist states – Japan, Germany and Italy – to highlight the weaknesses in Britain's global position. The Second World War then proved more destructive than the First to the country's situation and the most important event for exposing Britain's relative decline. It spent much and won little for itself other than a reputation for brave resistance in 1940, although it *did* win a say in how the post-war world was shaped and helped, alongside America, to foster liberal democracy and free trade in the Western world. Once again it was the US which gained most from the conflict, easily outstripping the Royal Navy and leading some British leaders to believe that their role was to 'guide' the new Anglo-Saxon giant along the wisest course. After all, it was felt that London had greater experience of world affairs than Washington and that the English-speaking peoples had a common interest in fostering liberal democracy, resisting Communism and encouraging freer world trade. The Americans had a more realistic view of the relationship and were well aware of differences with Britain on colonialism, trade preferences and European unity: on the last, ironically, the British long feared integration with Europe would harm their value in Washington, when actually the opposite was the case. In the post-war world leaders of both main parties persisted in a world role for decades, maintained the Empire long after India was lost and relied on prestige to offset increasingly obvious material failings. Even then the conclusion that it must commit itself to a European future provoked deep and lasting controversy. To a real extent Britain still *was* different from continental powers because of its island position, reliance on world commerce, tradition of free trade (in contrast to French and Italian protectionism), unwritten constitution and strong sense of nationality, as well as its triumphant survival in the Second World War, and it was frustrated at being unable to shape Europe in its own image. The result was a situation of growing dissatisfaction in which people and policy-makers oscillated between exaggerating their country's continuing power and overstating the scale of its decline. In this process myths about the past played a crucial part: was not Britain the Protestant champion who had triumphed against Louis XIV, the financial and commercial giant which had defeated Napoleon, the liberal victor over the Kaiser and Hitler? But in overcoming all these opponents Britain had required allies, some at least of which were as powerful as herself: in particular Russia had had a greater part to play in destroying Bonaparte and Nazism. Britain had never been able to ignore Europe, but relied either on balance of power or an active policy there. A more realistic, balanced appreciation would have recognised that there were always limits to the country's past greatness, that it could not ignore the wishes of its European partners, that its ability to maintain order beyond Europe was extremely limited, and that its government structure and diplomatic skill were no better than many others. But it was a substantial, stable and secure nation, as well as a wealthy one when measured against most states; by working through such multilateral structures as the EU, NATO and UN it could still influence global developments; and by making suitable alliances within those organisations it could hope to build the liberal, orderly, commercially 'open' world in which its own political beliefs and economic interests could best thrive, even if the relative greatness of the Victorians was gone forever. As one of the leading analysts of post-war British foreign policy wrote at the end of the Cold War, 'Britain should look forward, not back; and ... should match the ... rhetoric of British national life to the constraints of national capabilities and the limitations of the international context'.[8]

Notes

1 Darwin J., 'The Fear of Falling: British Politics and Imperial Decline Since 1900', *Transactions of the Royal Historical Society*, **36**, 1986, 41.

2 Newton S., *Profits of Peace: The Political Economy of Anglo-German Appeasement* (Oxford, 1996), 3.

3 Holland R., *The Pursuit of Greatness: Britain and the World Role, 1900–1970* (London, 1991), 19.

4 Kennedy P., *The Realities Behind Diplomacy: Background Influences on British External Policy, 1865–1980* (London, 1985), 23–4. Kennedy fails to differentiate sufficiently between financial and industrial capitalism in contributing to British power: on financial-commercial capital see Cain P.J. and Hopkins A.G., *British Imperialism: Crisis and Deconstruction* (London, 1993).

5 Porter B., *Britain, Europe and the World, 1850-1986*, 2nd edn (London, 1986), xi and xiv. See also the same author's *The Lion's Share: A Short History of British Imperialism* (London, 1975). A determinist view of British decline can actually be traced to the end of the Victorian Era and the geographer Halford Mackinder who, in *Britain and the British Seas* (1902), argued that swifter land communications were shifting power to such 'continental' states as Russia and America.
6 Barnett C., *The Collapse of British Power* (London, 1972), 15.
7 Reynolds D., *Britannia Overruled* (London, 1991), 1; and on the Canadian School's path-breaking ideas see the special edition of the *International History Review*, **13**(4), 1991.
8 Wallace W., 'Foreign Policy and National Identity in the United Kingdom', *International Affairs*, **67**(1), 1991, 80.

Bibliographical essay

This bibliography is intended to provide a brief pointer to some of the main books on British foreign policy in the twentieth century, including many of those used in the present study. Readers should note, however, that there are many articles in the field (which it has been impossible to list here for reasons of space), as well as such documentary collections as *British Documents on the Origins of the War* (for the years 1898–1914), *Documents on British Foreign Policy* (for the inter-war period) and *Documents on British Policy Overseas* (post-1945), all prepared by Foreign Office historians. Unless otherwise stated the place of publication of the works listed is London.

There are a number of stimulating texts which overlap with the current volume including Paul Hayes, *Modern British Foreign Policy: The Twentieth Century* (Black, 1978), a chronological account based mainly on published documents which, despite its title, ends in 1939. Paul Kennedy, *The Realities Behind Diplomacy: Background Influences on British External Policy, 1865–1980* (Fontana, 1985) was a path-breaking study, weak perhaps on the post-1945 period and rather mechanical in interpretation, but a challenging and stimulating analysis of Britain's decline from its Victorian heyday. Even more determinist about the country's 'inevitable' eclipse was Bernard Porter, *Britain, Europe and the World, 1850–1986* (2nd edn, George Allen and Unwin, 1986). C.J. Bartlett, *British Foreign Policy in the Twentieth Century* (Macmillan, 1989) is a short account, best for drawing out the debates between historians on the various phases of British policy. More recent general texts are Robert Holland, *The Pursuit of Greatness: Britain and the World Role, 1900–1970* (Fontana, 1991), strong on Imperial perspectives but also showing the pressures created by domestic social and economic policies, and David Reynolds, *Britannia Overruled* (Longman, 1991), which is detailed on the post-1945 years and emphasises that changes in British power have been relative, not absolute. Books which focus on Imperial decline are Bernard Porter, *The Lion's Share: A Short History of British Imperialism, 1850–1970* (Longman, 1975) and R.J.

Cain and A.G. Hopkins, *British Imperialism: Crisis and Deconstruction, 1914–90* (Longman, 1993) which helpfully emphasises the importance of financial capitalism in Imperial development. For a sympathetic and stimulating discussion of the transition to the Commonwealth see Nicholas Mansergh, *The Commonwealth Experience* (Weidenfeld and Nicolson, 1969). Two collections of essays by leading scholars, which look at a particular theme over the last century, are D.C. Watt, *Succeeding John Bull: America in Britain's Place, 1900–75* (Cambridge University Press, 1984) and Michael Howard, *The Continental Commitment: The Dilemma of British Defence Policy in the Era of Two World Wars* (reprint, Ashfield Press, 1989). And on the intelligence services see Christopher Andrew, *Secret Service: The Making of the British Intelligence Community* (Heinemann, 1985).

Well-established introductions to British diplomacy at the end of the nineteenth century, both of which are linked to documentary collections, are Kenneth Bourne, *The Foreign Policy of Victorian England, 1830–1902* (Oxford University Press, 1970) and C.J. Lowe, *The Reluctant Imperialists, Vol. I, British Foreign Policy, 1878–1902* and *Vol. II, The Documents* (Routledge and Kegan Paul, 1967), but on the growth of the Empire see Ronald Hyam, *Britain's Imperial Century, 1815–1914* (Batsford, 1976). More focused on Salisbury's period are J.A.S. Grenville, *Lord Salisbury and Foreign Policy: The Close of the Nineteenth Century* (Athlone Press, 1970) and the shorter interpretative essay by Christopher Howard, *Splendid Isolation: A Study of Ideas Concerning Britain's ... Foreign Policy During the Later Years of ... Salisbury* (Macmillan, 1967); whilst on the coming of the Japanese alliance see Ian Nish, *The Anglo-Japanese Alliance: The Diplomacy of Two Island Empires, 1894–1907* (Athlone Press, 1966), and on the *ententes* see George Monger, *The End of Isolation: British Foreign Policy 1900–1907* (Nelson, 1963), the first comprehensive work to be based on the documents for this period, and Christopher Andrew, *Theophile Delcassé and the Making of the Entente Cordiale* (Macmillan, 1968), which draws on French sources. Grey's period as Foreign Secretary is the focus of Zara Steiner, *Britain and the Origins of the First World War* (Macmillan, 1977), a well-established, lucid introduction to its topic, and the most readable, well-documented biography of Grey is Keith Robbins, *Sir Edward Grey* (Cassell, 1971). All the best-known historians in the field were gathered together for the comprehensive F.H. Hinsley (ed.), *British Foreign Policy under Sir Edward Grey* (Cambridge, University Press, Cambridge, 1977). On policy-making see Zara Steiner, *The Foreign Office and Foreign Policy, 1898–1914* (Ashfield, 1969), on military policies Samuel Williamson, *The Politics of Grand Strategy: Britain and France Prepare for War 1904–14* (Cambridge, Mass., Harvard University Press, 1969), and, on one main theme of these years, Paul Kennedy, *The Rise of Anglo-German Antagonism,*

1860–1914 (George Allen and Unwin, 1982). Obsession with the German menace has been offset in particular by Keith Wilson, *The Policy of the Entente: Essays on the Determinants of British Foreign Policy, 1904–14* (Cambridge, Cambridge University Press, 1985) and the importance of the Russian threat has recently been fully explored, with a thesis different to Wilson's, in Keith Neilson, *Britain and the Last Tsar: British Policy and Russia, 1894–1917* (Oxford, Clarendon Press, 1995).

The most comprehensive and stimulating introduction to wartime diplomacy is David Stevenson, *The First World War in International Politics* (Oxford University Press, 1988). On the impact of the war on Britain see J.M. Bourne, *Britain and the Great War, 1914–18* (Edward Arnold, 1989) and John Turner, *British Politics and the Great War* (New Haven, Yale University Press,1992), whilst G. Cassar, *Asquith as War Leader* (Hambledon Press, 1994) is a well-focused and sympathetic study of its subject. John Gooch, *The Prospect of War: Studies in British Defence Policy, 1847–1945* (Cass, 1981) includes a number of essays on pre-1914 and wartime military issues, whilst on war aims see Victor Rothwell, *British War Aims and Peace Diplomacy, 1914–18* (Oxford, Clarendon Press, 1971) and, on Anglo-American relations, Kathleen Burk, *Britain, America and the Sinews of War, 1914–18* (Allen and Unwin, 1985) or David Woodward, *Trial by Friendship: Anglo-American Relations, 1917–18* (Lexington, University of Kentucky Press, 1993). The Versailles conference is comprehensively introduced by Alan Sharp, *The Versailles Settlement: Peacemaking in Paris 1919* (Macmillan, 1991), but specifically British concerns are more fully explored in A. Lentin, *Lloyd George, Woodrow Wilson and the Guilt of Germany* (Leicester University Press, 1984) or Erik Goldstein, *Winning the Peace: British Diplomatic Strategy, Peace Planning and the Paris Peace Conference* (Oxford, Clarendon Press, 1991), and the wider difficulties bred by the peace settlement are discussed by Kenneth Morgan, *Consensus and Disunity: The Lloyd George Coalition, 1918–22* (Oxford, Clarendon Press, 1979) and Michael Dockrill and J. Douglas Goold, *Peace without Promise: Britain and the Peace Conferences, 1919–23* (Batsford, 1981). G.H. Bennett, *British Foreign Policy During the Curzon Period, 1919–24* (Macmillan, 1995) is a fresh, admirably objective analysis of its subject, emphasising the diversity of problems Britain faced in the wake of war. On more specific problems in this period see George Egerton, *Great Britain and the Creation of the League of Nations* (Scolar, 1979), Ian Nish, *Alliance in Decline: A Study in Anglo-Japanese Relations* (Athlone Press, 1972) and John Darwin, *Britain, Egypt and the Middle East, 1918–22* (Macmillan, 1981), whilst Anne Orde, *Great Britain and International Security, 1920–26* (Royal Historical Society, 1978) and John R. Ferris, *The Evolution of British Strategic Policy, 1919–26* (Macmillan, 1989) carry the story down to the mid-1920s.

One of the few attempts at a comprehensive account of inter-war foreign policy is F.S. Northedge, *The Troubled Giant: Britain and the Great Powers, 1916–39* (Bell, 1966) but important general themes are explored in Robert Holland, *Britain and the Commonwealth Alliance, 1918–39* (Macmillan, 1981), Brian Bond, *British Military Policy Between the Two World Wars* (Oxford, Clarendon Press, 1980) and Martin Ceadel, *Pacifism in Britain, 1914–45* (Oxford, Clarendon Press, 1980). The personalities who dominated foreign policy in the late 1920s are the focus of David Dutton, *Austen Chamberlain: Gentleman in Politics* (Ross Anderson, 1985) and David Carlton, *MacDonald versus Henderson: The Foreign Policy of the Second Labour Government* (Macmillan, 1970). One of the best detailed books on these years is B.J.C. McKercher, *The Second Baldwin Government and the United States, 1924–29* (Cambridge, Cambridge University Press, 1984), a theme explored again more recently in McKercher's edited collection, *Anglo-American Relations in the 1920s* (Macmillan, 1991). Dick Richardson, *The Evolution of British Disarmament Policy in the 1920s* (Pinter, 1989) highlights the lukewarm attitude of the British government to disarmament. Of the numerous books dealing with the 1930s and Appeasement, mention should be made first of A.J.P. Taylor, *The Origins of the Second World War* (Penguin, 1961), a controversial work much of which has now been debunked. One of the best early studies of Appeasement using government documents was Keith Middlemas, *Diplomacy of Illusion: The British Government and Germany, 1937–39* (Weidenfeld and Nicolson, 1972), though it is rather narrowly focused. Keith Middlemas and John Barnes, *Baldwin: A Biography* (Macmillan, 1970) is a remarkably thorough study, and the first great crisis of the decade is discussed in Christopher Thorne, *The Limits of Foreign Policy: The West, the League and the Far Eastern Crisis, 1931–33* (Hamish Hamilton, 1972). The best critique of Neville Chamberlain is now R.A.C. Parker, *Chamberlain and Appeasement* (Macmillan, 1993) but important aspects of his policy are also addressed in S. Newton, *Profits of Peace: The Political Economy of Anglo-German Appeasement* (Oxford, Clarendon Press, 1996) and Richard Cockett, *Twilight of Truth: Chamberlain, Appeasement and the Manipulation of the Press* (Weidenfeld and Nicolson, 1989). The fullest account of the final breakdown of peace, and a remarkable example of multi-archival research, is Donald Watt, *How War Came: The Immediate Origins of the Second World War* (Heinemann, 1989), whilst the seminal study of the emergence of British propaganda services by 1939 is Philip Taylor, *The Projection of Britain* (Cambridge University Press, 1981).

The Foreign Office historian Sir Llewellyn Woodward produced an official history of *British Foreign Policy in the Second World War* (5 vols, HMSO, 1970–76), as well as a one-volume abridged summary (HMSO,

1970). Churchill as a war leader is now the subject of widely different views. Martin Gilbert's *Churchill: A Life* (Heinemann, 1991) is predictably sympathetic, J. Charmley, *Churchill: The End of Glory* (Hodder and Stoughton, 1993) extremely critical, and Norman Rose, *Churchill: An Unruly Life* (Simon and Schuster, 1994) perhaps the most objective. The most important themes in wartime diplomacy are Anglo-Soviet and Anglo-American relations. The former are discussed both by Martin Kitchen, *British Policy Towards the Soviet Union During the Second World War* (Macmillan, 1986) and Victor Rothwell, *Britain and the Origins of the Cold War, 1941*–7 (Cape, 1982); and the latter are discussed by David Reynolds, *The Creation of the Anglo-American Alliance, 1937–41* (Europa, 1981) and Robert Hathaway, *Ambiguous Partnership: Britain and America, 1944*–7 (Columbia University Press, 1981). The post-war years down to 1973 were the subject of both F.S. Northedge, *Descent from Power: British Foreign Policy, 1945–73* (George Allen and Unwin, 1974) and Joseph Frankel, *British Foreign Policy, 1945–73* (Oxford University Press, 1975), but a longer perspective is taken by David Sanders, *Losing an Empire, Finding a Role: British Foreign Policy Since 1945* (Macmillan, 1990), which combines historical enquiry with theoretical analysis. The 'three circles' of British policy have all been the subject of individual studies covering the whole post-war period. On America see especially David Dimbleby and David Reynolds, *An Ocean Apart* (Hodder and Stoughton, 1988), C.J. Bartlett, *The Special Relationship* (Longman, 1992) and John Baylis, *Anglo-American Defence Relations, 1939–84* (Macmillan, 1984). On Imperial decline see especially John Darwin, *Britain and Decolonisation* (Macmillan, 1988), but also David Goldsworthy, *Colonial Issues in British Politics, 1945–61* (Oxford, Clarendon Press, 1971), and Nicholas Tarling, *The Fall of Imperial Britain in South-East Asia* (New York, Oxford University Press, 1993). And on the move to a European focus see either Sean Greenwood, *Britain and European Cooperation Since 1945* (Oxford, Blackwell, 1993) or John Young, *Britain and European Unity, 1945–92* (Macmillan, 1993).

Government sources for the years 1945–56 have now been open to historians for some time. The fullest discussion of foreign policy under the Labour government is Alan Bullock, *Ernest Bevin: Foreign Secretary, 1945–56* (Heinemann, 1983) but see also Ritchie Ovendale, ed., *The Foreign Policy of the British Labour Governments* (Leicester, Leicester University Press, 1984). Important detailed studies within the period include R.J. Moore, *Escape from Empire: The Attlee Government and the Indian Problem* (Oxford, Clarendon Press, 1983), John Kent, *British Imperial Strategy and the Origins of the Cold War* (Leicester, Leicester University Press, 1993), Anne Deighton, *The Impossible Peace: Britain, the Division of Germany and the Origins of the Cold War* (Oxford University

Press, 1990), Ritchie Ovendale, *The English-Speaking Alliance: Britain, the US, the Dominions and the Cold War* (Allen and Unwin, 1985) and Callum MacDonald, *Britain and the Korean War* (Oxford, Blackwell, 1990). On the Conservatives in office after 1945 see John Young, ed., *The Foreign Policy of Churchill's Peacetime Administration* (Leicester, Leicester University Press, 1988) and the same author's *Winston Churchill's Last Campaign: Britain and Russia 1951–5* (Oxford University Press, 1996). The official biography of *Anthony Eden* is by Robert Rhodes James (Weidenfeld and Nicolson, 1986). On the Suez crisis see especially Keith Kyle, *Suez* (Weidenfeld and Nicolson, 1991) and Scott Lucas, *Divided We Stand: Britain, the US and the Suez Crisis* (John Curtis, 1991). The importance of intelligence and propaganda is brought out in Richard Aldrich, ed., *British Intelligence, Strategy and the Cold War 1945–51* (Routledge, 1992). The years since 1956 are not yet well-covered by historical research but an early example of primary materials on the Macmillan government is Richard Aldous and Sabine Lee, eds, *Harold Macmillan and Britain's World Role* (Macmillan, 1996). On the period down to 1973 some of the best work has been done in the form of biographies. Alastair Horne's, *Macmillan, Vol. 2, 1957–86* (Macmillan, 1991) is quite detailed but a shorter introduction is John Turner, *Macmillan* (Longman, 1994). Ben Pimlott's, *Harold Wilson* (Harper Collins, 1992) was well-received by critics but Philip Ziegler's, *Wilson: The Authorised Life* (Weidenfeld and Nicholson, 1993) makes use of Wilson's private papers and American archival documents. John Campbell's *Edward Heath* (Jonathan Cape, 1993) shows what can be done by historians before the archives open, as does Stuart Ball and Anthony Seldon, eds, *The Heath Government, 1970–74* (Longman, 1996). Britain's role in Europe after 1973 is best covered by Stephen George's, *An Awkward Partner: Britain in the European Community* (Oxford University Press, 1990). On the Falklands crisis see Lawrence Freedman and V. Gamba-Stonehouse, *Signals of War* (Faber, 1990) and on Anglo-American relations in the 1980s Geoffrey Smith, *Reagan and Thatcher* (Bodley Head, 1990). Geoffrey Howe's, *Conflict of Loyalty* (Macmillan, 1994) is better than most memoirs by British foreign secretaries and very full on the years 1983–89, whilst the contemporary situation is best covered in Michael Clarke, *British External Policy-making in the 1990s* (Macmillan, 1992), though for an analysis of the present-day FCO see John Dickie, *Inside the Foreign Office* (Chapmans, 1992).

Index